Schola Latina
II
KEY

GlossaHouse
Wilmore, KY
www.glossahouse.com

Schola Latina II Key

© GlossaHouse, 2023

All rights reserved. No part of this work may be reproduced or transmitted in any form or by any means, electronic or mechanical, including photocopying and recording, or by means of any information storage or retrieval system, except as may be expressly permitted by the 1976 Copyright Act or in writing from the publisher. Requests for permission should be addressed in writing to:

GlossaHouse, LLC
110 Callis Circle
Wilmore, KY 40390

Publisher's Cataloging-in-Publication Data

Stephenson, Ken (revised by Thomas Caucutt and Ruth Baldwin)
  Schola Latina II KEY/ Wilmore, KY: GlossaHouse, 2023

xvi, 230 pages ; 22 cm.– (LAETA— Latin Ancient Educational Tools & Aids)

ISBN: 978-1-63663-066-3 (paperback)

Library of Congress Control Number:

Corrected Version, June 2024

Cover Design by T. Michael W. Halcomb

Book Layout and volume editing by Thomas Caucutt and Ruth Baldwin

Original content by Ken Stephenson who grants GlossaHouse the rights to publish *Schola Latina I & II*.

Select maps used with permission from Ancient World Mapping Center at https://awmc.unc.edu/.

Schola Latina II Key

BY

Ken Stephenson

Revised by

Thomas Caucutt   Ruth Baldwin

GlossaHouse
Wilmore, KY
www.glossahouse.com

LAETA
Latin Ancient Educational Tools & Aids

SERIES EDITOR
T. Michael W. Halcomb

LAETA

The Latin term LAETA is an adjective that means "fertile" or "welcoming," especially when describing land. It is also a term that captures the link between this series and its Hebrew (HA'ARETS) and Greek (AGROS) counterparts also bearing land-related names and published by GlossaHouse. In keeping with those series, LAETA functions as an acronym: Latin Ancient Educational Tools & Aids. This series exists because, while there are many great resources on Latin, more can and always will need to be created. Thus, LAETA welcomes new and innovative works, those that make a contribution, however big or small, to the journey of learning Latin. The long-term aim is to create a tiered curriculum suite featuring innovative readers, grammars, specialized studies, and similar resources that will both encourage and foster the use of Latin. Additionally, the LAETA series endeavors to facilitate the creation and publication of innovative and inexpensive print and digital resources within the context of the global community.

Table of Contents

Preface ix
Pronunciation x
At the Beginning of Class xii
Prayers, Creeds, and Hymns xiii

Lectiōnēs

I   Review of 1st Declension and 1st Conjugation . . . 2
II   Review of 2nd Declension and Adjectives; *ego* . . 8
III Review of 2nd Conjugation; Direct Objects; *tū*. 14
IV   More Direct Objects; Numbers. 17
V   3rd Declension. 23
VI   Adverbs; Infinitives; *is, ea, id* 29
VII   The Genitive, *ūnus* 37
VIII   Prepositions (+Acc.); *duo* 43
IX   The Dative Case; *trēs* 47
X   Prepositions (+Abl.); *hic, haec, hoc* 53
XI   2-Case Prepositions; *ille, illa, illud* 59
XII   Question Words 65
XIII   3rd Conjugation. 73
XIV   Imperfect Tense 79
XV   More Imperfect Tense 85
XVI   Vestīmenta 91
XVII Tempora Annī. 97
XVIII Mensēs 103
XIX   Quod Erit Erit 109
XX   Perfect Tense 115
XXI   3rd Conjugation -iō Verbs 121
XXII 4 Conjugation 127
XXIII 3rd Declension Adjectives. 133
XXIV Commands 139

Glossary (Latin to English) 145
Glossary (English to Latin) 153
Numbers 160
Vocabulary by Lectiō 161
Paradigms 165
Dicta 171
Colloquia 173
Timeline 177
Map of the Roman Empire 179
Historia. 181

SCHOLA LATINA II

by Ken Stephenson

revised by Ruth Baldwin
& Thomas Caucutt

Preface

Where did my Latin education, starting so well as it did, go wrong? ... I think it would have helped me very much if I had ever been got into the habit of speaking Latin, if only to say "Please" and "Thank you" and "Pass the mustard."

– Dorothy Sayers

The need for the present volume arises from my agreement with Dorothy Sayers' comments on learning Latin. In order for a language to become natural and spontaneous with a student, it must become a *language*, which means, as Latin scholars know, it must become a matter of the tongue, the *lingua*. It must be on the lips during the course of a normal day. In the first volume of this method, the student learned the names of familiar objects – animals, parts of the body, and household items – and everyday verbs, e.g., *to eat* rather than *to seize*. In this volume, the student will learn the Latin names of articles of clothing, foods, and fun activities, as well as some basic transitive verbs, e.g., *to know, to have, to hold*.

This book also continues with more useful conversational phrases that would put the language onto the tongue even before the mastery of grammar. Students will learn how to give the time and date, to talk about seasons, and to complain about a cold. And they'll learn how to say "Please pass the butter." Make these conversations a part of your routine at home, and soon Latin will become a living language for you, despite rumors you've heard to the contrary.

The history summaries correspond to stories from *Famous Men of Rome* by John H. Haaren and A. B. Poland and are meant for review only. The students should at least read the stories from the book or hear them read and should be encouraged, in order to reinforce the material and to make the learning more fun, to act the stories out or to illustrate them.

Make sure to do all the exercises: the tedious, the tough, and the fun. Above all, practice the forms – out loud. A list of all forms, by *lectiō,* is provided on pages 165-168. Practice saying them – out loud – at least twice a week. And have I mentioned that you should say them out loud? The student who faithfully rehearses the forms as if they were nonsense poetry will much more easily make his way down the road to mastery of Latin than will the student who thinks to himself that it all looks pretty straightforward. Take it from the voice of experience: say them out loud.

Eāmus!

Pronunciation

Several different methods of pronouncing Latin exist. The following notes correspond to what is known as "classical" pronunciation.

Vowels

If you were to say the word "no" very slowly, you would discover that your pronunciation of the vowel "o" probably started something like "uh" and ended something like "oo." Such glides do not occur in single vowels in Latin. There are six vowels in Latin, and these six vowels may be pronounced either long or short. A macron (a small horizontal mark above the vowel) indicates a long vowel. A short vowel has no macron. Below are each of the six Latin vowels, both short and long, with an English word to help guide your pronunciation:

Short vowels		**Long vowels**	
a	as in *a*lter	ā	as in f*a*ther (twice as long as short *a*)
e	as in p*e*t	ē	as in th*ey*
i	as in p*i*n	ī	as in sk*i*
o	as in *o*ff	ō	as in t*o*tal
u	as in p*u*t	ū	as in r*u*le
y	as in p*u*t	ȳ	as in r*u*le

Macrons

Macrons are small horizontal bars written above long vowels in Latin. Macrons indicate the proper pronunciation and length of vowels and give important clues to a word's use & meaning within a sentence.

Diphthongs

Diphthongs are vowel combinations. Below are some common to Latin:

ae	like *i* in k*i*te
au	like *ou* in l*ou*d
ei	like *e* in h*e*y
eu	like *eu* in f*eu*d
ui	like *uey* in gl*uey*

Consonants

The consonants are pronounced as in English with the following exceptions:

b	as in English (except before *s* and *t*, where it is pronounced *p*)
c	always like *c* in *c*ar
ch	always like *k* in *k*ite
g	always like *g* in *g*ap
i	like *y* in *y*et (only when it begins a word or precedes a vowel)
ph	like *ph* in *ph*one
r	trilled or rolled
s	always like *s* in *s*ing
th	like *t* in *t*ell
v	like *w* in *w*ine

Accents & Syllables

The Latin accent is a musical one: accented syllables are spoken with a higher pitch than are other syllables and not necessarily with any more force.

In two-syllable words, the first syllable is always accented. In longer words, the accent comes either on the next-to-last syllable (if that one is long) or on the third-to-last syllable (if the next-to-last isn't long). Latin words are never stressed or accented on the last syllable.

audēmus	au·ˈdē·mus
iūra	ˈiū·ra
nostra	ˈnos·tra
dēfendere	dē·ˈfen·de·re

A syllable is long if it contains a long vowel (with a macron) or if it contains a vowel is followed by two consonants.

At the Beginning of Class

Magister:	Salvēte, discipulī.	Hello, students.
Discipulī:	Salvē, magister.	Hello, teacher.
Magister:	Surgite. Ōrēmus.	Stand up. Let's pray.
Omnēs:	Domine Deus, adiūvā nōs	Lord God, help us
	linguam Latīnam discere. Amen.	to learn the Latin language. Amen.
Omnēs:	Pater noster, quī in caelī es,	Our Father, You who are in heaven,
	sanctificētur nōmen tuum;	may Your name be made holy;
	veniat rēgnum tuum;	may Your kingdom come;
	fiat voluntās tua	may Your will be done
	sicut in caelō et in terrā.	on earth just as in heaven.
	Pānem nostrum supersubstantiālem	Our daily bread
	dā nōbīs hodiē,	give us today,
	et dimitte nōbīs debita nostra	and forgive us our debts
	sicut et nōs dimissimus debitōribus nostrīs;	just as we also forgive our debtors;
	et nē indūcās nōs in temptātiōnem,	and lead us not into temptation,
	sed līberā nōs ā malō. Amen.	but deliver us from evil. Amen.
Magister:	Grātiās, discipulī. Sedēte.	Thank you, students. Sit down.

Prayers, Creeds, and Hymns

Christus Vincit

Glōria Patrī

Sanctus and Benedictus

Symbolum Apostolicum (The Apostles' Creed)

Crēdō in Deum Patrem omnipotentem;	I believe in one God the Father almighty;
Creatōrem caelī et terrae.	Creator of the heaven and the earth,
Et in Iēsum Christum,	And in Jesus Christ
Fīlium euis ūnīcum, Dominum nostrum;	His only Son, our Lord;
quī conceptus est dē Spīritū Sanctō,	who was conceived of the Holy Spirit,
nātus ex Mariā virgine;	born of the virgin Mary;
passus sub Pontiō Pilatō,	He suffered under Pontius Pilate,
crucifixus, mortuus, et sepultus;	was crucified, dead, and buried;
descendit ad īnferna;	He descended into hell;
tertia diē resurrexit ā mortuīs;	on the third day He rose again from the dead;
ascendit ad caelōs;	He ascended to the heavens;
sedet ad dexteram	and is seated at the right hand
Deī Patris omnipotentis;	of God the Father almighty;
inde ventūrus est iūdicāre	from thence He shall come to judge
vīvōs et mortuōs	both the quick and the dead.
Crēdō in Spīritum Sanctum;	I believe in the Holy Spirit;
sanctam ecclēsiam catholicam;	the holy catholic church;
sanctōrum commūniōnem;	the communion of the saints;
remissiōnem peccatōrum;	the forgiveness of sins;
carnis resurrectiōnem;	the resurrection of the body;
vītam aeternam. Amen.	and the life everlasting. Amen.

Tē Deum

Tē Deum laudāmus;	We praise you, O God;
Tē Dominum cōnfitēmur.	We acclaim you, O Lord.
Tē aeternum Patrem	You, eternal Father,
omnis terra venerātur.	all the world worships.
Tibi omnēs angelī,	To you all angels,
Tibi caelī et ūniversae potestātēs,	To you the powers of heaven and the universe,
Tibi cherubim et seraphim	To you cherubim and seraphim
incessābilī vōce proclamant:	proclaim with unceasing voice:
Sanctus Sanctus Sanctus	Holy, holy, holy,
Dominus Deus sabaoth.	Lord, God of Hosts,
Plenī sunt caelī et terra	heaven and earth are full
māiestātis glōriae tuae.	of the majesty of your glory.
Tē gloriōsus apostolōrum chorus,	You the glorious chorus of apostles,
Tē prophetārum laudābilis numerus,	You the noble fellowship of prophets,
Tē martyrum candidātus laudat exercitus.	You the white-robed army of martyrs praise.
Tē per orbem terrārum	You through the world
sancta cōnfitētur ecclēsia,	the holy Church acclaims,
Patrem immensae maiestātis.	Father, of majesty unbounded.
Venerandum	Worthy of worship
tuum vērum et ūnicum Fīlium;	is your true and only Son,
Sanctum quoque Paraclītum Spiritum.	and the Holy Spirit, Comforter.
Tū Rēx glōriae Christe.	You, Christ, are the King of glory.
Tū Patris sempiternus es Fīlius.	You are the eternal Son of the Father.
Tū ad liberandum susceptūrus hominem,	You when undertaking man's deliverance,
nōn horruistī virginis ūterum.	did not spurn the virgin's womb.
Tū dēvictō mortis aculeō,	You, having overcome the sting of death,
aperuistī crēdentibus rēgna caelōrum.	opened the kingdom of heaven to believers.
Tū ad dexteram Deī sedēs,	You sit at God's right hand
in glōria Patris.	in the glory of the Father.
Iūdex crēderis esse ventūrus.	You are believed to be coming as Judge.
Tē ergō quaesimus,	We ask you then,
tuīs famulīs subvenī,	come down to your servants,
quōs pretiōsō sanguine rēdemistī.	whom you have redeemed by your precious blood.
Aeternā fac cum sanctīs tuīs	Make us to be numbered with your saints in
in glōriā numerārī.	eternal glory

I – Prīma   Nōmen:

I – Prīma lectiō (1 – First lesson)   **REVIEW**

I. Dictum

Audēmus iūra nostra dēfendere.   *We dare to defend our rights*
    (Alabama state motto)

II. Colloquium   *Latīnē*   *Anglicē*

Sextus:	Salvē! Quōmodō aestās erat?	Hi! How was the summer?
Iūlia:	Optimē! Et quōmodō tē habēs?	Great! And how are you?
Sextus:	Bene mē habeō.	I'm well.
		(see page 173 for other answers)

III. Verba renovanda (Vocabulary for review) – 1st Conjugation and 1st Declension

Latīnē	*Anglicē*	*Latīnē*	*Anglicē*	*Latīnē*	*Anglicē*
ambulō, ambulāre	to walk	agricola, -ae, m.	farmer	nauta, -ae, m.	sailor
amō, amāre	to love, to like	aqua, -ae, f.	water	patella, -ae, f.	plate
arō, arāre	to plow	aquila, -ae, f.	eagle	patria, -ae, f.	fatherland, country
cantō, cantāre	to sing	charta, -ae, f.	paper		
cēnō, cēnāre	to dine, to eat	culīna, -ae, f.	kitchen	pecūnia, -ae, f.	money
cōgitō, cōgitāre	to think	corōna, -ae, f.	crown	puella, -ae, f.	girl
dubitō, dubitāre	to doubt, to be uncertain	culpa, -ae, f.	fault	rēgīna, -ae, f.	queen
		discipula, -ae, f.	student	Rōma, -ae, f.	Rome
dūrō, dūrāre	to endure	ecclēsia, -ae, f.	church	sella, -ae, f.	chair
errō, errāre	to err, to wander, to be mistaken	fēmina, -ae, f.	woman	silva, -ae, f.	forest
		fenestra, -ae, f.	window	stella, -ae, f.	star
festīnō, festīnāre	to hurry	fīlia, -ae, f.	daughter	terra, -ae, f.	land, earth
imperō, imperāre	to rule, to order	furca, -ae, f.	fork	ursa, -ae, f.	bear
intrō, intrāre	to enter	Gallia, -ae, f.	Gaul	via, -ae, f.	road, way
iudicō, iūdicāre	to judge	gallīna, -ae, f.	chicken	victōria, -ae, f.	victory
laborō, labōrāre	to work	glōria, -ae, f.	glory	vīta, -ae, f.	life
nāvigō, nāvigāre	to sail	herba, -ae, f.	plant, herb		
ōrō, ōrāre	to pray, to speak	Hispania, -ae, f.	Spain		
peccō, peccāre	to sin	hōra, -ae, f.	hour		
pugnō, pugnāre	to fight	iānua, -ae, f.	door		
recitō, recitāre	to recite	īnsula, -ae, f.	island		
rēgnō, rēgnāre	to reign	Ītalia, -ae, f.	Italy		
stō, stāre	to stand	lingua, -ae, f.	language, tongue		
superō, superāre	to overcome, to conquer	lūna, -ae, f.	moon		
		magistra, -ae, f.	teacher		
tardō, tardāre	to be slow	Maria, -ae, f.	Mary		
volō, volāre	to fly	mēnsa, -ae, f.	table		

1. What detail distinguishes 1st conjugation?   *the infinitive ending -āre*

2. What detail distinguishes 1st declension?   *the genitive singular ending -ae*

I – Prīma   Nōmen:

IV. Grammatica

Here are the forms you learned for present tense of 1ˢᵗ-conjugation verbs in Book I.

	Singular	Plural				Personal Endings		
						Singular	Plural	
1ˢᵗ person __amō__	amō	amāmus	amāmus	I		-ō	-mus	we
2ⁿᵈ person __amās__	amās	amātis	amātis	you		-s	-tis	you
3ʳᵈ person __amat__	amat	amant	amānt	he, she it		-t	-nt	they

A <u>verb</u> is a word that expresses action or state of being. The <u>subject</u> of a sentence tells who or what is acting or being. In Latin, <u>pronouns</u> (words that replace nouns) are built into the ends of verbs as <u>personal endings</u>. Pronouns are distinguished by <u>person</u> (1ˢᵗ, 2ⁿᵈ, or 3ʳᵈ) and <u>number</u> (singular or plural). <u>Conjugating a verb</u> means adding personal endings to a <u>stem</u> to indicate the person and number of the pronoun.

The second principal part of a verb is its infinitive, translated *to* + ____, e.g., *amāre* = *to love*.

Amāre is a 1ˢᵗ-<u>conjugation verb</u>. To find the stem of a 1ˢᵗ-conjugation verb, drop the *–re* from the <u>infinitive</u>. For example, the stem of *amō, amāre* is *amā-*. To conjugate a verb in present tense, add the personal endings to the stem. For 1ˢᵗ conjugation, remember that the first-person singular form drops the final *ā* of the stem, e.g.: *amō*, not *amāō*.

Here are the forms you learned for 1ˢᵗ declension in Book I.

	Singular	Plural	Case Endings Singular	Plural
nominative	ursa	ursae	-a	-ae
genitive	ursae	ursārum	-ae	-ārum
dative	ursae	ursīs	-ae	-īs
accusative	ursam	ursās	-am	-ās
ablative	ursā	ursīs	-ā	-īs

A <u>noun</u> is a word that names a person, place, thing, or idea. <u>Declining a noun</u> means adding <u>case endings</u> to a <u>stem</u>. *Ursa, -ae, f.* is a 1ˢᵗ-declension noun. To find the stem of any Latin noun, drop the <u>genitive singular case ending</u> (the second form in the <u>declension</u>). For example, the stem of **ursa, -ae, f.** above, would be **urs-**. To decline a noun, write the <u>nominative singular form</u>; then add the rest of the case endings to the stem, column by column, top to bottom.

A <u>sentence</u> must have a subject and a verb. In Latin, a complete sentence may have only one word since a pronoun is built into every conjugated verb form. Latin also uses two-word sentences: one <u>subject noun</u> and one verb. The subject noun must be in the nominative case; the noun and the verb must agree in person and number. In a sentence that has a subject noun, the verb will *always* be 3ʳᵈ person whether singular or plural, to agree with its subject noun, e.g. *Ursa stat. Ursae stant.* It is most common in Latin for the verb to be the last word in the sentence. A linking verb, however, may stand at the beginning or in the middle of a sentence, e.g.: *Est puella. Puella est rēgīna.*

I – Prīma   Nōmen:

V. Historia (*Famous Men of Rome*, Chapter XIV)

Between 264-241 BC, Rome begins the first of three wars with Carthage. These are known as the Punic Wars since the founders of Carthage were Phoenicians, a people the Romans called *Punicī*. The Roman general, Marcus Atilius Regulus, defeats a large Carthaginian navy, but he is then defeated in Africa and is captured by an army led by Xanthippus. He recommends that the Roman Senate reject peace terms, even though doing so means he must remain a prisoner.

VI. Dēlēgāta

A. *Scrībe* the conjugation of <u>amō, amāre</u> in present tense two times.

1.	amō	amāmus	2.	amō	amāmus
	amās	amātis		amās	amātis
	amat	amant		amat	amant

B. *Scrībe* the personal endings for present tense two times.

1.	-ō	-mus	2.	-ō	-mus
	-s	-tis		-s	-tis
	-t	-nt		-t	-nt

C. *Scrībe* the declension of <u>ursa, -ae, f.</u> two times.

1.	ursa	ursae	2.	ursa	ursae
	ursae	ursārum		ursae	ursārum
	ursae	ursīs		ursae	ursīs
	ursam	ursās		ursam	ursās
	ursā	ursīs		ursā	ursīs

D. *Variātiōnēs* (Variations): *Recitā* these sentences. Notice changes that make each one plural.

a. Ursa stat.   Ursae stant.   (The bear stands. The bears stand.)
b. Agricola stat.   Agricolae stant.   (The farmer stands. The farmers stand.)
c. Ecclēsia stat.   Ecclēsiae stant.   (The church stands. The churches stand.)
d. Discipula stat.   Discipulae stant.   (The student stands. The students stand.)
e. Iānua stat.   Iānuae stant.   (The door stands. The doors stand.)
f. Mēnsa stat.   Mēnsae stant.   (The table stands. The tables stand.)

I – Prīma   Nōmen: _____

E. Translate these sentences (from Latin to English or from English to Latin).

1. Puella ambulat. — *The girl walks.*
2. Aquila cēnat. — *The eagle eats.*
3. Fīliae cōgitant. — *The daughters are thinking.*
4. Rēgīna rēgnat. — *The queen reigns.*
5. Discipulae recitant. — *The students read aloud.*
6. Agricola arat. — *The farmer plows.*
7. Chickens fight. — *Gallīnae pugnant.*
8. The hours are slow. — *Hōrae tardant.*
9. The country conquers. — *Patria superat.*
10. The church speaks. — *Ecclēsia ōrat.*
11. Eagles are flying. — *Aquilae volant.*
12. Rome endures. — *Rōma dūrat.*

F. Fill in the blanks.

1. Personal endings indicate the __*person*__ and __*number*__ of the subject of a verb.
2. To find the stem of 1st-conjugation verbs, drop the __*-re*__ of the __*infinitive*__.
3. Adding personal endings to the stem of a verb is called __*conjugating*__.
4. Adding case endings to the stem of a noun is called __*declining*__.
5. To find the stem of any noun, drop the __*genitive*__ __*singular*__ case ending.
6. The subject and verb of a sentence must agree in __*person*__ and __*number*__.

G. Translate these *verba* and phrases.

1. prīma lectiō — *first lesson*
2. variātiōnēs — *variations*
3. verba renovanda — *vocabulary for review*

I – Prīma   Nōmen:

4. Audēmus iūra nostra dēfendere. _We dare to defend our rights._

H. *Scribe* **these sentences** *Latine.*

1. We are loving. _Amāmus._   6. You all are doubting. _Dubitātis._
2. You enter. _Intrās._   7. They do judge. _Iudicant._
3. We hurry. _Festīnāmus._   8. The road wanders. _Via errat._
4. The girl speaks. _Puella ōrat._   9. Mary works. _Maria labōrat._
5. They are slow. _Tardant._   10. The sailors sail. _Nauta nāvigant._

I. Conjugate these verbs in present tense. *Scribe* **the meaning of each in the blank by it.**

1. arō, arāre _to plow_   2. rēgnō, rēgnāre _to reign_

   arō   _arāmus_   _rēgnō_   _rēgnāmus_
   arās   _arātis_   _rēgnās_   _rēgnātis_
   arat   _arant_   _rēgnat_   _rēgnant_

3. dūrō, dūrāre _to endure_   4. peccō, peccāre _to sin_

   dūrō   _dūrāmus_   _peccō_   _peccāmus_
   dūrās   _dūrātis_   _peccās_   _peccātis_
   dūrat   _dūrant_   _peccat_   _peccant_

I – Prīma   Nōmen: _____

J. Crossword Puzzle. When you complete this puzzle, the shaded letters, when read row by row from top to bottom, will tell you for what you should aim: _____ STELLAE _____

¹S	²I	L	³V	A	E		⁴C	E	N	A	⁵S
	M		I				H				E
	⁶P	A	T	E	L	L	A	E			L
	E		A				R				L
	R						⁷T	E	R	R	A
⁸C	O	R	O	⁹N	A		A				E
U				A		¹⁰M	E	N	S	¹¹A	
¹²L	I	N	G	U	A					R	
I				T						A	
N			¹³N	A	¹⁴V	I	G	A	N	T	
A					I					I	
¹⁵E	R	R	A		¹⁶A	M	A	M	U	S	

RĒCTĒ
1. forests
4. you (sing.) eat
6. plates
7. land
8. crown
10. table
12. language
13. they sail
15. I err
16. we love

DEORSUM
2. I rule
3. life
4. papers
5. chairs
8. kitchens
9. sailor
11. you all plow
14. road

K. Historia. Review the history and fill in the blanks.

1. What are the three wars with Carthage called? _____ the Punic Wars _____

2. Why do they have this name? _____ They are called "Punic" because Carthage was founded by the Phoenicians, whom the Romans called "Punici". _____

3. What are the dates of the first of these wars? _The First Punic War lasts from 264-241 BC._

4. What Roman general lands in Africa to attack the Carthaginians? _____ Regulus _____

5. How does he show bravery after being taken prisoner? _Regulus sacrifices his own life for the good of Rome and even keeps his promises to his enemies._

II – Secunda lectiō (2 – Second lesson)   MORE REVIEW

I. Dictum

Hannibal ad portās!   *Hannibal [is] at the gates!*

II. Colloquium

Latīnē   *Anglicē*

Līvia:	Ubi habitās?	Where do you live?
Gāius:	In Alabāmā.	In Alabama.
		(See p. 173 for more states)

III. Verba nova

Latīnē	*Anglicē*	*Scrībe tōtum verbum Latīnum.*	*Dērīvātī*
angelus, -ī, m.	angel	*angelus, -ī, m.*	*angelic*
thronus, -ī, m.	throne	*thonus, -ī, m.*	*enthroned*

Verba renovanda – 2nd Declension and Adjectives

Latine	*Anglice*	*Latine*	*Anglice*	*Latine*	*Anglice*
agnus, -ī, m.	lamb	mendācium, -ī, n.	lie	verbum, -ī, n.	word
amīcus, -ī, m.	friend	mundus, -ī, m.	world	vīnum, -ī, n.	wine
annus, -ī, m.	year	mūrus, -ī, m.	wall		
bellum, -ī, n.	war	nāsus, -ī, m.	nose	**Adjectives**	
brācchium, -ī, n.	arm	nimbus, -ī, m.	cloud	aeternus, -a, -um	eternal
caelum, -ī, n.	sky, heaven	nuntius, -ī, m.	message, messenger	altus, -a, -um	high, deep
calamus, -ī, m.	pen			angustus, -a, -um	narrow
capillus, -ī, m.	hair	oculus, -ī. m.	eye	antīquus, -a, -um	old, ancient
Christus, -ī, m.	Christ	oppidum, -ī, n.	town	bellus, -a, -um	pretty
cubiculum, -ī, n.	bedroom	peccātum, -ī, n.	sin	bonus, -a, -um	good
culter, cultrī, m.	knife	pōculum, -ī, n.	cup	lātus, -a, -um	wide
Deus, -ī, m.	God	porcus, -ī, m.	pig	magnus, -a, -um	large, great
digitus, -ī, m.	finger, toe	praemium, -ī, n.	reward	malus, -a, -um	bad
discipulus, -ī, m.	student	puer, puerī, m.	boy	meus, -a, um	my
dominus, -ī, m.	lord, master	puteus, -ī, m.	well	multus, -a, -um	much, many
dōnum, -ī, n.	gift	rēgnum, -ī, n.	kingdom	novus, -a, -um	new
equus, -ī, m.	horse	servus, -ī, m.	slave	optimus, -a, -um	best
exedrium, -ī. n.	living room	signum, -ī, n.	sign, standard	parvus, -a, -um	small
fīlius, -ī, m.	son	solum, -ī, n.	floor	prīmus, -a, -um	first
focus, -ī, m.	fireplace, family	speculum, -ī, n.	mirror	sanctus, -a, -um	holy
gaudium, -ī, n.	joy	stīlus, -ī, m.	pencil	secundus, -a, um	second
gladius, -ī, m.	sword	stomachus, -ī, m.	stomach	tōtus, -a, -um	whole
lectus, -ī, m.	bed, couch	taurus, -ī, m.	bull	tūtus, -a, -um	safe
liber, librī, m.	book	tēlum, -ī, n.	weapon	tuus, -a, -um	your
magister, magistrī, m.	teacher	vallum, -ī, n.	wall, rampart		

II – Secunda   Nōmen: _____

IV. Grammatica

Here are the forms for 2nd-declension nouns from Book I:

				Case Endings	
Masculine	Singular	Plural		Singular	Plural
nominative	nimb<u>us</u>	nimb<u>ī</u>		-us	-ī
genitive	nimb<u>ī</u>	nimb<u>ōrum</u>		-ī	-ōrum
dative	nimb<u>ō</u>	nimb<u>īs</u>		-ō	-īs
accusative	nimb<u>um</u>	nimb<u>ōs</u>		-um	-ōs
ablative	nimb<u>ō</u>	nimb<u>īs</u>		-ō	-īs

				Singular	Plural
Neuter	Singular	Plural			
nominative	dōn<u>um</u>	dōn<u>a</u>		-um	-a
genitive	dōn<u>ī</u>	dōn<u>ōrum</u>		-ī	-ōrum
dative	dōn<u>ō</u>	dōn<u>īs</u>		-ō	-īs
accusative	dōn<u>um</u>	dōn<u>a</u>		-um	-a
ablative	dōn<u>ō</u>	dōn<u>īs</u>		-ō	-īs

Latin nouns are distinguished by <u>gender</u>, <u>number</u>, and <u>case</u>. Most 1st-declension nouns are feminine. (Exceptions such as *agricola* and *nauta* are masculine.) Latin nouns ending in –*us* and –*er* in the nominative singular are <u>2nd-declension masculine</u>. Latin nouns ending in –*um* in the nominative singular are <u>2nd-declension neuter</u>.

<u>Adjectives</u> modify or describe nouns, pronouns, or other adjectives. A Latin adjective *must* agree with the noun it modifies in gender, number, and case. Use 1st-declension case endings for feminine adjectives. Use 2nd-declension masculine or neuter case endings for masculine or neuter adjectives. Adjectives indicating size or quantity (number) usually come *before* the noun; other adjectives usually *follow* the noun.

So far, pronouns have been built into verbs, but the Romans also had separate pronouns. Here's the <u>form for *I*</u>.

	Singular	Plural		Translation	
nominative	ego	nōs		I	we
genitive	meī	nostrī		of me	of us
dative	mihi	nōbīs		to/for me	to/for us
accusative	mē	nōs		me	us
ablative	mē	nōbīs		by/with/from me	by/with/from us

II – Secunda   Nōmen:

And here's one more form for you to review, present tense of *sum, esse*:

	Singular	Plural	Translation:	
1st person	sum	sumus	I am	we are
2nd person	es	estis	you are	you all are
3rd person	est	sunt	he/she/it is	they are

V. Historia (*Famous Men of Rome*, Chapter XV, Parts I-II)

In the 2nd Punic War, 218-202 BC, Hannibal attacks Italy with an army and elephants. Quintus Fabius attempts a policy of delay, now known as a Fabian policy. The Romans lose 70,000 soldiers at the battle of Cannae. Publius Cornelius Africanus decides Rome has been too cautious, and he leads an army to Africa.

VI. Dēlēgāta

A. *Scrībe* the new Latin *verba* and their meanings.

	Latīnē		*Anglicē*
1.	angelus, -ī, m.	1.	angel
2.	thronus, -ī, m.	2.	throne

B. *Scrībe* the declensions of <u>nimbus, -ī, m.</u> (1) and <u>dōnum, -ī, n.</u> (2).

1.	nimbus	nimbī	2.	dōnum	dōna
	nimbī	nimbōrum		dōnī	dōnōrum
	nimbō	nimbīs		dōnō	dōnīs
	nimbum	nimbōs		dōnum	dōna
	nimbō	nimbīs		dōnō	dōnīs

C. *Scrībe* the present-tense conjugation of <u>sum, esse</u> two times.

1.	sum	sumus	2.	sum	sumus
	es	estis		es	estis
	est	sunt		est	sunt

II – Secunda   Nōmen: _____

D. *Variātiōnēs*. *Recita* these sentences several times, sometimes row by row and sometimes column by column. Pay close attention to the changes involved in making the adjective agree with its noun in gender, number, and case.

1. Furca est nova.   Furcae sunt novae.   (The fork is new. The forks are new.)
2. Furca est parva.   Furcae sunt parvae.   (The fork is small. The forks are small.)
3. Calamus est novus.   Calamī sunt novī.   (The pen is new. The pens are new.)
4. Calamus est parvus.   Calamī sunt parvī.   (The pen is small. The pens are small.)
5. Speculum est novum.   Specula sunt nova.   (The mirror is new. The mirrors are new.)
6. Speculum est parvum.   Specula sunt parva.   (The mirror is small. The mirrors are small.)
7. Nauta est bonus.   Nautae sunt bonī.   (The sailor is good. The sailors are good.)
8. Nauta bonus nāvigat.   Nautae bonī nāvigant.   (A good sailor sails. Good sailors sail.)

E. Translate these sentences (from Latin to English or from English to Latin).

1. Mūrus est altus.   *The wall is high.*
2. Oppidum est tūtum.   *The town is safe.*
3. Nimbī sunt magnī.   *The clouds are great.*
4. Nāsus meus est angustus.   *My nose is narrow.*
5. Multa verba sunt antīqua.   *Many words are old.*
6. The best gifts are small.   *Dōna optima sunt parva.*
7. Prīma mēnsa est magna.   *The first table is large.*
8. Prīma mēnsa magna est.   *The first table is large.*
9. Joy is a gift.   *Gaudium est donum.*
10. Many angels are singing.   *Multī angelī cantant.*
11. My sons are praying.   *Fīliī meī orant.*

F. Fill in the blanks.

1. Nouns with a nominative ending in __-us__ and __-er__ are 2nd-declension masculine nouns.

2. Nouns with a nominative ending in ____-um____ are 2nd-declension neuter nouns.

3. An adjective must agree with the noun it modifies in ____case____, ____number____, and ____gender____.

II – Secunda   Nōmen:

G. **Translate these Latin sentences (from Latin to English or from English to Latin).**

1. Amīcī sumus.   *We are friends.*

2. Tūta es.   *You are safe.*

3. Bonī estis.   *You all are good.*

4. I am small.   *[Ego] sum parvus/a.*

5. We are holy.   *[Nōs] sanctī/ae sumus.*

6. Your kingdom is wide. *Rēgnum tuum est lātum.*

Ex Scriptūrīs (from the Bible):

7. Dominus rēgnat. (Ps. 97:1, alt.)   *The Lord reigns.*

8. Caelum thronus meus est. (Is. 66:1, alt.) *Heaven is my throne.*

9. Rēgnat Deus tuus. (Is. 52:7, alt.)   *Your God reigns.*

10. Ego sum Dominus Deus tuus. (Ex. 20:5)   *I am the Lord your God.*

H. *Scrībe* the declensions of <u>annus, -ī, m.</u> (1) and <u>signum, -ī, n.</u> (2).

1.	*annus*	*annī*	2.	*signum*	*signa*
	annī	*annōrum*		*signī*	*signōrum*
	annō	*annīs*		*signō*	*signīs*
	annum	*annōs*		*signum*	*signa*
	annō	*annīs*		*signō*	*signīs*

I. **Translate these *verba* and phrases.**

1. secunda lectiō   *second lesson*   2. ex Scriptūrīs   *from the scriptures*

3. Ubi habitās?   *Where do you live?*

4. prīma   *first*   5. variātiōnēs   *variations*

II – Secunda   Nōmen:

J. Crossword Puzzle. All adjectives are in the nominative case, but watch carefully for gender and number. Unscramble the shaded letters to spell a two-word Latin sentence and its two-word English translation, an important name for God.

¹B	O	N	²A	E		³P	⁴A	R	V	A
E			N				N			
L			T		⁵M	A	G	N	A	E
⁶L	A	T	I		A		U			
U			Q		L		S			
⁷S	E	C	U	N	D	A	⁸T	O	⁹T	I
			U				U		U	
			¹⁰M	U	L	¹¹T	U	S	T	
						U			U	
						¹²A	L	T	U	M

RECTĒ
1. good (f. pl.)
3. small (f. sing.)
5. great (f. pl.)
6. wide (m. pl.)
7. second (n. pl.)
8. whole (m. pl.)
10. much (m. sing.)
12. (n. sing.)

DEORSUM
1. pretty (m. sing.)
2. ancient (n. sing.)
4. narrow (m. sing.)
5. bad (f. sing.)
9. safe (n. sing.)
11. your (n. pl.)

Hidden sentences:
  Latin: E G O   S U M.   English: I   A M.

K. Historia. Review the history and fill in the blanks.

1. What are the dates of the 2ⁿᵈ Punic War? _The 2ⁿᵈ Punic War lasted from 218-202 BC._

2. What Carthaginian general attacks Italy? _Hannibal_

3. What special feature does his army have? _Hannibal's army had elephants._

4. What is the name of Rome's first strategy in this war? _a Fabian policy_

5. In what battle do the Romans suffer great losses?
   The Romans suffered a terrible defeat at Cannae, where they lost 70,00 soldiers.

6. What Roman general leads an army to Africa?
   Scipio Africanus led an army to Africa to draw Hannibal away from Italy.

III – Tertia   Nōmen:

III – Tertia lectiō (3 – Third lesson)   DIRECT OBJECTS

I. Dictum

ē plūribus ūnum   _out of many, one_

II. Colloquium   *Latīnē*   *Anglicē*

Minister:	Salvē. Possumne tibi ministrāre?	Hello. Can I help you?
Marcus:	Velim mālum.	I'd like an apple.

III. Verba nova

Latīnē	*Anglicē*	*Scrībe tōtum verbum Latīnum.*	*Dērīvātī*
argentum, -ī, n.	silver	argentum, -ī, n.	Argentina
aurum, -ī, n.	gold	aurum, -ī, n.	Au
mālum, -ī, n.	apple	mālum, -ī, n.	
sapientia, -ae, f.	wisdom	sapientia, -ae, f.	insipid
dō, dare, dedī, datum	to give		data
dō	dare	dedī	datum
laudō, laudāre, laudāvī, laudātum	to praise		laud, laudible
laudō	laudāre	laudāvī	laudātum
habeō, habēre, habuī, habitum	to have, to possess		habit
habeō	habēre	habuī	habitum
videō, vidēre, vīdī, vīsum	to see		video
video	vidēre	vīdī	visum

IV. Verba renovanda – 2nd Conjugation

doceō, docēre	to teach	moveō, movēre	to move	timeō, timēre	to fear, be afraid
doleō, dolēre	to ache	pateō, patēre	to be open	valeō, valēre	to be strong
fleō, flēre	to weep, to cry	placeō, placēre	to please		
gaudeō, gaudēre	to rejoice	rīdeō, rīdēre	to laugh	**Other**	
lūceō, lūcēre	to shine	salveō, salvēre	to be well	et	and
maneō, manēre	to stay, to remain	sedeō, sedēre	to sit	nōn	not
misereō, miserēre	to be sorry	sileō, silēre	to be silent	spīritus, -ūs, m.	spirit

III – Tertia   Nōmen:

IV. Grammatica

Here is the form you learned in Book I for present tense of 2nd-conjugation verbs:

	Singular	Plural	Personal Endings Singular	Plural
1st person	maneō	manēmus	-ō	-mus
2nd person	manēs	manētis	-s	-tis
3rd person	manet	manent	-t	-nt

Second-conjugation verbs are recognizable because the infinitive ends in *-ēre*. To find the stem of a 2nd conjugation verb, simply drop the *–re* of the infinitive. (E.g., the stem of *maneō, manēre* is *manē-*.) To conjugate the verb, add *all* the personal endings to the stem.

Here is a new form to learn. It is for the Latin pronoun *you*:

	Singular	Plural	Translation	
nominative	tū	vōs	you	you all
genitive	tuī	vestrī	of you	of you all
dative	tibi	vōbīs	to/for you	to/for you all
accusative	tē	vōs	you	you all
ablative	tē	vōbīs	by/with/from you	b/w/f you all

Grammatica Nova

Until now, we have used only the nominative case in sentences, but now we will learn to use the other cases. Nominative case indicates the subject of a sentence. It reveals who or what the sentence is about, and may indicate who or what is doing the action of the verb. But there are other uses for nouns. For example, in Latin, the accusative case indicates the direct object of an action verb. A direct object receives the action of the verb. Consider this sentence:

"Mary sees the horse."

What is the verb in the sentence above? __sees__. Who or what is doing the action? __Mary__. Therefore, __Mary__ is the subject of the sentence. Who or what is being seen? __horse__. Therefore, __horse__ is the direct object of the sentence.

In English, the use of a noun is often indicated by word order: "The horse sees Mary" means something quite different from "Mary sees the horse"! Cases, rather than order, indicate the use of a noun in Latin. For instance,

*Maria **equum** videt.*
*Videt Maria **equum**.*   All mean the same thing: "Mary sees the **horse**."
***Equum** videt Maria.*

Word order in Latin can change a lot, but the *usual* order is **subject – direct object – adverb – verb**.

III – Tertia   Nōmen: _____

V. Historia (*Famous Men of Rome,* Chapter XV, Parts III and IV)

The Romans under Scipio defeat the Carthaginian army under Hasdrubal Gisco and invade Africa. Carthage calls Hannibal back from Italy, but at the battle of Zama, even the great Hannibal suffers defeat at the hands of Scipio, who is given the title "Africanus."

VI. Dēlēgāta

A. *Scrībe* the new Latin *verba* and their meanings.

	Latīnē		*Anglicē*
1.	argentum, -ī, n.	1.	silver
2.	aurum, -ī, n.	2.	gold
3.	mālum, -ī, n.	3.	apple
4.	sapientia, -ae, f.	4.	wisdom
5.	dō, dare, dedī, datum	5.	to give
6.	laudō, laudāre, laudāvī, laudātum	6.	to praise
7.	habeō, habēre, habuī, habitum	7.	to have, to possess
8.	video, vidēre, vīdī, vīsum	8.	to see

B. *Variātiōnēs.* *Recita* these sentence patterns several times. Pay close attention to the form used for the direct object of the sentence. Hint: The accusative case always ends in –*m,* just as in *hi<u>m</u>* and the<u>m</u> in English. *Recitā* the whole Latin line, including the nominative form before the sentence.

1. Pecūnia.   Maria pecūniam videt.   (Money. Mary sees the money.)
2. Stella.   Maria stellam videt.   (Star. Mary sees the star.)
3. Gladius.   Maria gladium videt.   (Sword. Mary sees the sword.)
4. Nimbus.   Maria nimbum videt.   (Cloud. Mary sees the cloud.)
5. Aurum.   Maria aurum videt.   (Gold. Mary sees the gold.)
6. Signum.   Maria signum videt.   (Sign. Mary sees the sign.)
7. Magna herba.   Maria magnam herbam videt.   (Large plant. Mary sees the large plant.)
8. Agnus bellus.   Maria agnum bellum videt.   (Pretty lamb. Mary sees the pretty lamb.)
9. Dōnum tuum.   Maria dōnum tuum videt.   (Your gift. Mary sees your gift.)

III – Tertia   Nōmen: _____

C. Translate these sentences.

1. Maria culīnam videt.   _Mary sees the kitchen._
2. Nautae terram vident.   _The sailor sees land._
3. Agricola porcum videt.   _The farmer sees the pig._
4. Puer puellam amat.   _The boy loves the girl._
5. Puella puerum nōn amat.   _The girl does not love the boy._
6. Deus mē amat.   _God loves me._
7. Magister librum habet.   _The teacher has a book._
8. Servus pōculum habet.   _The servant has a cup._
9. Gallia silvam habet.   _Gaul has a forest._
10. Rēgīna tē laudat.   _The queen praises you._
11. Puellae Deum laudant.   _The girls praise God._
12. Deum laudāmus.   _We praise God._
13. Magister dōnum dat.   _The teacher gives a gift._

D. Fill in the blanks.

1. A direct object tells who or what ___receives___ the ___action___ of the ___verb___.
2. In Latin, the ___accusative___ case is used for direct objects.
3. The usual word order in a Latin sentence is ___S___ - ___DO___ - ___adv.___ - ___V___.
4. The subject of 1st- and 2nd-person verbs is *always* the ___pronoun___ built into them.
5. All Latin sentences with subject nouns *must* have ___3rd___ - person verbs.
6. Accusative case endings are: 1st declension: ___-am___ (S) ___-ās___ (P)

   2nd declension (M):   ___-um___ (S) ___-ōs___ (P)

   2nd declension (N):   ___-um___ (S) ___-a___ (P)

III – Tertia   Nōmen:

E. Translate these Latin sentences.

1. Maria magnum mālum videt.   _Mary sees a big apple._
2. Tōta ecclēsia Deum laudat.   _The whole church praises God._
3. Tē multī magistrī laudant.   _Many teachers praise you._
4. Tē laudant multī magistrī.   _Many teachers praise you._
5. Multī magistrī tē laudant.   _Many teachers praise you._
6. Rēgīna multum argentum habet.   _The queen has much silver._
7. Agricola parvam mēnsam habet.   _The farmer has a small table._

Ex Scriptūrīs:

8. Fīlius meus es tū. (Ps. 2:7)   _you are my son._
9. Dominus dat sapientiam. (Pv. 2:6)   _The Lord gives wisdom._
10. Spīritus vītam dat. (II Cor. 3:6) _The spirit gives life._
11. Argentum et aurum nōn habeō.   _I do not have silver and gold._
    (Acts 3:6)

F. Conjugate fleō, flēre (1) and moveō, movēre (2) in present tense.

1.	_fleō_	_flēmus_	2.	_moveō_	_movēmus_
	flēs	_flētis_		_movēs_	_movētis_
	flet	_flent_		_movet_	_movent_

G. Derivati. Complete each sentence with an English *verbum* chosen from the following *verba* The italicized *verbum* in the sentence should help you think of the Latin root.

applause   data   vision   argentine

1. I have excellent ___vision___ ; I can *see* very well. Latin root: ___vidēo, vidēre___

2. ___Data___ are the *given* facts about something. Latin root: ___dō, dare___

3. The ___argentine___ color of the relic gave it a *silvery* hue. Latin root: ___argentum, -ī, n.___

III – Tertia   Nōmen: _____

4. The audience showed great *praise* with loud ___applause___. Latin root: ___laudō, laudāre___

H. Crossword Puzzle. Be sure to use the correct ending for the grammar indicated. Unscramble the shaded letters to find some good news (*Latīnē*).

RECTĒ
1. silver (acc. s.)
4. you (s.) laugh
6. chair (acc. s.)
8. apple (acc. s.)
11. I see
13. me (acc.)
15. wisdom (acc. s.)
17. and
19. land (acc. s.)

DEORSUM
1. gold (acc. s.)
2. nose (acc. s.)
3. bear (acc. s.)
5. we ache
7. you (pl.) praise
9. I give
10. son (acc. s.)
12. she has
14. you (s.) love
16. not
18. you (acc. s.)

Hidden message: D E U S   T E   A M A T.

I. Historia. Review the history and fill in the blanks.

1. What general first defends Carthage against Scipio? ___Hasdrubal Gisco___

2. In what battle does Scipio defeat Hannibal? ___The Battle of Zama___

3. What title is given to Scipio after his victory? ___He is called Africanus___

IV – Quarta   Nōmen:

IV – Quarta lectiō (4 – Fourth lesson)   MORE DIRECT OBJECTS

I. Dictum

    Carthāgō dēlenda est!   *Carthage must be destroyed!*
    — Cato the Censor

II. Colloquium   *Latīnē*   *Anglicē*

Claudia:	Velīsne lūdum facere?	Would you like to play a game?
Marcus:	Certē volō lūdum facere!	Sure, I want to play a game!

N.B.: *-ne* is a particle added to the end of the first word of a sentence. It asks a "yes or no" question.

III. Verba nova

Latīnē	*Anglicē*	*Scrībe tōtum verbum Latīnum.*	*Dērīvātī*
abacus, -ī, m.	gameboard	abacus, -ī, m.	abacus
ālea, -ae, f.	(game) die	ālea, -ae, f.	
calculus, -ī, m.	stone, game piece	calculus, -ī, m.	calculate
dextera, -ae, f.	right hand	dextera, -ae, f.	dexterous
lūdus, -ī, m.	game, school	lūdus, -ī, m.	ludicrous
spatium, -ī, n.	space	spatium, -ī, n.	spatious
teneō, tenēre, tenuī, tentum to hold			tentative
teneō	tenēre	tenuī	tentum

Verba renovanda – Numbers

Latine	**Anglice**				
		octō	eight	septendecim	seventeen
		novem	nine	duodēvīgintī	eighteen
ūnus	one	decem	ten	ūndēvīgintī	nineteen
duo	two	ūndecim	eleven	vīgintī	twenty
trēs	three	duodecim	twelve	vīgintī ūnus	twenty-one
quattuor	four	tredecim	thirteen	vīgintī duo	twenty-two (etc.)
quīnque	five	quattuordecim	fourteen	centum	one hundred
sex	six	quīndecim	fifteen	mīlle	one thousand
septem	seven	sēdecim	sixteen		

IV – Quarta   Nōmen:

IV. Grammatica

Here are the personal endings for future tense you learned in Book I.

                              Singular   Plural

1ˢᵗ person ___I will___   -bō   -bimus   ___We will___

2ⁿᵈ person ___You will___   -bis   -bitis   ___You all will___

3ʳᵈ person ___He, she, it will___ -bit   -bunt   ___They will___

To conjugate 1ˢᵗ- and 2ⁿᵈ-conjugation verbs in future tense, add the appropriate ending to the stem of the verb. Here are the forms for *amō, amāre* and *maneō, manēre* in future tense.

amābō	amābimus
amābis	amābitis
amābit	amābunt

manēbō	manēbimus
manēbis	manēbitis
manēbit	manēbunt

Here is the present tense of *possum, posse* to review.

                              Singular   Plural

1ˢᵗ person ___I am able.___   possum   possumus   ___We are able.___

2ⁿᵈ person ___You are able.___   potes   potestis   ___You all are able.___

3ʳᵈ person ___He, she, it is able.___ potest   possunt   ___They are able.___

Remember that a present-tense Latin verb can usually be translated three ways. Besides the *simple* present, there is the *progressive* (using the helping verbs *is, am,* or *are* and a form of the verb ending in *–ing*) and the *emphatic* (using the helping verbs verbs *does* or *do*).

Ursa mē terret.	The bear frightens me.	(simple)
	The bear is frightening me.	(progressive)
	The bear does frighten me.	(emphatic)
Lūdōs spectō.	I watch games.	(simple)
	I am watching games.	(progressive)
	I do watch games.	(emphatic)

Grammatica Nova

In this lesson, we'll use plural nouns as direct objects. Watch for *–ās* (1ˢᵗ declension), *-ōs* (2ⁿᵈ-declension masculine), and *–a* (2ⁿᵈ-declension neuter) at the end of these plural direct objects.

IV – Quarta   Nōmen:

V. Historia (*Famous Men of Rome,* Chapter XVI)

Plebeian farmers return after decades of war to farms ruined by neglect. The patricians, on the other hand, become richer and more decadent. Marcus Porcius Cato, the Censor, taxes luxuries to stop the moral decline, and he urges Rome to utterly destroy Carthage, which happens at the end of the third Punic War, in 146 BC.

VI. Dēlēgāta

A. *Scrībe* the new Latin *verba* and their meanings.

	Latīnē		*Anglicē*
1.	abacus, -ī, m.	1.	gameboard
2.	ālea, -ae, f.	2.	(game) die
3.	calculus, -ī, m.	3.	game piece, stone
4.	dextera, -ae, f.	4.	right hand
5.	lūdus, -ī, m.	5.	game, school
6.	spatium, -ī, n.	6.	space
7.	teneō, tenēre, tenuī, tentum	7.	to hold

B. *Variātiōnēs.* *Recitā* these sentence patterns several times. Pay close attention to the form used for the direct object of the sentence. Be sure to read the whole Latin line aloud, including the nominative form before the sentence.

1. Patella.   Marcus patellās tenet.   (Plate. Mark holds the plates.)
2. Ālea.   Marcus āleās tenet.   (Die. Mark holds the dice.)
3. Lūdus.   Marcus lūdōs tenet.   (Game. Mark holds the games.)
4. Calculus.   Marcus calculōs tenet.   (Stone. Mark holds the stones.)
5. Dōnum.   Marcus dōna tenet.   (Gift. Mark holds the gifts.)
6. Pōculum.   Marcus pōcula tenet.   (Cup. Mark holds the cups.)
7. Parva furca. Marcus parvās furcās tenet.   (Small fork. Mark holds the small forks.)
8. Stilus bonus. Marcus stilōs bonōs tenet.   (Good pencil. Mark holds the good pencils.)
9. Mālum bellum. Marcus māla bella tenet.   (Pretty apple. Mark holds the pretty apples.)

C. Translate these sentences (from Latin to English or English to Latin).

1. Maria lūdōs habet.   *Mary has games.*

2. Puellae lūdum habent.   *The girls have a game.*

IV – Quarta   Nōmen:

3. Marcus calculum movet.   *Marcus moves the game piece.*

4. Dextera tua āleās tenet.   *Your right hand holds the dice.*

5. Puerī abacōs movent.   *The boys move the game boards.*

6. Deus vōs amat.   *God loves you.*

7. Nautae tē vident.   *The sailors see you.*

8. Nautae nōs vident.   *The sailors see us.*

9. Servants are moving mirrors.   *Servī specula movent.*

10. The queen praises you all.   *Rēgīna vōs laudat.*

11. I see ramparts.   *Valla videō.*

12. You all see bears.   *Ursās vidētis.*

13. The teacher is giving rewards.   *Magistra praemia dat.*

D. Fill in the blanks.

1. *Scrībe* the accusative case endings for 1st- and 2nd-declension nouns.

    1st declension: *-am* (S)   *-ās* (P)

    2nd declension (M):   *-um* (S)   *-ōs* (P)

    2nd declension (N):   *-um* (S)   *-a* (P)

E. Translate these Latin sentences.

1. Iūlia quattuor lūdōs habet.   *Julia has four games.*

2. Abacus vīgintī spatia habet.   *The game board has twenty spaces.*

3. Magistrī nōs docēbunt.   *The teachers will teach us.*

4. Rēgīnās bonās laudābō.   *I will praise good queens.*

5. Nautās bonōs vidēbis.   *You will see the good sailors.*

6. Calculus meus calculum tuum superābit.   *My game piece will conquer your game piece.*

IV – Quarta   Nōmen:

7. Multa praemia dabimus. *We will give many prizes.*

Ex Scriptūrīs:

8. Dextera tua mē tenēbit. (Ps. 139:10, alt.) *Your right hand will hold me.*

9. Angelōs iūdicābimus. (I Cor. 6:3, alt.) *We will judge angels.*

F. Conjugate <u>teneō, tenēre</u> (1) and <u>laudō, laudāre</u> (2) in future tense.

1. *tenēbō*   *tenēbimus*   2. *laudābō*   *laudābimus*

   tenēbis   *tenēbitis*   *laudābis*   *laudābitis*

   tenēbit   *tenēbunt*   *laudābit*   *laudābunt*

G. Translate these *verba* and phrases.

1. quarta   *fourth*   2. second   *secundus, -a, -um*

3. first   *prīmus, -a, um* 4. variātiōnēs *variations*

5. Carthāgō dēlenda est!   *Carthage must be destroyed!*

6. How was the summer?   *Quōmodō aestās erat?*

7. Velīsne lūdum facere?   *Would you like to play a game?*

8. Velīsne mālum?   *Would you like an apple?*

H. **Dērīvatī.** Complete each sentence with an English *verbum* chosen from the following *verba*. The italicized *verbum* in the sentence should help you think of the Latin root.

ludicrous   dexterity   calculate   tenacity   spatial

1. *Stones* were used to *calculate* the total. Latin root: *calculus, -ī, m.*

2. *spatial* relationships define things in *space*. Latin root: *spatium, -ī, n.*

3. The athlete's *tenacity* helped her to *hold* on in pain. Latin root: *teneō, tenēre*

4. A *ludicrous* move quickly ended the *game*. Latin root: *lūdus, -ī, m.*

5. Manual *dexterity* requires careful *hand* movement. Latin root: *dextera, -ae, f.*

IV – Quarta   Nōmen: _____

I. Crossword Puzzle. Be sure to use the correct ending for the grammar indicated.

		¹T	R	E	D	E	C	I	²M	
		E							E	
		N		³D						
		E		U		⁴V	O	⁵S		
⁶A	B	A	C	O	S			P	⁷C	
	I			D		⁸T		A	A	
	⁹M	O	V	E	B	U	N	T	L	
	U			V				I	C	
	S			I				A	U	
				G		¹⁰A			L	
		¹¹T		I		¹²L	U	D	O	S
		R		N		E			S	
	¹³D	E	X	T	E	R	A			
¹⁴N	O	S		I		¹⁵S	E	X		

RĒCTĒ
1. novem + quattuor =
4. you all (acc. pl)
6. gamboards (acc.)
9. they will move
11. games (acc.)
12. right hand (nom.)
14. us
15. sēdecim − decem =

DEORSUM
1. we will hold
2. me (acc. s)
3. trēs x sex =
5. spaces (acc.)
7. game pieces (acc.)
8. you (nom. s)
10. dice (acc.)
11. quīndecim ÷ quīnque =
13. I give

J. Historia. Review the history and fill in the blanks.

1. Why do the plebians lose their farms? _because of poverty and neglect caused by war_

2. What problem does Cato see in Roman society? _luxury and decadence_

3. About what other great enemy does Cato warn Rome repeatedly? _Carthage_

4. In what year does the third and last Punic War end? _The 3rd Punic War ends in 146 BC._

5. How long do the Punic Wars last altogether? _The 1st Punic War (264-241 BC) was 23 years long, the 2nd Punic War (218-202 BC) lasted 17 years, and the 3rd Punic War (149-146) lasted 3 years (149-146 BC). Altogether the wars span 120 years!_

V – Quīnta　　　　　　　　　　Nōmen:

V – Quīnta lectiō (5 – Fifth lesson)　　　　3rd DECLENSION

I. Dictum

Senātus Populusque Rōmānus (__S.P.Q.R.__)　__The Roman Senate and People__

II. Colloquium　　*Latīnē*　　　　　　　*Anglicē*

| Magistra: | Silentium, quaesō. Aperīte librōs ad lectiōnem quīntam. | Silence, please. Open (your) books to lesson five. |

III. Verba nova

Latīnē	*Anglicē*	*Scrībe tōtum verbum Latīnum.*	*Dērīvātī*
cāritās, cāritātis, f.	love	*caritas, cāritātis, f.*	charity
dīves, dīvitis, m./f.	rich person	*dives, dīvitis, m./f.*	
humilitās, humilitātis, f.	humility	*humilitās, humilitātis, f.*	humility
pedāle, pedālis, n. (nom. pl. – pedālia)	sock	*pedāle, pedālis, n.*	pedal
portiō, portiōnis, f.	portion, snack	*portiō, portiōnis, f.*	portion
resurrectiō, resurrectiōnis, f.	resurrection	*resurrectiō, resurrectiōnis, f.*	resurrect

Verba renovanda – 3rd declension

Latīnē	*Anglicē*
auris, auris, f.	ear
avis, avis, f.	bird
bōs, bovis, m./f.	ox, cow
Caesar, -is, m.	Caesar
canis, canis, m./f.	dog
caput, capitis, n.	head
cochleāre, cochleāris, n.	spoon
collis, collis, m.	hill
corpus, corporis, n.	body
crūs, crūris, n.	leg
crux, crucis, f.	cross
dēns, dentis, m.	tooth
fēles, fēlis, f.	cat
flūmen, flūminis, n.	river
frāter, frātris, m.	brother
homō, hominis, m.	person, human
hostis, hostis, m./f.	enemy
ignis, ignis, m.	fire
imperātor, -is, m.	commander
lacūnar, -is, n.	ceiling
legiō, legiōnis, f.	legion
lēx, lēgis, f.	law
lūx, lūcis, f.	light
māter, mātris, f.	mother
mīles, mīlitis, m.	soldier
mōns, montis, m.	mountain
mors, mortis, f.	death
nāvis, nāvis, f.	ship
nōmen, nōminis, n.	name
nox, noctis, f.	night
ōs, ōris, n.	mouth
pars, partis, f.	part
pāstor, pāstōris, m.	shepherd
pater, patris, m.	father
pax, pācis, f.	peace
pēs, pedis, m.	foot
rēx, rēgis, m.	king
serpēns, serpentis, m./f.	snake
soror, sorōris, f.	sister
tempus, temporis, n.	time
urbs, urbis, f.	city
vēritās, vēritātis, f.	truth
virtūs, virtūtis, f.	courage, virtue
vōx, vōcis, f.	voice

V – Quīnta   Nōmen:

IV. Grammatica

Here are the forms for 3rd-declension nouns from Book I. The first two are an example of a noun declension and the case endings for most masculine and feminine nouns of 3rd declension.

	Singular	Plural	Singular	Plural
nominative	pater	patrēs	(varies)	-ēs
genitive	patris	patrum	-is	-um
dative	patrī	patribus	-ī	-ibus
accusative	patrem	patrēs	-em	-ēs
ablative	patre	patribus	-e	-ibus

And here is an example of a neuter of 3rd declension noun and its case endings.

	Singular	Plural	Singular	Plural
nominative	flūmen	flūmina	(varies)	-a
genitive	flūminis	flūminum	-is	-um
dative	flūminī	flūminibus	-ī	-ibus
accusative	flūmen	flūmina	(varies)	-a
ablative	flūmine	flūminibus	-e	-ibus

Here is a model declension and case endings for masculine and faminine *i*-stem nouns of 3rd declension. These nouns have either (1) a nominative and genitive singular of two syllables (e.g., *fēles, fēlis, f.*) or they have (2) stems ending with two consonants (e.g., *pars, part-*).

	Singular	Plural	Singular	Plural
nominative	fēles	fēlēs	(varies)	-ēs
genitive	fēlis	fēlium	-is	-ium
dative	fēlī	fēlibus	-ī	-ibus
accusative	fēlem	fēlēs	-em	-īs
ablative	fēle	fēlibus	-e	-ibus

V – Quīnta   Nōmen: _____

V. Historia (*Famous Men of Rome,* Chapter XVII)

   Cornelia, daughter of Scipio Africanus, has two sons, Tiberius Gracchus and Caius Gracchus, whom she calls her jewels. In 133 BC, Tiberius Gracchus is elected tribune, but jealous nobles kill him during a riot. In 123 BC, Caius Gracchus is elected tribune, but he has himself killed to avoid a second riot.

VI. Dēlēgāta

A. *Scrībe* the new Latin *verba* and their meanings.

	Latīnē		*Anglicē*
1.	caritas, cāritātis, f.	1.	love
2.	dīves, dīvitis, m./f.	2.	rich person
3.	humilitās, humilitātis, f.	3.	humility
4.	pedāle, pedālis, n.	4.	sock
5.	portiō, portiōnis, f.	5.	snack, portion
6.	resurrectiō, resurrectiōnis, f.	6.	resurrection

B. *Variātiōnēs.* *Recitā* these sentence patterns several times. Pay close attention to the form used for the direct object of the sentence. Be sure to read the whole line aloud, including the nominative form before the sentence.

   1. Ego.   Deus mē amat.   (I. God loves me.)
   2. Nōs.   Deus nōs amat.   (We. God loves us.)
   3. Tū.   Deus tē amat.   (You. God loves you.)
   4. Vōs.   Deus vōs amat.   (You all. God loves you all.)

C. Translate these sentences (from Latin to English or from English to Latin).

1. Avis volat.   The bird flies.
2. Avēs volant.   The birds fly.
3. Ōra silent.   The mouths are silent.
4. Mīlitēs hostīs vident.   The soldiers see the enemies.
5. Pastor agnōs videt.   The shepherd sees the lambs.

V – Quīnta   Nōmen: _____

6. Mōns altus est.   _The mountain is high._

7. Lacūnar est altum.   _The ceiling is high._

8. Large cities are safe.   _Urbēs magnae sunt tūtae._

9. Death is an enemy.   _Mors est hostis._

10. My father is king.   _Pater meus est rēx._

11. I move chairs.   _Sellās moveō._

12. We see stars.   _Stellās vidēmus._

13. My teacher is giving gifts. _Magistra mea dōna dat._

D. Fill in the blanks.

1. What are the accusative endings for 3rd-declension nouns?

   Masculine or feminine: sing.: __-em__   pl.: __-ēs__

   Neuter: sing.: _varies_ pl.: __-a__

E. Translate these sentences (from Latin to English or from English to Latin).

1. Humilitās est virtus.   _Humility is a virtue._

2. Dīves frātrem habet.   _The rich man has a brother._

3. Octō pedālia teneō.   _I hold eight socks._

4. Canis serpentēs videt.   _The dog sees the snakes._

5. My sister has a pretty voice. _Soror mea vōcem bellam habet._

6. The sailor will sail a ship. _Nauta nāvem nāvigābit._

7. A good man loves truth.   _Homō bonus virtūtem amat._

Ex Scriptūrīs:

8. Ego sum resurrectiō et vīta. (Jn. 11:25)   _I am the resurrection and the life._

9. Lingua ignis est. (James 3:6)   _The tongue is a fire._

V – Quīnta   Nōmen: _____

10. Deus lūx est. (I Jn. 1:5) _____ *God is light* _____

11. Deus cāritas est. (I Jn. 4:8) _____ *God is love.* _____

12. Cāritās nōn cōgitat malum. (I Cor. 13:5) _____ *Love does not think evil.* _____

F. Decline lēx, lēgis, f. (1), caput, capitis, n. (2), fēles, fēlis, m./f (3), and ōs, ōris, n. (4)

1.	lēx	lēgēs	2.	fēles	fēlēs
	lēgis	lēgum		fēlis	fēlium
	lēgī	lēgibus		fēlī	fēlibus
	lēgem	lēgēs		fēlem	fēlīs
	lēge	lēgibus		fēle	fēlibus
3.	caput	capita	4.	ōs	ōra
	capitis	capitum		ōris	ōrum
	capitī	captibus		ōrī	ōribus
	caput	capita		ōs	ōra
	capite	capitibus		ōre	ōribus

G. Translate these *verba* and phrases.

1. quīnta _____ *fifth* _____   2. fourth _____ *quartus, -a, -um* _____

3. Senātus Populusque Rōmānus _____ *The Roman Senate and People* _____

4. Hannibal is at the gates! _____ *Hannibal ad portās!* _____

5. Where do you live? _____ *Ubi habitās?* _____

H. Dērīvātī. Complete each sentence with an English *verbum* chosen from the following *verba*. The italicized *verbum* in the sentence should help you think of the Latin root.

proportionate   humiliation   charity

1. *Humility* is not the same as _____*humiliation*_____. Latin root: _____*humilitās, humilitātis, f.*_____

2. _____*charity*_____ is a sign of *love* in a Christian. Latin root: _____*caritas, cāritātis, f.*_____

V – Quīnta Nōmen: _____

3. The meal *portions* were ___*proportionate*___ to his size. Latin root: ___*portiō, portiōnis, f.*___

I. Crossword Puzzle. Be sure to use the correct ending for the grammar indicated. Unscramble the shaded letters to find the name of a Roman *dīves*: _____*CORNELIA*_____

```
 ¹C  O  ²R  P  ³O  R  A
 A      E      R         ⁴N      ⁵P
 R      S      A         ⁶N  O  M  E  N
 I      U                X        D
 T      R         ⁷P              A
 A      R         A      ⁸F       L
 T      E         ⁹C  O  L  L  E  S
 E      C         E      U
¹⁰M  A  T  R  E  M       M    ¹¹P
        I                I       E
       ¹²P  O  R  T  I  O  N  E  S
        N                A
        E
       ¹³H  U  M  I  L  I  T  A  T  E  M
```

RECTĒ
1. bodies (acc. pl)
6. name (acc.)
9. hills (nom.)
10. mother (acc.s)
12. snacks (acc.)
13. humility (acc.)

DEORSUM
1. love (acc.)
2. resurrection (acc.s)
3. mouths (nom.)
4. night (nom.)
5. sock (nom.)
7. peace (acc.)
8. rivers (nom.)
11. foot (nom.)

J. Historia. Review the history story and fill in the blanks.

1. Who is Cornelia's father? ___*Scipio Africanus was Cornelia's father.*___

2. What are Cornelia's jewels? ___*Cornelia's jewels were her sons, Tiberius and Caius.*___

3. What power did Roman tribunes have? ___*Roman tribunes had "veto" power.*___

4. If the Gracchi both died so young, why do you think they are still remembered?

VI – Sexta lectiō (6 – Sixth lesson) ADVERBS and INFINITIVES

I. Dictum

sine quā nōn — *essential ingredient (lit. without which not)*

II. Colloquium

	Latīnē	*Anglicē*
Aemīlia:	Quid amās facere?	What do you like to do?
Publius:	Lūdōs facere amō.	I like to play games.

III. Verba nova

Latīnē	*Anglicē*	*Scrībe tōtum verbum Latīnum.*	*Dērīvātī*
dīgnus, -a, -um	worthy	dīgnus, -a, -um	dignity
faba, -ae, f.	bean	faba, -ae, f.	
holus, holeris, n.	vegetable	holus, holeris, n.	
nummus, -ī, m.	coin	nummus, -ī, m.	numismatist
pōmum, -ī, n.	fruit	pōmum, -ī, n.	
spectāculum, -ī, n.	sight, show	spectāculum, -ī, n.	spectacle
spectō, spectāre, spectāvī, spectātum	to look at, to watch		inspect
	spectō	spectāre	spectāvī	spectātum
terreō, terrēre, terruī, territum	to frighten		terrify
	terreō	terrēre	terruī	territum

1. Label each *verbum* as noun (N), verb (V), or adjective (Adj) to its left (in the margin).

2. Which nouns are from 1st declension? Which are from 2nd? Which are from 3rd?

3. Which verb is from 1st conjugation? Which is from 2nd?

Verba renovanda – Adverbs

Latīnē	*Anglicē*						
bene	well	male	badly	nunc	now		
hīc	here	multum	a lot	parum	a little		
ibi	there	nōn	not	saepe	often		
		numquam	never	semper	always		

VI – Sexta   Nōmen: _____

IV. Grammatica

An adverb is a word that modifies a __verb__, an __adjective__, or another __adverb__. An adverb is normally placed before the word it modifies. Best of all, because adverbs never change their endings, they cannot be __declined__ or __conjugated__.

Spectācula numquam spectō.	I never watch shows.
Spectācula saepe spectō.	I often watch shows.

Here is a new form to learn – It is the Latin demonstrative pronoun that means *he, she, it, they*. Memorize this paradigm horizontally rather than vertically. (NB: b/w/f = by/with/from)

singular

	is (he)	ea (she)	id (it)		Translation	
nominative	is	ea	id	he	she	it
genitive	eius	eius	eius	of him/his	of her/her	of it/its
dative	eī	eī	eī	to/for him	to/for her	to/for it
accusative	eum	eam	id	him	her/her	it
ablative	eō	eā	eō	b/w/f him	b/w/f her	b/w/f it

plural

					Translation	
nominative	eī	eae	ea	they	they	they
genitive	eōrum	eārum	eōrum	of them/their	of them/their	of them/their
dative	eīs	eīs	eīs	to/for them	to/for them	to/for them
accusative	eōs	eās	ea	them	them	them
ablative	eīs	eīs	eīs	by/w/f them	b/w/f them	b/w/f them

The second principal part of a verb is its __infinitive__. It is translated "*to* ____." E.g., *amāre* = __to love__; *ambulāre* = __to walk__; *rīdēre* = __to laugh__. The infinitive can also be used to complete the meaning of verbs like *amō*, *possum*, and *velisne*.

Amō ambulāre.	I like to walk.
Possum ambulāre.	I am able to walk. (I can walk.)
Velisne ambulāre?	Would you like to walk?

VI – Sexta   Nōmen: _____

V. Historia (*Famous Men of Rome,* Chapter XVIII, Parts I and II)

Caius Marius defeats the Teutones and Cimbri in 102 BC. He takes the side of the plebeians in the civil debates, but the patricians dare not harm him because of his great military skill.

VI. Dēlēgāta

A. *Scrībe* the new Latin *verba* and their meanings.

	Latīnē		*Anglicē*
1.	dīgnus, -a, -um	1.	worthy
2.	faba, -ae, f.	2.	bean
3.	holus, holeris, n.	3.	vegetable
4.	nummus, -ī, m.	4.	coin
5.	pōmum, -ī, n.	5.	fruit
6.	spectāculum, -ī, n.	6.	sight, show
7.	spectō, -āre, -āvī, -ātum	7.	to look at, to watch
8.	terreō, -ēre, -uī, -itum	8.	to frighten

B. *Variātiōnēs.* *Recita* these sentence patterns several times.

1. Velīsne holera?   (Would you like vegetables?)
2. Velīsne cēnāre?   (Would you like to eat?)
3. Velīsne holera cēnāre?   (Would you like to eat vegetables?)
4. Velīsne sedēre?   (Would you like to sit?)
5. Velīsne cantāre?   (Would you like to sing?)
7. Cantāre amāmus.   (We like to sing.)
8. Cantāre possum.   (I am able to sing. / I can sing.)
9. Cantāre possumus.   (We are able to sing. / We can sing.)

C. Translate these sentences (from Latin to English or from English to Latin).

1. Faba est holus.   *A bean is a vegetable.*

2. The apple is fruit.   *Mālum est pōmum.*

3. The Lamb is worthy.   *Agnus est dīgnus.*

| VI – Sexta | Nōmen: |

4. Nummus est parvus. _The coin is small._

5. Now he is holding coins. _[Is] nummōs nunc tenet._

6. Is multōs nummōs tenet. _He is holding many coins._

7. Ea nummōs novōs dabit. _She will give new coins._

8. Eī spectāculum spectant. _They watch the show._

9. Eae spectācula spectābunt. _They will watch shows._

10. Spectācula placēbunt. _The shows will be pleasing._

11. An eagle frightens the snake. _Aquila serpentem terret._

12. The eagle is not frightening the snake. _Aquila serpentem nōn terret._

D. Fill in the blanks.

1. An adverb modifies a __verb__, an __adjective__, or another __adverb__.

2. The infinitive of a verb is its __second__ principal part; it is translated __to__ + (verb).

1. There are no *verba Latina* for __article adjectives__ or __helping verbs__.

E. Translate these sentences (from Latin to English or from English to Latin).

1. Angelī cantāre amant. _The angels love to sing._

2. Dīves cantāre nōn amat. _The rich man doesn't like to sing._

3. Velisne portiōnem cēnāre? _Would you like to eat a snack?_

4. Calculōs movēre nunc potest. _Now he is able to move the game pieces._

5. Nautae vidēre terram possunt. _The sailors are able to see the land._

6. She is looking at a coin. _[Ea] nummum spectat._

7. She is able to look at coins here. _[Ea] nummōs spectāre hīc potest._

8. He likes to look at coins. _[Is] nummōs spectāre amat._

VI – Sexta　　　　　　　　　　　　　　Nōmen:

Ex Scriptūrīs:

9. Quī (= he who) habet Fīlium habet vītam; quī nōn habet Fīlium vītam nōn habet.
　　　　　　　　　　　　　　　　　　　　　　　　(I Jn. 5:12, alt)

　　He who has the son has life; he who does not have the son does not have life.

F. Decline faba, -ae, f. (1) and holus, holeris, n. (2).

1.	faba	fabae	2.	holus	holera
	fabae	fabārum		holeris	holerum
	fabae	fabīs		holerī	holeribus
	fabam	fabās		holus	holera
	fabā	fabīs		holere	holeribus

G. Translate these *verba* and phrases.

1. sexta　　_sixth_　　　　　　2. fifth　　_quīntus, -a, -um_

3. sine quā nōn　_essential ingredient_　　4. Out of many, one　_ē plūribus ūnum_

5. Certē!　_Sure!_　　　　　　6. please　　_quaesō_

7. I would like an apple.　　_Velim mālum._

8. Quid amās facere?　　_What do you like to do?_

9. Velīsne spectāre?　　_Would you like to watch?_

10. We are not able to laugh.　_[Nōs] rīdēre nōn possumus._

11. She loves to pray.　　_Amat orāre._

H. Dērīvātī. Complete each sentence with an English *verbum* chosen from the following *verba*. The italicized *verbum* in the sentence should help you think of the Latin root.

　　　　spectacles　　spectacle　　terrified　　dignity

1. Someone with _dignity_ is *worthy* of respect. Latin root: _dīgnus, -a, -um_

2. The _spectacle_ was a *sight* to behold. Latin root: _spectāculum, -ī, n._

VI – Sexta   Nōmen:

3. ___spectacles___ are lenses through which one *looks*. Latin root: ___spectō, spectāre___

4. People don't like to be *frightened* or ___terrified___. Latin root: ___terreō, terrēre___

I. *Verbum* Search. *Verba* listed below can be found in the nominative or accusative form (singular or plural), reading forward, backward, up, down, or diagonally. Unused letters in the box spell pairs of opposites when read left to right, top to bottom.

In the grid to the right of the list, circle the letter corresponding to the form found in the word search. The circled letters in the grid will spell good news.

Opposites: ___numquam___ and ___semper___, ___hic___ and ___ibi___, ___bene___ and ___male___

H	N	A	M	O	P	O	R	T	I	O
U	E	U	M	Q	P	N	U	M	M	I
M	A	I	T	N	E	I	P	A	S	T
I	E	U	A	M	D	S	C	A	P	C
L	L	E	M	A	A	A	P	U	A	E
I	A	E	B	E	L	R	H	R	T	R
T	I	A	G	C	I	C	I	U	I	R
A	F	I	U	N	A	T	B	M	A	U
T	I	L	B	E	A	B	A	C	O	S
E	U	N	E	S	O	D	U	L	M	E
M	E	T	I	V	I	D	A	L	E	R

	nom		acc	
	s	pl	s	pl
ABACUS	R	E	L	A
ALEA	S	D	H	P
ANGELUS	D	V	M	K
AURUM	E	G	E	J
CALCULUS	P	O	R	X
CARITAS	B	N	U	Q
DIVES	A	C	S	T
FABA	D	F	Y	N
HUMILITAS	A	O	O	I
LUDUS	I	L	M	N
NUMMUS	X	T	F	R
PEDALE	E	C	E	C
POMUM	R	H	R	H
PORTIO	A	S	N	B
RESURRECTIO	N	D	E	R
SAPIENTIA	L	O	G	H
SPATIUM	D	E	D	E

Good news: ___Adverbs don't change!___

J. Historia. Review the history and fill in the blanks.

1. What tribes does Marius defeat? ___Marius defeats the Teutones and Cimbri___

2. In what year does he defeat them? ___Marius defeats them in 102 BC.___

3. Whose side does he take in the civil unrest? ___Marius sides with the Plebeians___

VII – Septima   Nōmen:

VII – Septima lectiō (7 – Seventh lesson)   THE GENITIVE

I. Dictum

id est (_i.e._)   _that is_

II. Colloquium   *Latīnē*   *Anglicē*

Lūcius:	Salvē, Claudia.	Hello, Claudia.
	Quid est tibi?	What's the matter?
Claudia:	Mē male habeō.	I feel poorly.

(For more names, see p. 174)

III. Verba

Latīnē	*Anglicē*	*Scrībe tōtum verbum Latīnum.*	*Dērīvātī*
cerasum, -ī, n.	cherry	_cerasum, -ī, n._	
clāvis, clāvis, f.	key	_clāvis, clāvis, f._	_clavicle_
fīnis, fīnis, m.	end, border	_fīnis, fīnis, m._	_finish_
infernus, -ī, m.	hell, underworld	_infernus, -ī, m._	_hell, underworld_
lampas, lampadis, f.	lamp, torch	_lampas, lampadis, f._	_lamp_
principium, -ī, n.	beginning	_principium, -ī, n._	_principle_
scientia, -ae, f.	knowledge	_scientiae, -ae, f._	_scientific_
timor, timōris, m.	fear	_timor, timōris, m._	_timorous_

1. What kind of *verba* are these? _All these verba are nouns._

2. *Scrībe* the declension (1, 2, or 3) of each *verbum* to its left.

3. How do you know the declension of each noun? _____
   The genitive singular ending (in the 2nd principle part) indicates a noun's declension.

4. We must _____memorize_____ the gender of each noun.

5. ___clāvis___ and ___fīnis___ are *i*-stem nouns of 3rd declension.

VII – Septima   Nōmen: _____

IV. Grammatica

In this *lectiō*, we'll begin using the <u>genitive case</u> as a possessive form, and in other phrases which use the preposition *of* in English.

patria rēg<u>is</u>	the country *of* the king **or** the king's country
lūdus puell<u>ae</u>	the game *of* the girl **or** the girl's game
lūdus puell<u>ārum</u>	the game *of* the girls **or** the girls' game
librī discipul<u>ōrum</u>	the books *of* the students **or** the students' books
dentēs serpent<u>is</u>	the teeth *of* the snake **or** the snake's teeth
timor De<u>ī</u>	the fear *of* God

The genitive case is the possessive form of a noun. It modifies another noun, and it usually comes *after* the word it modifies. Notice that the genitive need not agree with the noun it modifies in gender, number, case, or declension.

<u>Numbers</u> can be adjectives, too. Most numbers are not declined (They behave themselves – like adverbs!), but *ūnus, duō,* and *trēs* must be declined. Here's the form for <u>*ūnus, -a, um*</u>.

	masculine	feminine	neuter
nominative	ūnus	ūna	ūnum
genitive	ūnīus	ūnīus	ūnīus
dative	ūnī	ūnī	ūnī
accusative	ūnum	ūnam	ūnum
ablative	ūnō	ūnā	ūnō

1. What two cases have different endings from those you already know? __*gen. and dat.*__

2. Why are there no plural forms in this declension? __*The number one is singular.*__

3. Numbers express quantity and should therefore __*precede*__ the nouns they modify.

V. Historia (*Famous Men of Rome,* Chapter XVIII, Part II)

General Sulla achieves great victories during the Social War between 91-89 BC. The patricians, believing they no longer need Marius, elect Sulla to be consul in 88 BC, and send Marius into exile. While Sulla goes off to war against Mithridates, Marius returns to Rome and slaughters many nobles.

VII – Septima   Nōmen: _____

VI. Dēlēgāta

A. *Scrībe* the new Latin *verba* and their meanings.

	Latīnē		*Anglicē*
1.	cerasum, -ī, n.	1.	cherry
2.	clāvis, clāvis, f.	2.	key
3.	fīnis, fīnis, m.	3.	end, border
4.	infernus, -ī, n.	4.	hell, underworld
5.	lampas, lampadis, f.	5.	lamp, torch
6.	principium, -ī, n.	6.	beginning
7.	scientia, -ae, f.	7.	knowledge
8.	timor, timōris, m.	8.	fear

B. *Variātiōnēs*. *Recita* these sentence patterns several times.

1. Librōs puellae teneō.   (I am holding the books of the girl / the girl's books.)
2. Librōs puellārum teneō.   (I am holding the books of the girls / the girls' books.)
3. Librōs magistrī teneō.   (I am holding the books of the teacher / the teacher's books.)
4. Librōs magistrōrum teneō.   (I am holding the books of the teachers / the teachers' books.)
5. Librōs puerī teneō.   (I am holding the books of the boy / the boy's books.)
6. Librōs puerōrum teneō.   (I am holding the books of the boys / the boys' books.)
7. Librōs mīlitis teneō.   (I am holding the books of the soldier / the soldier's books.)
8. Librōs mīlitum teneō.   (I am holding the books of the soldiers / the soldiers' books.)

C. Translate these Latin sentences.

1. Ūna rēgīna sedet.   *One queen sits.*
2. Ūnus equus stat.   *One horse stands.*
3. Ūnum dōnum patet.   *One gift is open.*
4. Principium librī est bonum.   *The beginning of the book is good.*
5. Fīnis librī est malus.   *The end of the book is bad.*
6. Fīnēs patriae sunt tūtī.   *The borders of the country are safe.*

VII – Septima   **Nōmen:** _____

7. Scientia rēgis magna est. _____ *The knowledge of the king is great.*

8. Crūra sellārum sunt alta. _____ *The chairs' legs are tall.*

9. Oculī aquilae valent. _____ *The eagle's eyes are strong.*

10. Ignis infernī est aeternus. _____ *The fire of hell is eternal.*

11. Vōcēs puerōrum numquam silent. _____ *The boys' voices are never silent.*

12. Pars flūminis est angusta. _____ *Part of the river is narrow.*

13. Gladiī hostium sunt magnī. _____ *The enemies' swords are large.*

14. Nummī dīvitum sunt multī. _____ *The rich mens' coins are many.*

D. Fill in the blanks.

1. The genitive case in Latin corresponds to the _____*possessive*_____ (case) in English.

2. Genitive forms can be translated by placing the word ___*of*___ in front of the noun.

3. A noun in the genitive case usually _____*follows*_____ the noun it modifies.

1. Genitive case endings are: 1st: __*-ae*__ (S) __*-ārum*__ (P)   2nd: __*-ī*__ (S) __*-ōrum*__ (P)

   3rd: __*-is*__ (S) __*-um*__ (P)   3rd *i*-stem: __*-is*__ (S) __*-ium*__ (P).

5. The _____*accusative*_____ case is used for direct objects.

E. Translate these sentences (from Latin to English or from English to Latin).

1. Cerasum est pōmum. _____ *The cherry is a fruit.*

2. Cerasa cēnāre amō. _____ *I love to eat cherries.*

3. Ūnam lampadem habēmus. _____ *We have one lamp.*

4. Ūnam clāvem habēbimus. _____ *We will have one key.*

5. The slave will hold one coin. _____ *Servus ūnum nummum tenēbit.*

6. Mary is the mother of Christ. _____ *Maria est māter Christī.*

7. Timōrem serpentium habeō. _____ *I have a fear of snakes.*

VII – Septima   Nōmen:

8. Lūx ūnīus lampadis est magnus. ___The light of one lamp is great.___

9. I have the teacher's key. ___Ego clāvem magistrī habeō.___

10. You have the teachers' keys. ___Tū clāvīs magistrōrum habēs.___

11. Love is the end of fear. ___Cāritās est fīnis timōris.___

Ex Scriptūrīs:

12. Habeō clāvīs mortis et infernī. (Rev. 1:18) _____

___I have the keys of death and hell.___

13. Magna [est] glōria Dominī. (Ps. 138:5) ___Great is the glory of the Lord.___

14. Tū es Christus, Fīlius Deī. (Matt. 16:16) ___You are the Christ, the son of God.___

15. Timor Dominī est principium scientiae. (Prov. 1:7, alt.) _____

___The fear of the Lord is the beginning of wisdom.___

F. Decline <u>cerasum, -ī, n.</u> (1) and <u>clāvis, clāvis, f.</u> (2).

1.	cerasum	cerasa	2.	clāvis	clāvēs
	cerasī	cerasōrum		clāvis	clāvium
	cerasō	cerasīs		clāvī	clāvibus
	cerasum	cerasa		clāvem	clāvīs
	cerasō	cerasīs		clāve	clāvibus

G. Translate these *verba* and phrases.

1. septima ___seventh___   2. sixth ___sextus, -a, -um___

3. id est ___that is___   4. third ___tertius, -a, -um___

5. Carthage must be destroyed! ___Carthāgō dēlenda est!___

6. Ubi habitās? ___Where do you live?___

7. Quid est tibi? ___What is the matter with you?___

VII – Septima   Nōmen:

H. Dērīvātī. Complete each sentence with an English *verbum* chosen from the following *verba*. The italicized *verbum* in the sentence should help you think of the Latin root.

finite   principle   clavier   timidity   scientist

1. A _____principle_____ is a *beginning* assumption. Latin root: _____principium, -ī, n._____

2. _____timidity_____ and *fear* are synonyms. Latin root: _____timor, timōris, m._____

3. People are _____finite_____; they have an *end*. Latin root: _____fīnis, fīnis, m._____

4. A _____scientist_____ seeks *knowledge*. Latin root: _____scientia, -ae, f._____

5. A _____clavier_____ was an early *keyboard* instrument. Latin root: _____clāvis, clāvis, f._____

I. Alphabet Code. *Scrībe* the genitive singular of each *verba Latīna* in the spaces. A code letter is under each blank. Use the code to fill in the blanks in the shaded box.

FINIS	F	I	N	I	S		CERASUM	C	E	R	A	S	I	
	y	k	f	k	u			x	m	d	q	u	k	
TIMOR	T	I	M	O	R	I	S	INFERNUS	I	N	F	E	R	N	I
	h	k	b	g	d	k	u		k	f	y	m	d	f	k
CLAVIS	C	L	A	V	I	S		SCIENTIA	S	C	I	E	N	T	I	A	E
	x	w	q	e	k	u			u	x	k	m	f	h	k	q	m
LAMPAS	L	A	M	P	A	D	I	S	PRINCIPIUM	P	R	I	N	C	I	P	I	I
	w	q	b	z	q	j	k	u		z	d	k	f	x	k	z	k	k

Now you know how to use the P O S S E S S I V E In Latin!
                                  z g u u m u u k e m

J. Historia. Review the history story and fill in the blanks.

1. In what year is Sulla elected consul? _____Sulla is elected consul in 88 BC._____

2. Which side does he take in the civil unrest? _____He sides with the patricians._____

3. What happens while he fights Mithridates? _____Marius returns and murders many nobles._____

VIII – Octāva   Nōmen: _____

VIII – Octāva lectiō (8 – Eighth lesson)   PREPOSITIONS (+ Ac)

I. Dictum

ad nauseam   ___too long___   (lit.: ___to the point of seasickness___)

II. Colloquium   *Latīnē*   *Anglicē*

Claudia:	Multum sternuō et caput mihi dolet.	I am sneezing a lot and my head hurts.
Lūcius:	Gravēdine labōrās! Vīse medicum.	You have a cold! Go see a doctor. (See p. 174 for more illnesses)

III. Verba

Latīnē	*Anglicē*	*Scrībe tōtum verbum Latīnum.*	*Dērīvātī*
ad (+ Acc.)	to, toward, near, at	ad (+ acc.)	advance
ante (+ Acc.)	before, in front of	ante (+ acc.)	ante bellum
circum (+ Acc.)	around, about	circum (+ acc.)	circumference
per (+ Acc.)	through	per (+ acc.)	perforate
secundum (+ Acc.)	beside, according to	secundum (+ acc.)	second
super (+ Acc.)	above, over	super (+ acc.)	super man
trāns (+ Acc.)	across	trans (+ acc.)	transport
evangelium, -ī, n.	gospel	evangelium, -ī, n.	evangelist

natō, natāre, natāvī, natātum to swim

___natō___   ___natāre___   ___natāvī___   ___natātum___

1. Which *verbum* is a verb? ___natō, natāre___   Which conjugation? ___first___

2. What kind of *verbum* are most of the *verba*? ___Most of the verba are prepositions.___

VIII – Octāva   Nōmen:

IV. Grammatica

Most of the new *verba* in this *lectiō* are prepositions. A preposition is followed by a noun (the object of the preposition) and tells the relationship in space or time between that noun and another noun, verb, or adjective in the sentence.

In Latin, prepositions are very particular about the case of the nouns that follow them. All prepositions take either the accusative (Acc.) and/or the ablative (Abl.) case. In this *lectiō*, all the prepositions are followed by nouns in the accusative case. We normally say that these prepositions *take the accusative*. When we memorize prepositions and their meanings, we must also memorize the case(s) that each preposition takes.

Note that prepositions that take the accusative case don't necessarily have anything to do with direct objects. The accusative case simply has two uses.

The prepositions themselves have no endings, but their objects *must* be written in either the accusative (Acc.) or the ablative (Abl.) case, depending upon which case a preposition takes.

What case is used in the *dictum*? __accusative__   Why? __ad takes only the acc. case__

Here are the forms for *duō*:

	masculine	feminine	neuter
nominative	duo	duae	duo
genitive	duōrum	duārum	duōrum
dative	duōbus	duābus	duōbus
accusative	duōs	duās	duo
ablative	duōbus	duābus	duōbus

1. Why are there no singular forms in this declension?

2. Because numbers express __quantity__, they should *precede* the nouns they modify.

N.B.: Latin sentences usually have this order:

   S (and its modifiers) IO (and its modifiers) DO (and its modifiers) ADV and finally V!

V. Historia (*Famous Men of Rome,* Chapter XIX)

In 83 BC, Sulla returns to Rome after defeating Mithridates. He attacks Marius and his followers. He declares himself dictator and kills thousands of real and suspected enemies.

VIII – Octāva   Nōmen: _____

VI. Dēlēgāta

A. *Scrībe* the new Latin *verba* and their meanings.

        Latīnē   *Anglicē*

1. _____ad (+ Acc.)_____   1. _____to, toward, near, at_____

2. _____ante (+ Acc.)_____   2. _____before, in front of_____

3. _____circum (+ Acc.)_____   3. _____around, about_____

4. _____per (+ Acc.)_____   4. _____through_____

5. _____secundum (+ Acc.)_____   5. _____beside, according to_____

6. _____super (+ Acc.)_____   6. _____above, over, upon_____

7. _____trāns (+ Acc.)_____   7. _____across_____

8. _____evangelium, -ī, n._____   8. _____gospel_____

9. _____natō, nature, natāvī, natātum_____   9. _____to swim_____

B. *Variātiōnēs.* *Recitā* these sentence patterns several times.

1. Ad iānuam ambulābit.   (He will walk to the door.)
2. Circum iānuam ambulābit.   (He will walk around the door.)
3. Per iānuam ambulābit.   (He will walk through the door.)
4. Ante iānuam stābit.   (He will stand in front of the door.)
5. Secundum iānuam stābit.   (He will stand beside the door.)
6. Sellae ante mēnsās sunt.   (The chairs are in front of the tables.)
7. Sellae circum mēnsās sunt.   (The chairs are around the tables.)
8. Sellae secundum mēnsās sunt.   (The chairs are beside the tables.)

C. Translate these sentences.

1. Lampas secundum mēnsam est.   _The lamp is beside the table._

2. Duae lampadēs secundum mēnsam sunt.   _Two lamps are beside the table._

3. Avis per fenestram volat.   _The bird flies through the window._

4. Duae avēs per fenestram volant.   _Two birds fly through the window._

5. Ea bene natāre potest.   _She is able to swim well._

VIII – Octāva   Nōmen: _____

6. Is multum natāre amat.   *He loves to swim a lot.*

7. Is trāns flūmen natat.   *He swims across the river.*

8. Ea trāns flūmen natābit.   *She will swim across the river.*

9. Eī trāns flūmen natābunt.   *They will swim across the river.*

10. Eae trāns flūmen natābunt.   *They will swim across the river.*

11. Hostēs circum collem movent.   *The enemies move around the hill.*

12. Bōs holera ante puteum cēnat.   *The ox eats vegetables near the well.*

13. Duo hominēs ad puteum stant.   *Two men stand near the well.*

14. Mīlitēs super signum pugnant.   *The soldiers fight over the standard.*

D. Fill in the blanks.

1. The objects of Latin prepositions must be written in either the __abl.__ or the __acc.__ case.

2. The prepositions in this *lectiō* all take the _____accusative_____ case.

3. We must _____memorize_____ the case(s) each preposition takes.

4. The _____accusative_____ case is also used for direct objects.

5. Accusative case endings are: 1st: __-am__ (S) __-ās__ (P); 2nd M: __-um__ (S) __-ōs__ (P);

   2nd N: __-um__ (S); __-a__ (P); 3rd M/F: __-em__ (S) __-ēs__ (P); 3rd N: __varies__ (S) __varies__ (P).

E. *Scrībe* these English sentences *Latīnē*.

1. The king will sit upon the throne.   *Rēx super thronum sedēbit.*

2. He moves the stone through two spaces.   *Is calculum per duo spatia movēbit.*

3. Legions are standing around two hills.   *Legiōnēs circum duōs collīs stant.*

4. The teacher teaches two students.   *Magister duās discipulās docet.*

5. An angel holds two swords.   *Angelus duōs gladiōs tenet.*

VIII – Octāva   Nōmen:

6. I see the walls of two towns.   _Mūrōs duōrum oppidōrum video._

7. I recite words of two languages.   _Duārum linguārum verba recitō._

8. The queen will eat two cherries.   _Rēgina duo cerasa cēnābit._

9. The boy stands near the church.   _Puer ad ecclēsiam stat._

10. She will walk through the door.   _Ea per iānuam ambulābit._

11. He will walk to the door.   _Is ad iānuam ambulābit._

Ex Scriptūrīs:

12. Et septem lampadēs ante thronum sunt septem spīritūs Deī. (Rev. 4:5, alt., spīritūs = nom. pl.)

    And the seven lamps before the throne are the seven spirits of God.

13. Vidēmus nunc per speculum. (I Cor. 13:12, alt.)   _We see now through a mirror._

14. Deus iūdicābit hominēs secundum evangelium meum per Christum. (Rom. 2:16, alt.)

    God will judge men according to my gospel through Christ.

F. Decline **evangelium, -ī, n.** (1), and conjugate **natō, natāre** in future tense (2).

1.	evangelium	evangelia	2.	natābō	natābimus
	evangeliī	evangeliōrum		natābis	natābitis
	evangeliō	evangeliīs		natābit	natābunt
	evangelium	evangelia			
	evangeliō	evangeliīs			

G. Translate these *verba* and phrases.

1. octāva   _eighth_   2. seventh   _septimus, -a, -um_

3. ad nauseam   _too long_   4. Vīse medicum.   _Go see a doctor._

5. The Roman Senate and People   _Senātus Populusque Rōmānus_

6. Audēmus iūra nostra dēfendere.   _We dare to defend our rights._

VIII – Octāva   Nōmen: _____

7. Quid amās facere?   _____*What do you like to do?*_____

8. Lūdōs facere amō.   _____*I like to play games.*_____

H. Derivati. Complete each sentence with an English *verbum* chosen from the following *verba*. The italicized *verbum* in the sentence should help you think of the Latin root.

    translucent   superb   antebellum   natatorium   evangelist

1. An ___evangelist___ preaches the *gospel*. Latin root: ___evangelium, -ī, n.___

2. A ___natatorium___ is an indoor *swimming* pool. Latin root: ___natō, natāre___

3. ___translucent___ materials permit *light* to pass *across*. Latin root: ___trans &___

4. His ___superb___ performance was far *above* our expectations. Latin root: ___super___

5. ___ante bellum___ homes were built *before* the *war*. Latin root: ___ante & bellum___

I. *Verbum* Ladder.
If you write the *octō verba* from this lesson on the right rows, the shaded spaces, read from top to bottom, should show the *quīntum verbum* from this *lectiō*'s list: ___secundum___

above | | | | T | R | A | N | S |
across | | | | | | P | E | R |
around | | | | | C | I | R | C | U | M
before | | | N | A | T | A | B | U | N | T
gospel | | | | | | | A | N | T | E
they will swim | | | | | | | A | D
through | | | | | | | S | U | P | E | R
toward | | E | V | A | N | G | E | L | I | U | M

J. Historia. Review the history and fill in the blanks.

1. What office does Sulla take when he returns? ___He declares himself dictator of Rome.___

2. What else does he do after he returns? ___He slaughters thousands.___

IX – Nōna lectiō (9 – Ninth lesson)   THE DATIVE

I. Dictum

ante merīdiem / post merīdiem   _before noon (a.m.) / after noon (p.m.)_

II. Colloquium   *Latīnē*   *Anglicē*

Claudia:	Salvē medice.	Hello, doctor.
Medicus:	Salvē. Quid est?	Hello. What's up?
Claudia:	Ego sum aeger!	I am sick!
Medicus:	Manē in lectō trīs diēs.	Stay in bed three days.
	(aeger, aegra, aegrum – sick)	

III. Verba

Latīnē	*Anglicē*	*Scrībe tōtum verbum Latīnum.*	*Dērīvātī*
beātus, -a, -um	happy, blessed	_beātus, -a, -um_	_beatific_
cāseus, -ī, m.	cheese	_cāseus, -ī, m._	_cheese_
flōs, flōris, m.	flower	_flōs, flōris, m._	_Florida_
pānis, pānis, m.	bread	_pānis, pānis, m._	
pilleus, -ī, m.	hat	_pilleus, -ī, m._	
portō, portāre, portāvī, portātum to carry			_porter_
portō	_portāre_	_portāvī_	_portātum_
sapientia, -ae, f.	wisdom	_sapientia, -ae, f._	_homo sapiens_
studeō, studēre, studuī to be eager for, to study			_studious_
studeō	_studēre_	_studuī_	
vērus, -a, -um	true	_vērus, -a, -um_	_veritable_

1. *Scrībe* N (noun), V (verb), Adj (adjective), or P (preposition) to the left of each *verbum*.

2. Identify the declension of each noun by writing a 1, 2, or 3 next to each.

3. Why do the adjectives have three endings?   _There is one ending for each gender._

IX – Nōna   Nōmen: _____

IV. Grammatica

We begin to use the <u>dative case</u> in this *lectiō*. The dative case is usually translated with the words *to* or *for* before the noun and is used to indicate the <u>indirect object</u> of a sentence. An indirect object tells *to whom* or *for whom* an action is done.

Puer <u>puellae</u> flōrēs dat.	The boy is giving flowers to the girl.
Puella <u>puerō</u> flōrēs dat.	The girl is giving flowers to the boy.
Puer <u>sorōribus</u> flōrēs dat.	The boy is giving flowers to (his) sisters.

The indirect object *usually* comes before the direct object in a Latin sentence, but it can appear anywhere in a sentence, because in Latin, the endings indicate the function of the word in the sentence. If something besides the subject comes first in a Latin sentence, or if something besides the verb comes last, that word is emphasized.

Puer flōrēs puellīs dat.	The boy is giving flowers to the girls.
Flōrēs puer puellīs dat.	The boy is giving *flowers* to the girls.
Puellīs puer flōrēs dat.	The boy is giving flowers to the *girls*.

What case is used in the *dictum*? __acc.__   Why? __Ante and post take the accusative.__

Here's the <u>form for *trēs*</u>.

	masculine	feminine	neuter
nominative	**trēs**	**trēs**	**tria**
genitive	**trium**	**trium**	**trium**
dative	**tribus**	**tribus**	**tribus**
accusative	**trīs**	**trīs**	**tria**
ablative	**tribus**	**tribus**	**tribus**

Why are there no singular forms in this declension? __Three is always plural.__

V. Historia (*Famous Men of Rome*, Chapter XX)

In 70 BC, Cneius Pompey is elected consul, and he restores power previously taken from the citizens by Sulla. In 67, he clears the Mediterranean Sea of pirates, and in 66, he goes to Asia to defeat Mithridates and to increase the size of the Empire. After this, he retains the people's favor by funding spectacles with animals and violent fighting.

IX – Nōna   Nōmen:

VI. Dēlēgāta

A. *Scrībe* the new Latin *verba* and their meanings.

         Latīnē   *Anglicē*

1. *beātus, -a, -um* — 1. *happy, blessed*
2. *cāseus, -ī, m.* — 2. *cheese*
3. *flōs, flōris, m.* — 3. *flower*
4. *pānis, pānis, m.* — 4. *bread*
5. *pilleus, -ī, m.* — 5. *hat*
6. *portō, portāre, portāvī, portātum* — 6. *to carry*
7. *sapientia, -ae, f.* — 7. *wisdom*
8. *studeō, studēre, studuī* — 8. *to be eager for, to study*
9. *vērus, -a, -um* — 9. *true*

B. *Variātiōnēs. Recitā* these sentence patterns several times. Pay attention to the form used for the indirect object of the sentence. Be sure to read the whole Latin line aloud, including the nominative form before the sentence.

1. Puella.   Puer puellae māla dat.   (The boy is giving apples to the girl.)
2. Puellae.   Puer puellīs māla dat.   (The boy is giving apples to the girls.)
3. Magister.   Puer magistrō māla dat.   (The boy is giving apples to the teacher.)
4. Magistrī.   Puer magistrīs māla dat.   (The boy is giving apples to the teachers.)
5. Canis.   Puer canī māla dat.   (The boy is giving apples to the dog.)
6. Canēs.   Puer canibus māla dat.   (The boy is giving apples to the dogs.)

C. Translate these sentences.

1. Servus rēgīnae pānem portat.   *The servant carries bread to the queen.*

2. Servus rēgī pānem portat.   *The servant carries bread to the king.*

3. Servī dominō pānem portābunt.   *The servants will carry bread to their master.*

4. Discipulus magistrō librōs portat.   *The student carries books for the teacher.*

IX – Nōna   Nōmen:

5. Iūlia āvibus pānem dat.   *Julia gives bread to the birds.*

6. Maria tribus āvibus pānem dabit.   *Mary will give bread to three birds.*

7. Anna duābus āvibus pānem dat.   *Anna gives bread to two birds.*

8. Pater fīliō pilleum dabit.   *The father will give his son a hat.*

9. Verbum est vērum.   *The word is true.*

10. Verba Deī semper sunt vēra.   *The words of God are always true.*

11. Rēgīna beāta est.   *The queen is blessed.*

12. Agricola est beātus.   *The farmer is happy.*

13. Amō cāseum et pānem.   *I love cheese and bread.*

D. Fill in the blanks.

1. The dative case is used for the ___*indirect object*___ of a sentence.

2. The accusative case is most often used for the ___*direct object*___ in a sentence; it can also be used for the object of a ___*preposition*___.

3. The ___*nominative*___ case is used for the subject noun in a sentence.

4. The ___*genitive*___ case shows possession in Latin. It can be translated into English using the preposition ___*of*___.

5. Dative case endings: 1ˢᵗ: ___*-ae*___ (S) ___*-īs*___ (P); 2ⁿᵈ ___*-ō*___ (S) ___*-īs*___ (P); 3ʳᵈ: ___*-ī*___ (S) ___*-ibus*___ (P).

E. Translate these sentences (from Latin to English or from English to Latin).

1. Sellam per iānuam portābō.   *I will carry the chair through the door.*

2. Mīlitēs bonī aurum et argentum trāns patriam portābunt.
   The good soldiers will carry gold and silver across the country.

3. Pānis mihi placet.   *I like bread (lit. : Bread is pleasing to me).*

4. Placentne flōrēs tibi?   *Do you like flowers (lit.: Are flowers pleasing to you)?*

IX – Nōna   **Nōmen:**

5. The mother is giving a small book to her pretty daughter.

   Māter parvum librum puellae pulchrae dat.

6. The boy is giving a hat to the girl. *Puer puellae pilleum dat.*

7. The boy will give flowers to two girls. *Puer duābus puellīs flōrēs dabit.*

Ex Scriptūrīs:

8. Dabō tibi corōnam vītae. (Rev. 2:10) *I will give you a crown of life.*

9. Pater meus dat vōbīs pānem vērum. (Jn. 6:32)

   My father will give you the true bread.

10. Beātus es, Simon. Tū es Petrus et tibi dabō clāvīs regnī caelōrum. (Matt. 16:17-19)

    Blessed are you, Simon

    You are Peter and I will give you the keys of the kingdom of heaven.

F. Conjugate <u>terreō, terrēre</u> (1) and <u>portō, portāre</u> (2) in future tense.

1. *terrēbō*   *terrēbimus*   2. *portābō*   *portābimus*

   terrēbis   *terrēbitis*   *portābis*   *portābitis*

   terrēbit   *terrēbunt*   *portābit*   *portābunt*

G. Translate these *verba* and phrases.

1. nōna — *ninth*   2. eighth — *octāvus, -a, -um*

3. ante merīdiem — *before noon*   4. post merīdiem — *after noon*

5. essential ingredient — *sine quā nōn*   6. ad nauseam — *too long*

7. Velīsne lūdum facere? — *Would you like to play a game?*

8. Velīsne pānem? — *Would you like bread?*

9. Dēlenda est Carthāgō! — *Carthage must be destroyed!*

H. **Dērīvātī.** Complete each sentence with an English *verbum* chosen from the following *verba*. The italicized *verbum* in the sentence should help you think of the Latin root.

IX – Nōna   Nōmen: _____

                Beatitudes   veracity   Panera   portable   florist

1. ___*portable*___ objects can be *carried*. Latin root: ___*portō, portāre*___

2. A ___*florist*___ sells and arrange *flowers*. Latin root: ___*flōs, flōris, m.*___

3. The ___*Beatitudes*___ describe *blessed* people. Latin root: ___*beātus, -a, -um*___

4. ___*Panera*___ *Bread* is a restaurant with sandwiches. Latin root: ___*panis, panis, m.*___

5. The man's ___*veracity*___ convinced us he spoke *truth*. Latin root: ___*vērus, -a, -um*___

I. Crossword Puzzle. Be sure to use the correct form for the grammar indicated. Unscramble the shaded letters to complete the secret message.

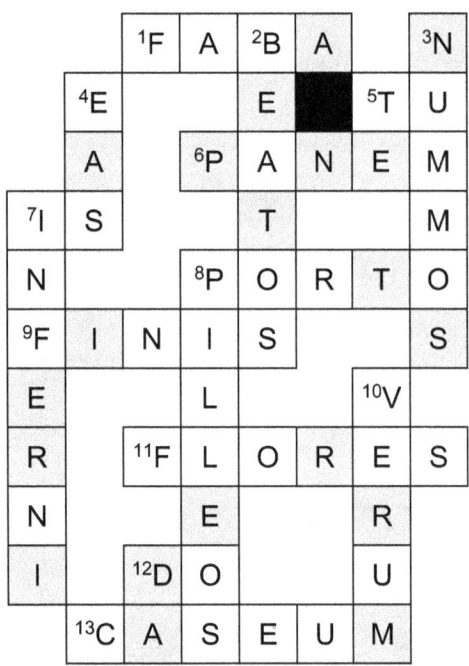

RĒCTĒ
1. bean (nom.)
5. you (acc. s.)
6. bread (acc. s.)
7. he
8. I carry
9. end (nom. s.)
11. flowers (acc.)
12. by him (abl. s.)
13. cheese (acc. s.)

DEORSUM
2. happy (m. acc. pl.)
3. coins (acc.)
4. them (f. acc. pl.)
5. you (acc. s.)
7. of hell
8. hats (acc.)
10. true (n. nom.)
12. I give

> If Disneyland made a ride based on Pompey's victories in 67 BC, it could be called:
>
> The P I R A T E S of the M E D I T E R R A N E A N

J. Historia. Review the history and fill in the blanks.

1. Whom does Pompey defeat in the Mediterranean Sea? ___*Pompey deafeats pirates.*___

2. Whom does Pompey defeat in Asia? ___*Pompey defeats Mithridates in Asia.*___

3. What does Pompey start in order to retain popularity? ___*He hosts games and spectacles.*___

X – Decima   Nōmen:

X – Decima lectiō (10 – Tenth lesson)   PREPOSITIONS (+ Ab)

I. Dictum

cum laude
(magnā cum laude; summā cum laude)   (with great praise; with highest praise)

II. Colloquium   *Latīnē*   *Anglicē*

Tiberius:	Quid velis?	What would you like?
Tullia:	Trāde mihi būtyrum quaesō.	Pass me the butter, please.
Tiberius:	Ecce.	Here it is. (lit., Behold!)

III. Verba

Latīnē	*Anglicē*	*Scrībe tōtum verbum Latīnum.*	*Dērīvātī*
ā / ab (+ Abl.)	from, away from	ā / ab (Abl.)	absent
būtyrum, -ī, n.	butter	būtyrum, -ī, n.	butter
cum (+ Abl.)	with	cum (+ Abl.)	consent
dē (+ Abl.)	about, concerning, down from	dē (+ Abl.)	describe
ē / ex (+ Abl.)	out of, out from	ē / ex (+ Abl.)	exit
laus, laudis, f.	praise	laus, laudis, f.	laudible
oleum, -ī, n.	oil	oleum, -ī, n.	petroleum
patientia, -ae, f.	patience	patientia, -ae, f.	patience
sine (+ Abl.)	without	sine (+ Abl.)	sinecure

1. *Scrībe* N (noun), V (verb), Adj (adjective), or P (preposition) to the left of each *verbum*.

2. *Scrībe* the declension (1, 2, or 3) of each noun to its right.

3. Objects of prepositions take the _____*Acc.*_____ or _____*Abl.*_____ case.

4. What case is used for indirect objects? ___*Dative gives the indirect object.*___

X – Decima   Nōmen:

IV. Grammatica

The new prepositions in this *lectiō* <u>always</u> take nouns in the <u>ablative</u> case as their objects. What case are all the nouns in the dictum? Why?

All languages have funny quirks. One of Latin's oddities is that when *cum* is used with a <u>pronoun</u>, it is attached to the <u>end</u> of the pronoun! So instead of saying *cum mē* or *cum vōbīs*, Latin uses compound words such as *mēcum* (= with me) or *vōbīscum* (= with you all).

In English we use *an* before a vowel and *a* before a consonant: **_an_** orange but **_a_** banana. Similarly, in Latin, use *ab* before a vowel and *ā* before a consonant: **_ab_** oppidō but **_ā_** silvā. Likewise, *ex* is generally used before a vowel, but *ē* before a consonant: **_ex_** oppidō but **_ē_** silvā.

Below are the forms for the very useful Latin pronoun *hic, haec, hoc*, which means *this / these*. Memorize this word horizontally (case by case, left to right). Try not to get the hiccups!

		masculine	feminine	neuter
this (S)	nominative	hic	haec	hoc
	genitive	huius	huius	huius
	dative	huic	huic	huic
	accusative	hunc	hanc	hoc
	ablative	hōc	hāc	hōc
these (P)	nominative	hī	hae	haec
	genitive	hōrum	hārum	hōrum
	dative	hīs	hīs	hīs
	accusative	hōs	hās	haec
	ablative	hīs	hīs	hīs

V. Historia (*Famous Men of Rome,* Chapter XXI, Part I)

Caius Julius Caesar (100 – 44 BC), a patrician, befriends the plebeians and works his way up Rome's political ladder. In 60 BC, he is given an army and proves to be a successful general, invading and conquering Gaul and part of Britain, and growing rapidly in popularity.

X – Decima   Nōmen: _____

VI. Dēlēgāta

A. *Scrībe* the new Latin *verba* and their meanings.

	Latīnē		*Anglicē*
1.	ā / ab (+ Abl.)	1.	from, away from
2.	būtyrum, -ī, n.	2.	butter
3.	cum (+ Abl.)	3.	With
4.	dē (+ Abl.)	4.	about, concerning; down from
5.	ē / ex (+Abl.)	5.	out of, out from
6.	laus, laudis, f.	6.	praise
7.	oleum, -ī, n.	7.	oil
8.	patientia, -ae, f.	8.	patience
9.	sine (+ Abl.)	9.	without

B. *Variātiōnēs.* *Recitā* these sentence patterns several times. Pay attention to the form used for the object of the preposition. Be sure to read the whole Latin line aloud, including the nominative form before the sentence.

1. Pilleus.   Marcus sine pilleō ambulat.   (Mark is walking without a hat.)
2. Oppidum.   Marcus ab oppidō ambulat.   (Mark is walking away from the town.)
3. Amīcus.   Marcus cum amīcō ambulat.   (Mark is walking with a friend.)
4. Collis.   Marcus dē colle ambulat.   (Mark is walking down from the hill.)
5. Culīna.   Marcus ē culīnā ambulat.   (Mark is walking out of the kitchen.)
6. Gladiī.   Mīlitēs sine gladiīs pugnant. (The soldiers fight without swords.)
7. Montēs.   Mīlitēs dē montibus movent.   (The soldiers move down from the mountains.)

C. Translate these sentences (from Latin to English or from English to Latin).

1. Servus cum patientiā labōrat.   *The slave works without patience.*
2. Legiō ex Italiā movēbit.   *The legion will move out of Italy.*
3. Tēla dē vallīs volābunt.   *The weapons will fly down from the walls.*
4. Scientia sine cāritate est mala.   *Knowledge without love is bad.*

X – Decima   Nōmen: _____

5. Nautae ā nāvibus ambulant.   _The sailors walk from the ships._

6. Mīlitēs sine timōre pugnant.   _The sailors fight without fear._

7. We give praise to God.   _Deō laudem dāmus._

8. Julia is giving bread to birds.   _Iūlia avibus panem dat._

9. The words of the law are holy.   _Verba lēgis sunt sancta._

10. I like cheese and bread.   _Panem et cāseum amō._

11. Marcia pānem cum būtyrō amat.   _Marcia loves bread with butter._

12. Titus pānem sine būtyrō cēnāre amat.   _Titus likes bread without butter._

13. Agricola lampadem cum oleō tenet.   _The farmer is holding a lamp with oil._

14. Many books of the teachers are large.   _Multī librī magistrōrum sunt magnī._

D. Fill in the blanks.

1. *Sine, cum,* and *ex* always take the _____Ablative_____ case.

2. Use *ab* or *ex* before a *verbum* that begins with a _____consonant_____.

3. List three prepositions that take the accusative case: _____sine, ab, ex, dē, cum_____

4. Ablative case endings for each noun declension are:

   1st: __-ā__ (S) __-īs__ (P); 2nd: __-ō__ (S) __-īs__ (P); 3rd: __-e__ (S) __-ibus__ (P).

E. Translate these sentences (from Latin to English or from English to Latin).

1. Canis meus mēcum ambulābit.   _My dog will eat with me._

2. Deus est nōbīscum.   _God is with us._

3. Hic parvus flōs est bellus.   _This little flower is pretty._

4. Haec clāvis est magna.   _This key is large._

5. Hoc lātum flūmen tardat.   _This wide river is slow._

6. Angelī pugnāre sine gladiīs possunt.   _Angels are able to fight without swords._

X – Decima   Nōmen:

7. Mary prays with humility.   _Maria cum humilitāte ōrat._

8. I like bread with lots of cheese.   _Panem cum multō cāseō amō._

9. The legion moves out of Gaul.   _Legiō ē Galliā movet._

Ex Scriptūrīs:

10. Nōn timeō malum quoniam tū mēcum es. (Ps. 23:4; *quoniam* = because)

    I do not fear evil because you are with me.

11. Pānis Deī est quī descendit dē caelō et dat vītam mundō.

(Jn. 6:33, alt.; *quī* = he who; *descendit* = descends)

    The bread of God is he who descends from heaven and gives life to the world.

F. Decline <u>laus, laudis, f.</u> (1) and <u>būtyrum, -ī, n.</u> (2).

1.	laus	laudēs	2.	būtyrum	būtyra
	laudis	laudum		būtyrī	būtyrōrum
	laudī	laudibus		būtyrō	būtyrīs
	laudem	laudēs		būtyrum	būtyra
	laude	laudibus		būtyrō	būtyrīs

G. Translate these *verba* and phrases.

1. decima   _tenth_   2. ninth   _nōnus, -a, -um_

3. cum laude   _with praise_   4. Quid velis?   _What is the matter with you?_

5. Aperīte librōs.   _Open [your] books._   6. too long   _ad nauseam_

7. Trāde mihi pānem quaesō.   _Please pass me the bread._

8. Trāde mihi holera quaesō.   _Please pass me the vegetables._

9. Trāde mihi cāseum quaesō.   _Please pass me the cheese._

10. Hannibal ad portās!   _Hannibal is at the gates!_

X – Decima   Nōmen: _____

H. Dērīvātī. Complete each sentence with an English *verbum* chosen from the following *verba*. The italicized *verbum* in the sentence should help you think of the Latin root.

laud   sinecure   impatient

1. "All Glory, __Laud__, and Honor" is a hymn *praising* God. Latin root: ___laud, laudis, f.___

2. His *patient* mother was seldom ___impatient___. Latin root: ___patientia, -ae, f.___

3. A ___sinecure___ gave income *without* the *care* of souls. Latin root: ___sine___

I. Crossword Puzzle. Be sure to use the correct form for the grammar indicated.

Across (RĒCTĒ)
2. away from
4. with
5. patience (abl. s.)
7. oil (abl. s.)
9. toward
10. down from
11. out of
12. without

Down (DEORSUM)
1. humility (abl. s.)
3. butter (abl. s.)
5. snack (nom. s.)
6. I swim
8. praise (abl. s.)

Crossword answers:
- 2A: AB
- 3B: BUTYRO
- 4C: CUM
- 1H: HUMM (HUMILITATE down)
- 5P: PATIENTIA (across); POTIO/PORTIO
- 6N: NATATIO (down: N, A, T, A, T, I, O)
- 7O: O (OLEO across starts here)
- 8L: LAUDE (down)
- 9A: AD
- 10D: DE
- 11E: EX
- 12S: SINE

J. Historia. Review the history and fill in the blanks.

1. In what year is Julius Caesar born? ___Julius Caesar was born in 100 BC.___

2. Whose side does he take in the civil unrest? ___Caesar sides with the Plebeians.___

3. What two provinces does he conquer? ___Caesar conquered Gaul and part of Britain.___

XI – Ūndecima   Nōmen:

XI – Ūndecima lectiō   2-CASE PREPOSITIONS
(11 – Eleventh lesson)

I. Dictum

Vēnī, vīdī, vīcī.   <u>*I came; I saw; I conquered*</u>
— Julius Caesar

II. Colloquium   *Latīnē*   *Anglicē*

Magister:	Claudite librōs.	Close your books.
	Hōra est quaestiunculae.	It's time for a quiz.
Discipulus:	Oiei!	Ouch!

III. Verba

Latīnē	*Anglicē*	*Scrībe tōtum verbum Latīnum.*	*Dērīvātī*
ager, agrī, m.	field	ager, agrī, m.	agriculture
cīvitās, cīvitātis, f.	state	cīvitās, cīvitātis, f.	civilization
gemma, -ae, f.	gem, jewel	gemma, -ae, f.	gem
in (+ Acc.)	into, onto	in (+ Acc.)	in
in (+ Abl.)	in, on	in (+ Abl.)	in
margarīta, -ae, f.	pearl	margarita, -ae, f.	Margaret
porta, -ae, f.	gate	porta, -ae, f.	portal
similis, simile (adj. + Dat.)	similar to, like	similis, simile (+ Dat.)	simile
sub (+ Acc. / Abl.)	under, up to, up under	sub (+ Acc. / Abl.)	submarine
thēsaurus, -ī, m.	treasure	thēsaurus, -ī, m.	thesaurus

1. *Scrībe* N (noun), V (verb), Adj (adjective), or P (preposition) to the left of each *verbum*.

2. *Scrībe* the declension (1, 2, or 3) of each noun to its right.

3. How does one find the stem of a noun?   <u>*To find the stem, drop the gen. sing. ending.*</u>

4. How does one find the stem of a verb?   <u>*To find the stem, drop the infinitive ending -re.*</u>

IV. Grammatica

The two new prepositions are tricky because their meaning depends on the case used as object. In general, when they indicate motion *toward* something, they take the accusative; when they indicate motion *within* something or lack of motion, they take the ablative. So, when used with the accusative, *in* means *into* or *onto*, expressing motion toward something. When used with the ablative, it means *in* or *on*, expressing action *within* something or an absence of motion.

Māter in exedrium ambulat.	Mother is walking *into* the living room.
Māter in exedriō ambulat.	Mother is walking *in* the living room.
Māter in exedriō stat.	Mother is standing *in* the living room.

The preposition *sub* operates in the same way, but it's a little harder to see in English, because our language doesn't have two different forms for *under* with which to make the distinction.

Here is the Latin pronoun meaning *that / those*. Memorize it across (like *hic, haec, hoc*).

		masculine	feminine	neuter
that (S)	nominative	ille	illa	illud
	genitive	illīus	illīus	illīus
	dative	illī	illī	illī
	accusative	illum	illam	illud
	ablative	illō	illā	illō
those (P)	nominative	illī	illae	illa
	genitive	illōrum	illārum	illōrum
	dative	illīs	illīs	illīs
	accusative	illōs	illās	illa
	ablative	illīs	illīs	illīs

V. Historia (*Famous Men of Rome,* Chapter XXI, Part IIa)

Caesar, wanting to be master of Rome, gives fortunes to the poor. Pompey, fearing Caesar's popularity, orders Caesar to disband his army. In 49 BC, Caesar crosses the Rubicon River into Italy with his illegal army. He defeats Pompey and the army of the Republic at Pharsalia.

XI – Ūndecima   Nōmen:

VI. Dēlēgāta

A. *Scrībe* the new Latin *verba* and their meanings.

                Latīnē   *Anglicē*

1. ager, agrī, m. — 1. field
2. cīvitās, cīvitātis, f. — 2. state
3. gemma, -ae, f. — 3. gem, jewel
4. in (+ Acc.) — 4. into, onto
5. in (+ Abl.) — 5. in, on
6. margarita, -ae, f. — 6. pearl
7. porta, -ae, f. — 7. gate
8. similis, simile (+ Dat.) — 8. similar to, like
9. sub (+ Acc. / Abl.) — 9. under, up to, up under
10. thēsaurus, -ī, m. — 10. treasure

B. *Variātiōnēs*. *Recitā* these sentence patterns several times. Be sure to read the whole Latin line aloud, including the nominative form before the sentence. Pay special attention to the form used for *ager, agrī, m* and *porta, portae, f.*

1. Ager.   Ager est magnus.   (The field is large.)
2. Ager.   Flōrēs agrī sunt bellī.   (The flowers of the field are pretty.)
3. Ager.   Rēgnum caelōrum est simile agrō. (The kingdom of heaven is similar to a field.)
4. Ager.   Agricola agrum arābit.   (The farmer will plow the field.)
5. Ager.   Servus in agrum ambulat.   (The slave is walking into the field.)
6. Ager.   Equus in agrō stat.   (The horse is standing in the field.)
7. Portae. Portae sunt magnae.   (The gates are large.)
8. Portae. Dominus portārum nōn est dīves. (The master of the gates is not a rich man.)
9. Portae. Portās vidēmus.   (We see the gates.)
10. Portae. Legiōnēs in portās intrant.   (Legions enter into the gates.)
11. Portae. Mīlitēs in portīs stant.   (Soldiers stand in the gates.)

C. **Translate these sentences (from Latin to English or from English to Latin).**

1. Alabāma est cīvitās optima.   *Alabama is the best state.*

XI – Ūndecima   Nōmen: _____

2. Portae urbis patent. _____ *The gates of the city are open.*

3. Illa margarīta est bella. _____ *That pearl is pretty.*

4. Ille thēsaurus est parvus. _____ *That treasure is small.*

5. Lūcius sub aquā natat. _____ *Lucius swims under water.*

6. Augustus sub aquā natāre potest. _____ *Augustus is able to swim under water.*

7. Margarīta rēgīnae est bella. _____ *The queen's pearl is pretty.*

8. Aemīlia is holding a large pearl in [her] right hand.

   _____ *Aemilia magnam margarītam in dexterā [eius] tenet.*

9. Many gems are in that treasure. _____ *Multae gemmae sunt in illō thēsaurō.*

10. Great treasure is under the earth. _____ *Magnus thēsaurus sub terrā est.*

11. We are watching the city's gates. _____ *Portās urbis spectāmus*

12. Deus nōbīs lēgem bonam dat. _____ *God gives us a good law.*

13. Verba eius sunt sancta et vēra. _____ *Its words are holy and true.*

D. Fill in the blanks.

1. When *in* and *sub* indicate motion *toward* something, use the _____ *Acc.* _____ case.

2. When *in* and *sub* indicate motion *within* or lack of motion, use the _____ *Abl.* _____ case.

E. Translate these sentences (from Latin to English or from English to Latin).

1. Urbs duās portās habet. _____ *The city has two gates.*

2. Rēx magnum thēsaurum videt. _____ *The king sees a great treasure.*

3. Nauta magnās margarītās tenet. _____ *The sailor holds large pearls.*

4. Hic thēsaurus multum aurum et multōs nummōs habet cum paucīs gemmīs.

   _____ *This treasure has much gold and many coins with a few gems.*

5. Duōs equōs in agrō vidēmus. _____ *We see two horses in the field.*

XI – Ūndecima   **Nōmen:**

6. Illī equī in agrō agricolae stant.   *Those horses are standing in the farmer's field.*

7. The keys of the large gates are small.

    Clāvēs magnārum portārum sunt parvae.

8. A holy man is entering into the narrow gate.

    Sanctus homō in portam angustam intrat.

9. A pretty woman is walking on the narrow road.

    Fēmina bella in viā angustā ambulat.

10. The queen holds a large gem.   *Rēgīna magnam gemmam tenet.*

11. That pearl is in this treasure.   *Illa margarita est in hōc thēsaurō.*

Ex Scriptūrīs:

12. Et urbs sancta Hierusalem habet mūrum magnum et altum et duodecim portās et in portīs duodecim angelōs. (Rev. 21:12, alt.)   *And the holy city Jerusalem has a great and high wall and twelve gates and in the gates twelve angels.*

13. Simile est rēgnum caelōrum thēsaurō in agrō. (Matt. 13:44)   *The kingdom of heaven is like a treasure in a field.*

14. Et vōs Dominum habētis in caelō. (Col. 4:1)   *And you have a Master in heaven.*

F. Translate these *verba* and phrases.

1. ūndecima   *eleventh*   2. tenth   *decimus, -a, -um*

3. Oiei!   *Ouch!*   4. cum laude   *with praise*

5. Claudite librōs. *Close your books*   6. ad nauseam   *too long*

7. Hōra est quaestiunculae.   *It's time for a quiz.*

8. Ē plūribus ūnum   *Out of many, one.*

9. Repetītiō māter memoriae.   *Repetition is the mother of memory.*

XI – Ūndecima   Nōmen: _____

G. **Dērīvātī.** Complete each sentence with an English *verbum* chosen from the following *verba*. The italicized *verbum* in the sentence should help you think of the Latin root.

gemologist   thesaurus   civilian   agriculture   subterranean

1. __agriculture__ is the *cultivation* of *fields*. Latin root: __ager, agrī, m.__

2. __subterranean__ mines are *under* the *earth*. Latin root: __sub (+ Acc / Abl.)__

3. A __thesaurus__ is a *treasure* of words. Latin root: __thēsaurus, -ī, m.__

4. A __civilian__ is a citizen of the *state*. Latin root: __cīvitās, cīvitātis, f.__

5. A __gemolosgist__ is an authority on *gems*. Latin root: __gemma, -ae, f.__

H. **Alphabet Code.** Unscramble the letters given to form the *verba Latīna* from this *lectiō*. A code letter is under each blank. Use the code to fill in the secret message in the box.

Scrambled	Answer		Scrambled	Answer
NI	I N / b v		MIILSSI	S I M I L I S / h b a b t b h
BSU	S U B / h g d		VSIITCA	C I V I T A S / j b z b l k h
RGAE	A G E R / k n c q		AARRGITMA	M A R G A R I T A / a k q n k q b l k
MGAEM	G E M M A / n c a a k		RTUEHSASU	T H E S A U R U S / l u c h k g q g h
ATOPR	P O R T A / x i q l k			

> C A E S A R   C R O S S E S   T H E
> j k c h k q   j q i h h c h   l u c
>
> R U B I C O N   Doesn't mean "The emperor angers the river!"
> q g d b j i v

I. **Historia.** Review the history and fill in the blanks.

1. What does Pompey order Caesar to do? __to disband his army and resign__

2. What illegal act does Caesar commit? __Contrary to the law and to the orders of the Roman senate and people, without authority, he brings his army into Italy.__

XII – Duodecima   Nōmen:

XII – Duodecima lectiō (12 – Twelfth lesson)   QUESTION WORDS

I. Dictum

Et tū, Brūte?   *And you too, Brutus ?*
– *Julius Caesar*, Shakespeare

II. Colloquium   *Latīnē*   *Anglicē*

| **Popilia:** | Quota hōra est? | What time is it? |
| **Brūtus:** | Octāva hōra est. | It's eight o'clock. |

III. Verba

Latīnē	*Anglicē*	*Scrībe tōtum verbum Latīnum.*	*Dērīvātī*
cūr	why	cūr	
quandō	when	quandō	
quantus, -a, -um	how much	quantus, -a, -um	quantity
quid	what	quid	quid pro quo
quis	who	quis	
quōmodō	how	quōmodō	
quot	how many	quot	quota
quotus, -a, -um	which	quotus, -a, -u	
ubi	where	ubi	ubiquitous
servō, servāre, servāvī, servātum	to save, to keep, to guard		preserve
servō	servāre	servāvī	servātum

Nōtā bene (N.B.):
1. *Quantus* and *quotus* are adjectives that decline. They must agree with nouns they modify.
2. *Quot* is a special adjective that cannot be declined and never changes form.
3. *Quid* can be either the subject or the object of a question. *Quis* must be the subject of the question; it does not mean *whom*. You'll learn more about *quis* and *quid* another year.
4. The rest of the *verba* (except for *servō, servāre*) are adverbs and never change endings.

IV. Grammatica

You already know how to write a question that can be answered by *yes* or *no*: write the verb first and add the enclitic *–ne* to it. Another way to ask a question in Latin is simply to use the interrogatives, or question words, in this *lectiō*.

Cūr flēs?	Why are you crying?
Quis cantat?	Who is singing?
Quid Marcus habet?	What does Mark have?
Ubi Hanna est?	Where is Hannah?
Quotus pilleus est optimus?	Which hat is best?

The Romans used ordinal numbers (*prīma, secunda, tertia,* etc.) to express time. Now that you know the first twelve ordinal numbers, you can tell time too! Don't forget to specify *ante merīdiem* (before noon) or *post merīdiem* (after noon).

Prīma hōra est.	It's 1 o'clock.	(It's the 1st hour)
Secunda hōra est.	It's 2 o'clock.	(It's the 2nd hour)
Tertia hōra est.	It's 3 o'clock.	(It's the 3rd hour)
Quarta hōra est.	It's 4 o'clock.	(It's the 4th hour)

To be more specific you can add minutes too:

Est prīma hōra et decem minūtae.	It's 1:10	(minūta, -ae, f. = minute)
Est prīma hōra et quadrāns.	It's 1:15	(quadrans, quadrantis, f. = ¼)
Est prīma hōra et dimidia.	It's 1:30	(dimidia, -ae, f. = ½)
Est prīma et dodrāns.	It's 1:45	(dodrāns, dodrantis, f. = ¾)

Some times of day or night have special names:

Est <u>mānē</u>.	It's morning/dawn.	(mānē, adv. = morning)
Est <u>merīdiē</u>.	It's the middle of the day.	(merīdiē, adv. = noon)
Est <u>vesper</u>.	It's evening.	(vesper, vesperī, m. = evening)
Est <u>nox</u>.	It's night.	
Est <u>mediā nocte</u>.	It's the middle of the night.	
Tē <u>mox</u> vidēbō.	I will see you soon.	(mox, adv. = soon)
Tē <u>crās</u> vidēbō.	I will see you tomorrow.	(crās, adv. = tomorrow)
Tē <u>herī</u> vīdī.	I saw you yesterday.	(herī, adv. = yesterday)

V. Historia (*Famous Men of Rome,* Chapter XXI, Part IIb)

After more victories, Julius Caesar is named dictator for life. He improves the city and corrects the calendar. However, some of the nobles fear that he will become a king. He is stabbed to death in Pompey's theatre on March 15, 44 BC (the Ides of March).

XII – Duodecima   Nōmen: _____

VI. Dēlēgāta

A. *Scrībe* the new Latin *verba* and their meanings.

	Latīnē		*Anglicē*
1.	cūr	1.	why
2.	quandō	2.	when
3.	quantus, -a, -um	3.	how much
4.	quid	4.	what
5.	quis	5.	who
6.	quōmodō	6.	how
7.	quot	7.	how many
8.	quotus, -a, -um	8.	which
9.	ubi	9.	where
10.	servō, -āre, -āvī, -ātum	10.	to save, keep, guard

B. *Variatiōnēs.* *Recitā* these sentence patterns several times.

1. Quota hōra est?   Quīnta hōra est.   (What time is it? It's 5 o'clock.)
2. Quota hōra est?   Sexta hōra est.   (What time is it? It's 6 o'clock.)
3. Quota hōra est?   Septima hōra est.   (What time is it? It's 7 o'clock.)
4. Quota hōra est?   Octāva hōra est.   (What time is it? It's 8 o'clock.)
5. Quota hōra est?   Ūndecima hōra est.   (What time is it? It's 11 o'clock.)
6. Quota hōra est?   Duodecima hōra est.   (What time is it? It's 12 o'clock.)
7. Quota hōra est?   Prīma hōra post merīdiem.   (What time is it? It's 1:00 pm.)
8. Quota hōra est?   Prīma hōra ante merīdiem.   (What time is it? It's 1:00 am.)
9. Quota hōra est?   Est prīma hōra et dimidia. (What time is it? It's 1:30.)
10. Quota hōra est? Est prīma hōra et dodrante. (What time is it? It's 1:45.)

C. Translate these sentences.

1. Cūr festīnās?   *Why are you hurrying?*

2. Quis rīdet?   *Who is laughing?*

3. Quid dolet?   *What hurts?*

XII – Duodecima   Nōmen:

4. Ubi cāseus est?   _Where is the cheese?_

5. Quōmodō mīles pugnat?   _How does a soldier fight?_

6. Quandō natābis?   _When will you swim?_

7. Quot evangelia sunt?   _How many gospels are there?_

8. Quotus liber est optimus? _Which book is best?_

9. Cūr ursa puerōs terret?   _Why does the pear frighten the boys?_

10. Quis natāre potest?   _Who is able to swim?_

11. Quot spatia habet abacus? _How many spaces does the game board have?_

12. Quid Gāius in dexterā tenet? _What does Gaius hold in his right hand?_

13. Quantum aurum in thēsaurō est? _How much gold is in the treasure?_

D. Translate these sentences. Then find the question in Part C for which each could be an answer. *Scrībe* the question number in the short blank next to the sentence number.

__7__ 1. Sunt quattuor evangelia.   _There are four gospels._

__4__ 2. Cāseus est in culīnā.   _The cheese is in the kitchen._

__5__ 3. Mīles bene pugnat.   _The soldier fights well._

__8__ 4. Tertius liber est optimus. _The third book is best._

__13__ 5. Multum aurum in thēsaurō est. _There is much gold in the treasure._

__9__ 6. Ursa terret puerōs quod est magna (*quod* = because).

The bear frightens the boys because it is large.

E. Translate these sentences (from Latin to English of from English to Latin).

1. Sapientia, cāritās, humilitās, et patientia sunt quattuor virtūtēs.

Wisdom, love, humility, and patience are four virtues.

2. Ubi pilleus agricolae est?   _Where is the farmer's hat?_

3. Cūr librōs magistrō portant? _Why do they carry books for the teacher?_

XII – Duodecima Nōmen:

4. Quis flōrem puellae bellae dabit? _Who will give the pretty girl a flower?_

5. Quot gemmās rēx in thēsaurō habet?

   How many jewels does the king have in his treasure?

6. How many gems are in the king's treasure?

   Quot gemmae sunt in thēsaurō rēgis?

7. Who will walk through fire? _Quis per ignem ambulāvit?_

8. Quis hunc gladium mīlitī portābit? _Who will carry this sword to the soldier?_

9. Quis illam mēnsam et hanc sellam in culīnam movēre potest?

   Who is able to move that table and this chair into the kitchen?

10. Which man is happy? _Quotus vi rest beātus?_

11. Who has the third jewel? _Quis tertiam gemmam habet?_

Ex Scriptūrīs:

12. Ubi humilitās, ibi est sapientia. (Prov. 11:2) _Where there is humility, there is wisdom._

13. Quis est hic rēx glōriae? (Ps. 23:8 alt.) _Who is this king of glory?_

F. Translate these *verba* and phrases.

1. duodecima _twelfth_
2. eleventh _ūndecimus, -a, -um_
3. Et tū, Brūte? _And you too, Brutus?_
4. before noon _ante merīdiem (a.m.)_
5. after noon _post merīdiem (p.m.)_
6. Close your books. _Claudite librōs._
7. Quota hōra est? _What time is it?_
8. Quarta hōra est. _It's four o'clock._
9. Dēlenda est Carthāgō! _Carthage must be destroyed!_
10. Vēnī, vīdī, vīcī. _I came, I saw, I conquered._

G. Dērīvātī. Complete each sentence with an English *verbum* chosen from the following *verba*. The italicized *verbum* in the sentence should help you think of the Latin root.

XII – Duodecima   Nōmen: _____

                    quantity   quota   ubiquitous

1. Cell phones are __ubiquitous__; they're every*where*. Latin root: ____ubi____

2. State troopers may be given a __quota__ because they are asked *how many* speeding drivers

   they have arrested. Latin root: __quot__

3. A measure of __quantity__ shows *how much* one has. Latin root: __quantus, -a, -um__

H. *Verbum* Search. Each of the *verba* listed below can be found in this grid, reading forward, backward, up, down, or diagonally. Can you find them all? The unused letters will spell a crazy message. *Quid est? Scrībe* the crazy message on this line.

_____ saeegms = message _____

```
A  X  S  O  D  N  A  U  Q
T  H  E  S  A  U  R  U  S
I  A  E  A  S  O  B  C
R  E  S  G  T  M  I  I  U
A  D  U  M  O  R  M  N  R
G  I  T  D  U  B  O  E  E
R  U  O  M  Q  C  U  P  G
A  Q  U  A  N  T  U  S  A
M  S  Q  U  I  S  U  A  L
```

WORD LIST

AGER   QUID
CUM   QUIS
CUR   QUOMODO
QUANTUS   QUOT
GEMMA   QUOTUS
LAUS   SINE
MARGARITA   SUB
PORTA   UBI
THESAURUS   EX
QUANDO

I. Historia. Review the history and fill in the blanks.

1. What office do the people give Caesar? __Caesar is appointed dictator for life.__

2. What does Caesar do with his power? __He makes many improvements.__

3. What do the patricians fear? __The patricians fear he will become a king.__

4. How does Caesar die? __Caesar is assassinated by his opponents.__

5. On what date does he die? __Julius Caesar dies on March 15th, 44 BC.__

6. What is that date called? __That date is also known as the "Ides of March".__

XIII – Tertia Decima   Nōmen:

XIII – Tertia decima lectiō   3ᴿᴰ CONJUGATION
(13 – Thirteenth lesson)

I. Dictum

Silent lēgēs inter arma.   *Laws are silent among arms.*
— Marcus Tullius Cicero

II. Colloquium   *Latīnē*   *Anglicē*

Discipulī:	Blā, blā, blā.	Blah, blah, blah.
Magistra:	Silēte. Nunc attendite.	Be quiet. Now pay attention.

III. Verba

Latīnē   *Anglicē*   *Scrībe tōtum verbum Latīnum.*   *Dērīvātī*

ascendō, ascendere, ascendī, ascensum to ascend   *ascent*

    ascendō   *ascendere*   *ascendī*   *ascensum*

crēdō, crēdere, crēdidī, crēditum to believe   *creed*

    credo   *crēdere*   *crēdidī*   *crēditum*

dēscendō, dēscendere, dēscendī, dēscensum to descend   *descent*

    dēscendō   *dēsendere*   *dēscensī*   *dēscensum*

dīcō, dīcere, dīxī, dictum to say, to tell, to speak   *diction*

    dīcō   *dīcere*   *dīxī*   *dictum*

legō, legere, lēgī, lectum to read   *legible*

    legō   *legere*   *lēgī*   *lectum*

mittō, mittere, mīsī, missum to send   *missile*

    mittō   *mittere*   *mīsī*   *missum*

trādō, trādere, trādidī, trāditum to pass, hand over   *traitor*

    trādō   *trādere*   *trādidī*   *trāditum*

XIII – Tertia Decima   **Nōmen:** _____

1. What kind of *verba* are these? _____*All of them are verbs.*_____

2. How can you tell that these *verba* do not belong to 1st or 2nd conjugation?

   ___*The second principle part, or infinitive, does not end with -āre or -ēre but -ere.*___

IV. Grammatica

The new verbs in this *lectiō* belong to 3rd conjugation. In 3rd conjugation, the infinitive ends in –ere (*without* a macron), and it is pronounced with a short, rather than a long *e*. You will know to which conjugation a verb belongs by paying close attention to its infinitive and to the stem vowel within the infinitive:

1st conjugation:	**amāre**	(long *ā* stem vowel in the infinitive)
2nd conjugation:	**vidēre**	(long *ē* stem vowel in the infinitive)
3rd conjugation:	**dīcere**	(short *e* stem vowel in the infinitive)

Because the stem vowel of 3rd conjugation is short (not long as in 1st and 2nd conjugations), it changes. The first three forms ought to be *crēdeō, crēdes, crēdet*, but the stem vowel is so short that it gets bullied – and changes to *ō, i,* and *u* just to fit in!

		Singular	Plural	
1st person	*I believe*	crēdō	crēdimus	*We believe*
2nd person	*You believe*	crēdis	crēditis	*You all believe*
3rd person	*He, she, it believes*	crēdit	crēdunt	*They believe*

The endings are all familiar, so this conjugation should be easy to learn. Only the stem is odd.

Future tense works differently for 3rd conjugation. You'll learn about it later. For now, you should just know that the future-tense personal endings for 1st and 2nd conjugations don't work for 3rd conjugation.

When used with the verb *dīcō, dīcere*, the preposition *dē* means *about*.

Another way to write *and* in Latin: *-que* is an enclitic that means *and* when added to the second of two words to be joined, e.g., *soror frāterque* = *sister and brother*.

V. Historia (*Famous Men of Rome,* Chapter XXII)

Marcus Tullius Cicero (106-43 BC) lives through the times of Marius, Sulla, Pompey, and Julius Caesar. He is the greatest orator of ancient Roman times. He saves Rome from the conspiracy of Cataline, but also sees the Republic crumble and the beginning of the Empire.

XIII – Tertia Decima   Nōmen:

VI. Dēlēgāta

A. *Scrībe* the new Latin *verba* and their meanings.

        Latīnē   *Anglicē*

1. ascendō, ascendere, ascend, ascensum — 1. to ascend
2. credo, crēdere, crēdidī, crēditum — 2. to believe
3. dēscendō, -scendere, -scendī, -scensum — 3. to descend
4. dīcō, dīcere, dīxī, dictum — 4. to say, to tell, to speak
5. legō, legere, lēgī, lectum — 5. to read
6. mittō, mittere, mīsī, missum — 6. to send
7. trādō, trādere, trādidī, trāditum — 7. to pass, to hand over

B. *Variātiōnēs.* *Recitā* these sentence patterns several times. Pay special attention to the use of the dative case and of ordinal numbers.

1. Aemilia amīcō prīmum librum dat.   (Amelia gives the first book to a friend.)
2. Aemilia amīcae secundum librum legit.   (Amelia reads the second book to a friend.)
3. Aemilia sorōrī tertium librum mittit.   (Amelia sends the third book to her sister.)
4. Aemilia frātrī quartum librum servat.   (Amelia keeps the fourth book for her brother.)
5. Aemilia magistrō quīntum librum portat.   (Amelia carries the fifth book to the teacher.)
6. Aemilia mātrī sextum librum tradit.   (Amelia passes the sixth book to her mother.)

C. Translate these sentences (from Latin to English or from English to Latin).

1. Angelus in caelum ascendit. — The angel ascends into heaven.
2. Angelus dē caelō dēscendit. — The angel descends from heaven.
3. Crēdō amīcum meum. — I believe my friend.
4. Crēdō in ūnum Deum. — I believe in one God.
5. A soldier guards the treasure. — Mīlēs thēsaurum servat.
6. My brother is reading a book. — Frāter meus librum legit.
7. Dīvitēs argentum student. — Rich people are eager for silver.

XIII – Tertia Decima   **Nōmen:**

8. The good woman studies wisdom.   *Fēmina bona sapientiam studet.*

9. Pastor dē cāritāte dīcit.   *The shepherd speaks about love.*

10. Aemilia amīcae dōnum mittit.   *Aemilia sends a gift to her friend.*

11. Rēx fīliō corōnam trādit.   *The king passes the crown to his son.*

12. Cūr Gāius illum librum legit?   *Why does Gaius read that book?*

13. Quotum librum magister legit?   *Which book does the teacher read?*

14. Quis cīvitātem servābit?   *Who will save the state?*

15. Servābitne Cicero cīvitātem?   *Will Cicero save the state?*

D. Fill in the blanks.

1. With what three letters do infinitives of 1st-conjugation verbs end? *-āre* 2nd? *-ēre* 3rd? *-ere*

2. What is the difference between 2nd- and 3rd-conjugation infinitives? *A single macron!*

3. Latin prepositions take the *accusative* or *ablative* case.

4. The dative case is used for *the indirect object*.

E. Translate these Latin sentences (from Latin to English or from English to Latin).

1. Soror mea legere amat.   *My sister loves to read.*

2. Servus legere nōn potest.   *The servant is not able to read.*

3. Via circum montem dēscendit.   *The road descends around the mountain.*

4. Mīles glōriam et victōriam studet.   *The soldier is eager for glory and victory.*

5. A new queen ascends to the throne.   *Rēgīna nova ad thronum ascendit.*

6. Frāter tuus tibi magna dōna saepe mittit.   *Your brother often sends you large gifts.*

XIII – Tertia Decima   Nōmen:

7. Mīlitēs glōriam victōriamque in bellō semper student. _____

Soldiers are always eager for glory and victory in war.

8. Amīcus mihi clāvem parvae iānuae trādit. _____

A friend passes me the small door's key.

9. Caesar hostibus gladiōs nōn mittit. _____

Caesar does not send swords to the enemies.

10. Mark is reading a good book.   _Marcus librum bonum legit._

11. Livia believes in God.   _Livia in Deum crēdit._

12. A slave guards the queen's jewels.   _Servus gemmās rēgīnae servat._

Ex Scriptūrīs:

13. Amen dīcō vōbīs, dīves difficile intrābit in rēgnum caelōrum. (Matt. 19:23, alt.; *amen* – truly; *difficile* – with difficulty) _____

Truly, I tell you, a rich man will enter into the kingdom of heaven with difficulty.

F. Conjugate (1) *dīcō, dīcere* and (2) *mittō, mittere* in present tense.

1. _dīcō_   _dīcimus_   2. _mittō_   _mittimus_

    dīcere   _dīcitis_   _mittis_   _mittitis_

    dīcit   _dīcunt_   _mittit_   _mittunt_

G. Translate these *verba* and phrases.

1. tertia decima _thirteenth_   2. twelfth _duodecimus, -a, -um_

3. with praise _cum laude_   4. Ouch! _Oiei!_

5. Silēte. _Be silent._   6. Et tū, Brūte? _And you too, Brutus?_

7. Silent lēgēs inter arma. _Laws are silent among arms._

8. What time is it? _Quota hōra est?_

9. id est _that is_   10. eleventh _ūndecimus, -a, -um_

XIII – Tertia Decima   Nōmen: _____

H. Dērīvātī. Complete each sentence with an English *verbum* chosen from the following *verba*. The italicized *verbum* in the sentence should help you think of the Latin root.

predict   missionary   legible   creed   dictates   traditions

1. A __missionary__ is one who is *sent* to share the gospel. Latin root: __mittō, mittere__

2. Our forefathers have passed down __traditions__. Latin root: __trādō, trādere__

3. The Apostles' __creed__ states what Christian *believe*. Latin root: __crēdō, crēdere__

4. If a teacher __dictates__ sentences, she *speaks* them aloud. Latin root: __dīcō, dīcere__

5. __legible__ penmanship is easy to *read*. Latin root: __legō, legere__

6. To __predict__ is to *say* or *tell before*. Latin root: __dīcō, dīcere__

I. Crossword Puzzle. Be careful! One answer is very tricky!

	1H		2S	3T	U	4D	E	5M	U	6S
	O		I			E		I		E
	7C	R	E	D	I	S		T		R
			N			C		T		V
8L	9E	G	E	R	E		10O	R	A	
	X		C		N				N	
			S		11D	12I	C	13I	T	
	14T	R	A	D	I	S		B		
	E				T		15H	I	C	

RĒCTĒ
2. we are eager for
7. you (s.) believe
8. to read
10. mouths (nom. or acc.)
11. he says
14. you (s.) pass
15. this (m.)

DEORSUM
1. this (n.)
3. it ascends
4. it descends
5. I send
6. they save
9. out of
12. he
13. there
14. you (acc. s.)

J. Historia. Review the history and fill in the blanks.

1. Who is the greatest orator of Roman times? __Marcus Tullius Cicero__

2. What conspiracy does he stop? __Cicero foils the conspirace of Cataline__

XIV – Quarta Decima   Nōmen: _____

XIV – Quarta decima lectiō   IMPERFECT TENSE
(14 – Fourteenth lesson)

I. Dictum

Diēs Īrae   _Day of Wrath_

II. Colloquium   *Latīnē*   *Anglicē*

| Magister: | Līvia, converte hanc sententiam ex Anglicā in Latīnam: I prepare. | Livia, translate this sentence from English into Latin: I prepare. |
| Līvia: | Latīnē dīcimus: Parō. | In Latin we say: I prepare. |

III. Verba

Latīnē	*Anglicē*	*Scrībe tōtum verbum Latīnum.*	*Dērīvātī*
albus, -a, -um	white	albus, -a, -um	albino
avia, -ae, f.	grandmother	avia, -ae, f.	
flāvus, -a, -um	yellow	flāvus, -a, -um	
līberō, līberāre, līberāvī, līberātum	to free, to set free		liberty
līberō	līberāre	līberāvī	līberātum
niger, nigra, nigrum black		niger, nigra, nigum	Nigeria
parō, parāre, parāvī, parātum to prepare			prepare
parō	parāre	parāvī	parātum
quī	who, he who	quī	
rūfus, -a, -um	red	rūfus, -a, -um	Rufus
salūtō, salūtāre, salūtāvī, salūtātum to greet			salute
salūtō	salūtāre	salūtāvī	salūtātum

1. To what conjugation do the verbs belong? _All these verbs belong in 1st conjugation_

NB: *niger* has the less common -*er* ending in the masculine singular nominative (like the nouns *magister, puer, culter, ager,* and *liber*). Find its stem in the feminine or neuter form, i.e., *nigr-*.

XIV – Quarta Decima   Nōmen: _____

IV. Grammatica

You know how to talk about the present and the future in Latin, but in this *lectiō*, you'll learn how to speak about the past. Latin has several past tenses, but the easiest is the imperfect tense.

Here are the personal endings for the imperfect tense. The imperfect tense sign is __-bā__.

	singular	plural
1st person	-bam	-bāmus
2nd person	-bās	-bātis
3rd person	-bat	-bant

And here are the forms for 1st conjugation and 2nd conjugation in imperfect tense. The imperfect is easy! Simply add the imperfect personal endings to the stem.

The *im*perfect tense expresses action that occurred in the past but was *not* completed all at one time. Translate it using the helping verbs *was* or *were* with *–ing* at the end of the verb. It can also be translated using the helping verbs *used to* or *kept*.

		singular	plural	
1st person	I was loving	amābam	amābāmus	We were loving
2nd person	You were loving	amābās	amābātis	You all were loving
3rd person	He, she, it was loving	amābat	amābant	They were loving
1st person	I was staying	manēbam	manēbāmus	We were staying
2nd person	You were staying	manēbās	manēbātis	You all were staying
3rd person	He, she, it was staying	manēbat	manēbant	They were staying

Ambulābam.	I was walking.	I kept walking.	I used to walk.
Festīnābat.	He was hurrying.	He kept hurrying.	He used to hurry.
Cantābāmus.	We were singing.	We kept singing.	We used to sing.

V. Historia (*Famous Men of Rome,* Chapter XXIII)

Octavius Caesar, grandnephew of Julius Caesar, forms a triumvirate with Mark Antony and Lepidus. Octavius defeats Lepidus in Sicily and defeats Mark Antony at the Battle of Actium in 31 BC. Rejecting the title of king, he is named Emperor and given the title *Augustus* in 27 BC.

XIV – Quarta Decima   Nōmen:

VI. Dēlēgāta

A. *Scrībe* the new Latin *verba* and their meanings.

Latīnē *Anglicē*

1. albus, -a, -um — 1. white
2. avia, -ae, f. — 2. grandmother
3. flāvus, -a, -um — 3. yellow
4. līberō, līberāre, līberāvī, līberātum — 4. to free
5. niger, nigra, nigrum — 5. black
6. parō, parāre, parāvī, parātum — 6. to prepare
7. quī — 7. who, he who
8. rūfus, -a, -um — 8. red
9. salūtō, salūtāre, salūtāvī, salūtātum — 9. to greet

B. *Variātiōnēs.* *Recita* these sentence patterns several times.

1. Hic equus stābat. (This horse was standing.)
2. Ille equus cēnābat. (That horse was eating.)
3. Equus rūfus pugnābat. (The red horse was fighting.)
4. Equus niger labōrābat. (The black horse was working.)
5. Equus albus natābat. (The white horse was swimming.)
6. Equus flāvus ambulābat. (The yellow horse was walking.)
7. Prīmus equus aquilam spectābat. (The first horse was looking at an eagle.)
8. Tertius equus mīlitem portābat. (The third horse was carrying a soldier.)

C. *Converte hās sententiās.*

1. Avia mātrem salūtābat. — Grandma was greeting mother.
2. Soror holera parābat. — Sister was preparing vegetables.
3. Servī fabās rūfās parābant. — The servants were preparing red beans.
4. Capillī aviae sunt albī. — Grandma's hairs are white.
5. Dominus servōs līberābat. — The master was freeing the slaves.

XIV – Quarta Decima　　　　　　　　　**Nōmen:**

6. Hic flōs est flāvus.　　　*This flower is yellow.*

7. Illud cerasum est rūfum.　　　*That cherry is red.*

8. Quī cāritātem habet pācem habet.　　　*He who has love has peace.*

9. Ubi in urbe ambulābās?　　　*Were you walking in the city?*

10. Christum laudābāmus.　　　*We were praising Christ.*

11. Nauta margarītam nigram spectābat.　　　*The sailor was looking at the black pearl.*

12. Quotus rēx imperābat?　　　*Which king was ruling?*

13. Quot discipulī rīdēbant?　　　*How many students were laughing?*

14. Quandō frāter tuus tē terrēbat?　　　*When was your brother frightening you?*

D. *Converte* these imperfect verbs in three different ways.

1. Servābam.　　　*I was guarding, I used to guard, I kept guarding.*

2. Dolēbat.　　　*It was aching, it kept aching, it used to ache.*

3. Stābātis.　　　*You were standing, you kept standing, you used to stand.*

E. *Converte hās sententiās aut (aut = or) scrībe illās Anglicē.*

1. Spectābātisne eōs?　　　*Were you watching them?*

2. Cēnābantne canēs?　　　*Were they eating dogs? / Were the dogs eating?*

3. Beātus est quī Deum amat.　　　*Happy is he who loves God.*

4. Calculum flāvum movēbam in illō lūdō.
　　　I was moving the yellow gamepiece in that game.

5. Soror mea calculum rūfum movet.　　　*My sister moves the red gamepiece.*

6. Calculum movēbō ē tertiō spatiō ad octāvum spatium.
　　　I will move the game piece from the third space to the eighth space.

7. Soror mihi āleās trādit.　　　*My sister passes the dice to me.*

XIV – Quarta Decima　　　　　　　　　　**Nōmen:**

8. I was giving a red apple to the black horse in the long field.

    Equō nigrō in longō agrō mālum rubrum dabam.

9. *He* was carrying the girls' books.　　*Is librōs puellārum portābat.*

10. This cat is white.　　*Hic fēles est albus.*

11. I have a black dog.　　*Habeō canem nigrum.*

12. We were sitting in chairs.　　*In sellīs sedēbāmus.*

Ex Scriptūrīs:

13. Servābant eum. (Matt. 27:36)　　*They were serving him.*

14. Angelī et serpēns pugnābant. (Rev. 12:7, alt.)　*The angels and the sepent were fighting.*

15. Beātus est quī legit librum sanctum. (Rev. 1:3, alt.)

    Blessed is he who read the holy book.

F. Conjugate (1) *parō, parāre* **and (2)** *studeō, studēre* **in imperfect tense.**

1.	parābam	parābāmus	2. studēbam	studēbāmus
	parābās	parābātis	studēbās	studēbātis
	parābat	parābant	studēbat	studēbant

G. *Converte* **these** *verba* **and phrases.**

1. quarta decima　*fourteenth*　　2. thirteenth　*tertius decimus, -a, -um*

3. Diēs Īrae　*Day of Wrath*　　4. sine quā nōn　*essential ingredient*

5. summā cum laude　*with highest praise*　6. that is　*id est (i.e.)*

7. Converte hanc sententiam ex Anglicā in Latīnam.

    Translate this sentence from English into Latin.

8. Silent lēgēs inter arma.　　*Laws are silent among arms.*

9. Pay attention now.　　*Nunc attendite.*

10. The Roman Senate and People　　*Senātus Populusque Rōmānus*

XIV – Quarta Decima   **Nōmen:** _____

H. Dērīvātī. Complete each sentence with an English *verbum* chosen from the following *verba*. The italicized *verbum* in the sentence should help you think of the Latin root.

liberty   salutation   albino

1. An __albino__ rabbit is all *white*. Latin root: __albus, -a, -um__

2. __liberty__ is *freedom* we enjoy in America. Latin root: __līberō, līberāre__

3. "Dear Grandma" is an example of a letter's __salutation__, where the writer *greets* the person to whom he/she is writing. Latin root: __salūtō, salūtāre__

I. Anagram. In the spaces provided, *scribe* the *verbum Latinum* corresponding to the clue. Rearrange the shaded letters to spell something Caesar Augustus made and then destroyed.

clue									
he who	Q	U	I						
you were greeting	S	A	L	U	T	A	B	A	S
he was preparing	P	A	R	A	B	A	T		
I was freeing	L	I	B	E	R	A	B	A	M
black (f. nom. s.)	N	I	G	R	A				
red (m. nom. s.)	R	U	F	U	S				
yellow (n. nom. s.)	F	L	A	V	U	S			
white (m. nom. s.)	A	L	B	U	S				
grandmother	A	V	I	A					

Caesar Augustus made and then destroyed a:
T R I U M V I R A T E

J. Historia. Review the history and fill in the blanks.

1. How is Octavius related to Caesar? __Octavian is Caesar's grand nephew.__

2. With whom does he form a triumvirate? __He joins with Mark Antony and Lepidus.__

3. In what battle does he defeat Mark Antony? __Mark Antony is defeated at Actium.__

4. In what year does the Roman Empire officially begin? __The empire begins in 27 BC.__

XV – Quīnta Decima   Nōmen: _____

XV – Quīnta decima lectiō   MORE IMPERFECT
(15 – Fifteenth lesson)

I. Dictum

exemplī grātiā (_e.g._)   _for the sake of example_

II. Colloquium   *Latīnē*   *Anglicē*

Magister:	Confēcistīsne dēlēgātum vestrum?	Did you finish your assignment?
Discipulī:	Certē confēcimus!	Of course we finished!

III. Verba

Latīnē	*Anglicē*	*Scrībe tōtum verbum Latīnum.*	*Dērīvātī*
arcus, -ī, m.	bow, rainbow	arcus, -ī, m.	arch
aurantius, -a, -um	orange	aurantius, -a, -um	orange
avus, -ī, m.	grandfather	avus, -ī, m.	
caeruleus, -a, -um	blue	caeruleus, -a, -um	caerulean
ecce	behold!	ecce	
fulvus, -a, -um	brown	fulvus, -a, -um	
mālum aurantium, -ī, n.	(an) orange	mālum aurantium, -ī, n.	
purpureus, -a, -um	purple	purpureus, -a, -um	purple

1. Why do the *verba* for colors have three endings? _So they can modify all genders._

2. Which *verba* are nouns? _arcus, avus, mālum aurantium_   What declension? _2nd_

3. The genitive singular case ending for these declensions is:

   a. 1st _-ae_   b. 2nd _-ī_   c. 3rd _-is_

4. What is the nominative plural for these *verba*?

   a. arcus _arcī_   b. avus _avī_   c. avia _aviae_   d. ager _agrī_

XV – Quīnta Decima   Nōmen:

IV. Grammatica

Here is the <u>imperfect tense of *sum, esse*</u> and the <u>imperfect tense of *possum, posse*</u>. if you know the imperfect tense of *sum, esse*, the imperfect of *possum, posse* will be easy. Because these are irregular verbs, they must be carefully memorized.

	singular	plural	
1st person — *I was*	eram	erāmus	*We were*
2nd person — *You were*	erās	erātis	*You all were*
3rd person — *He, she, it was*	erat	erant	*They were*
1st person — *I was able*	poteram	poterāmus	*We were able*
2nd person — *You were able*	poterās	poterātis	*You all were able*
3rd person — *He, she, it was able*	poterat	poterant	*They were able*

Remember: *esse* is <u>not</u> a helping verb and <u>cannot</u> be used with another verb in a sentence.

Conjugate: (a) *sum, esse*; (b) *habeō, habēre*; (c) *possum, posse*; (d) *amō, amāre* in imperfect.

a.	*eram*	*erāmus*	b.	*habēbam*	*habēbāmus*
	erās	*erātis*		*habēbās*	*habēbātis*
	erat	*erant*		*habēbat*	*habēbant*
c.	*poteram*	*poterāmus*	d.	*amābam*	*amābāmus*
	poterās	*poterātis*		*amābās*	*amābātis*
	poterat	*poterant*		*amābat*	*amābant*

V. Historia (*Famous Men of Rome*, Chapter XXIV, Parts I and II)

After Augustus dies in 14 AD, the Empire sees three cruel emperors: Tiberius, Caligula, and Claudius. The fifth emperor, Nero, is even worse. In 54 AD, Nero's mother, Agrippina, kills emperor Claudius after making him name Nero his successor rather than his own son, Britannicus. Nero becomes emperor, but out of fear, he kills Britannicus and then Agrippina.

XV – Quīnta Decima   Nōmen:

VI. Dēlēgāta

A. *Scrībe* the new Latin *verba* and their meanings.

Latīnē	*Anglicē*
1. arcus, -ī, m.	1. bow, rainbow
2. aurantius, -a, -um	2. orange
3. avus, -ī, m.	3. grandfather
4. caeruleus, -a, -um	4. blue
5. ecce	5. behold!
6. fulvus, -a, -um	6. brown
7. mālum aurantium, -ī, n.	7. an orange
8. purpureus, -a, -um	8. purple

B. *Variātiōnēs.* *Recitā* these sentence patterns several times.

1. Avus huic puerō dōna dat.   (Grandfather is giving gifts to this boy.)
2. Avus huic puellae dōna dat.   (Grandfather is giving gifts to this girl.)
3. Avus illī puerō dōna dat.   (Grandfather is giving gifts to that boy.)
4. Avus illī puellae dōna dat.   (Grandfather is giving gifts to that girl.)
5. Avus eī dōna dat.   (Grandfather is giving gifts to him / her.)
6. Avus mihi dōna dat.   (Grandfather is giving gifts to me.)
7. Oculī huius puerī fulvī sunt.   (This boy's eyes are brown.)
9. Oculī illīus puellae caeruleī sunt.   (That girl's eyes are blue.)
10. Oculī eius caeruleī sunt.   (His / Her eyes are blue.)

C. *Converte hās sententiās.*

1. Hic flōs est aurantius.   *This flower is orange.*
2. Illud vīnum est purpureum.   *That wine is purple.*
3. Caelum est caeruleum.   *The sky is blue.*
4. Capillī meī sunt fulvī.   *My hairs are brown.*
5. Ōs meum est rūfum.   *My mouth is red.*

XV – Quīnta Decima　　　　　　Nōmen: _____

6. Dentēs meī sunt albī. _____ *My teeth are white.*

7. Stellae lūcēbant. _____ *The stars were shining.*

8. Ioannes ad mēnsam sedēbat. _____ *John was sitting at the table.*

9. Fēles in bracchiīs meīs erat. _____ *The cat was in my arms.*

10. Pānem in mēnsā habēbāmus. _____ *We used to have bread on the table.*

11. Cūr flōrem huic puellae dabās? _____ *Why were you giving a flower to this girl?*

12. Suntne capillī illīus puellae fulvī? _____ *Are this girl's hairs brown?*

13. Erantne capillī huius puerī flāvī? _____ *Were this boy's hairs yellow?*

D. *Converte* these imperfect verbs in three different ways.

1. Habēbāmus. _____ *We used to have, we kept having, we were having.*

2. Vidēbant. _____ *They were seeing, they used to see, they kept seeing.*

3. Movēbās. _____ *You were moving, you kept moving, you used to move.*

E. *Converte hās sententiās aut scrībe illās Anglicē.*

1. Avus capillōs fulvōs habēbat. _____ *Grandfather used to have brown hairs.*

2. Avus capillōs albōs nunc habet. _____ *Grandfather has white hairs now.*

3. Arcum mīlitis tenēre poteram. _____ *I was able to hold the soldier's bow.*

4. Arcus in caelō est aurantius et purpureus et caeruleus. _____
_____ *The bow in heaven is orange and purple and blue.*

5. Tarquinia ūnum canem habēbat. _____ *Tarquinia used to have one dog.*

6. Anna duōs canēs habēbat. _____ *Anna used to have two dogs.*

7. Septimus trīs canēs habēbat. _____ *Septimus used to have three dogs.*

8. That orange was good. _____ *Illud mālum aurantium erat bonum.*

9. She was able to carry the gems. _____ *Illa gemmās portāre poterat.*

XV – Quīnta Decima   Nōmen:

10. That flower is purple.   *Ille flōs est purpureus.*

11. The sailor used to have a blue jewel.   *Nauta gemmam caeruleam habēbat.*

Ex Scriptūrīs:

12. Et ille tenēbat in dexterā eius stellās septem et ecce: in ōre eius gladius erat. (Rev. 1:16, alt.)

    And he was holding seven stars in his right hand and behold: a sword was in his mouth.

13. Ecce equus albus et quī sedēbat in illō tenēbat arcum. (Rev. 6:2)

    Behold: a white horse, and he who was sitting on it was holding a bow.

14. Ecce equus rūfus et quī sedēbat in illō tenēbat gladium magnum. (Rev. 6:4, alt.)

    Behold: a red horse, and he who was sitting on it was holding a great sword.

F. Conjugate (1) *sum, esse* and (2) *possum, posse* in imperfect tense.

1. eram   erāmus   2. poteram   poterāmus
    erās   erātis   poterās   poterātis
    erat   erant   poterat   poterant

G. *Converte* these *verba* and phrases.

1. quīnta decima *fifteenth*   2. fourteenth *quartus decimus, -a, -um*
3. exemplī grātia *for example* 4. You, too, Brutus? *Et tū, Brūte?*
5. Claudite librōs. *Close your books.* 6. Diēs Īrae *Day of Wrath.*
7. Confēcistīne dēlēgātum tuum? *Did you finish your assignment?*
8. Quid est tibi? *What is the matter with you?*
9. Hōra est quaestiunculae. *It's time for a quiz.*
10. Translate this sentence. *Converte hanc sententiam.*
11. Where do you live? *Ubi habitās?*

H. Dērīvātī. Complete each sentence with an English *verbum* chosen from the following *verba*. The italicized *verbum* in the sentence should help you think of the Latin root.

arch   caerulean

XV – Quīnta Decima   Nōmen:

1. ___Caerulean___ is a shade of *blue*. Latin root: ___caeruleus, -a, -um___

2. An ___arch___ is a *bow*-shaped, curved opening. Latin root: ___arcus, -ī, m.___

I. Crossword Puzzle. When the puzzle is completed, the letters in the shaded squares can be rearranged to show what Roman history taught President James Madison to do with political powers. *Nōtā bene (N.B.)*: All adjectives in this puzzle are masculine singular.

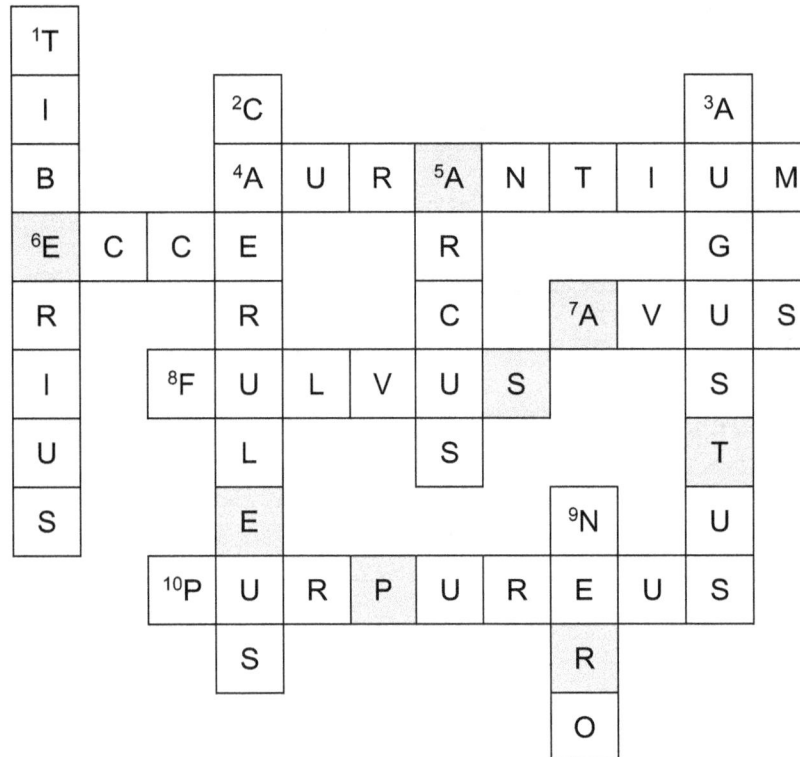

RĒCTĒ:
4. orange (the color)
6. behold
7. grandfather
8. brown
10. purple

DEORSUM
1. secundus imperātor
2. blue
3. prīmus imperātor
5. bow
9. quīntus imperātor

S E P A R A T E them!

J. Historia. Review the history and fill in the blanks.

1. Who is the second emperor of Rome?   ___Tiberius was Rome's second emperor.___

2. Quis tertius imperātor Romae est?   ___Tertius imperātor erat Caligula.___

3. Quis quartus imperātor Romae est?   ___Claudius erat quartus imperātor.___

4. In what year does Nero become emperor?   ___Nero became emperor in 54. AD___

XVI – Sexta Decima Nōmen: _____

XVI – Sexta decima lectiō   VESTĪMENTA
(16 – Sixteenth lesson)   (Clothes)

I. Dictum

Tē Deum laudāmus.   *We praise you, O God.*

II. Colloquium   *Latīnē*   *Anglicē*

| **Semprōnia:** | Ubi sunt calceī meī? | Where are my shoes? |
| **Catō:** | Hīc sunt! | Here they are! |

III. Verba

Latīnē	*Anglicē*	*Scrībe tōtum verbum Latīnum.*	*Dērīvātī*
brācae, brācārum, f.	pants	brācae, brācārum, f.	breeches
calceus, -ī, m.	shoe	calceus, -ī, m.	
camisia, -ae, f.	shirt	camisia, -ae, f.	camisole
cingulum, -ī, n.	belt	cingulum, -ī, n.	cinch

claudō, claudere, clausī, clausum to close — clause

| claudō | claudere | clausī | clausum |

gerō, gerere, gessī, gestum to wear — gestation

| gerō | gerere | gessī | gestum |

induō, induere, induī, indūtum to put on — endue

| induō | induere | induī | indūtum |

petō, petere, petīvī, petītum to seek, to beg, to ask for — petition

| petō | petere | petīvī | petītum |

scrībō, scrībere, scrīpsī, scriptum to write — script

| scrībō | scrībere | scrīpsī | scriptum |

Why do you think that *bracae* is plural, when a pair of pants is *one* piece of clothing?

XVI – Sexta Decima   Nōmen: _____

IV. Grammatica

The imperfect is almost as easy for 3rd conjugation as it is for 1st and 2nd conjugations. In this tense the stem vowel becomes an ē (remember that it changes quite a bit in the present tense too), and then add the imperfect personal endings to the stem.

	singular	plural	
1st person _I was believing_	crēdēbam	crēdēbāmus	_We were believing_
2nd person _You were believing_	crēdēbās	crēdēbātis	_You all were believing_
3rd person _He/she/it was believeing_	crēdēbat	crēdēbant	_They were believing_

1. How do you find the imperfect stem for 1st- and 2nd-conjugation verbs?
   Drop -re from the infinitive of the verb

2. What does the imperfect tense express? _It expresses past unclompleted action_

3. The two best helping verbs to use when translating the imperfect tense are _was_ and _were_.

4. Conjugate (a) dīcō, dīcere; (b) scrībō, scrībere; (c) claudō, claudere; and (d) mittō, mittere in imperfect tense.

a.	_dīcēbam_	_dīcēbāmus_	b.	_scrībēbam_	_scrībēbāmus_
	dīcēbās	_dīcēbātis_		_scrībābās_	_scrībābātis_
	dīcēbat	_dīcēbant_		_scrībēbat_	_scrībēbant_
c.	_claudēbam_	_claudēbāmus_	d.	_mittēbam_	_mittēbāmus_
	claudēbās	_claudēbātis_		_mittēbās_	_mittēbātis_
	claudēbat	_claudēbant_		_mittēbat_	_mittēbant_

V. Historia (*Famous Men of Rome,* Chapter XXIV, Parts III and IV)

Nero becomes even worse than before. He kills his friends and his wife, and, probably after setting the fire himself, he plays the harp as he watches Rome burn! He then blames Christians for the blaze and has many of them killed. A first plot to kill him fails. Then, in 68 AD, hiding in fear from a revolt by the army, Emperor Nero dies at the hand of a slave.

XVI – Sexta Decima   Nōmen:

VI. Dēlēgāta

A. *Scrībe* the new Latin *verba* and their meanings.

Latīnē	*Anglicē*
1. _brācae, brācārum, f._	1. _pants_
2. _calceus, -ī, m._	2. _shoe_
3. _camisia, -ae, f._	3. _shirt_
4. _cingulum, -ī, n._	4. _belt_
5. _claudō, claudere, clausī, clausum_	5. _to close_
6. _gerō, gerere, gessī, gestum_	6. _to wear_
7. _induō, induere, InduI, indūtum_	7. _to put on_
8. _petō, petere, petīvī, petītum_	8. _to seek, to beg, to ask for_
9. _scrībō, scrībere, scrīpsī, scrīptum_	9. _to write_

B. Variātiōnēs. *Recita* these sentence patterns several times. Be sure to read the whole Latin line aloud, including the nominative at the beginning.

1. Brācae.   Lūcius brācās induit.   (Pants. Lucius is putting on pants.)
2. Calceī.   Lūcius calceōs induit.   (Shoes. Lucius is putting on shoes.)
3. Camisia.   Lūcius camisiam induit.   (Shirt. Lucius is putting on a shirt.)
4. Cingulum.   Lūcius cingulum induit.   (Belt. Lucius is putting on a belt.)
5. Pedālia.   Lūcius pedālia induit.   (Socks. Lucius is putting on socks.)
6. Pilleus.   Lūcius pilleum induit.   (Hat. Lucius is putting on a hat.)
7. Brācae.   Stella brācās gerēbat.   (Pants. Stella was wearing pants.)
8. Calceī.   Stella calceōs gerēbat.   (Shoes. Stella was wearing shoes.)
9. Camisia.   Stella camisiam gerēbat.   (Shirt. Stella was wearing a shirt.)
10. Cingulum.   Stella cingulum gerēbat.   (Belt. Stella was wearing a belt.)
11. Pedālia.   Stella pedālia gerēbat.   (Socks. Stella was wearing socks.)
12. Pilleus.   Stella pilleum gerēbat.   (Hat. Stella was wearing a hat.)

C. Converte hās sententiās.

1. Antōnius calceōs induēbat.   _Antōnius was putting on shoes._

2. Vitellius calceōs fulvōs gerit.   _Vitellius wears brown shoes._

XVI – Sexta Decima   Nōmen: _____

3. Cornēlia brācās fulvās gerēbat. _____Cornelia used to wear brown pants._____

4. Iūlia duo pedālia induit. _____Julia puts on two socks._____

5. Sextus duōs pilleōs habēbat. _____Sextus used to have two hats._____

6. Lydia used to have two blue hats. _____Lydia duōs pilleōs caeruleōs habēbat._____

7. Marcus trīs camisiās flāvās habēbit. _____Marcus used to have three yellow shirts._____

8. Quis camisiam purpuream gerit? _____Who is wearing a purple shirt?_____

9. Cūr Aemilia duās camisiās aurantiās habet?

_____Why does Aemilia have two orange shirts?_____

D. *Converte* **these imperfect verbs in three different ways.**

1. Petēbant. _____They were asking, They kept asking, They used to ask._____

2. Scrībēbās. _____You were writing, You kept writing, You used to write._____

3. Claudēbātis. _____You all were closing. You all kept closing. You all used to close._____

E. *Converte hās sententiās aut scrībe illās Latīnē.*

1. Claudēbam fenestram. _____I was closing the window._____

2. Servī calceōs petunt. _____The servants were asking for shoes._____

3. Ille puer portiōnem petēbat. _____That boy kept asking for a snack._____

4. Hic magister librum scrībit. _____This teach is writing a book._____

5. The good student was able to write books.

_____Discipulus bonus poterat librōs scrībere._____

6. Mīlitēs illī rēgī scrībere poterant. _____The soldiers were able to write to the king._____

7. Avis super nimbōs ascendēbat. _____The bird was ascending above the clouds._____

8. The king was sending the legion across the country.

_____Rēx legiōnēs trans patriam mittēbat._____

XVI – Sexta Decima   Nōmen:

9. Augustus mēcum ambulābat.   _Augustus used to walk with me._

10. I was wearing a wide hat.   _Pilleum lātum gerēbam._

11. Titus was writing to Livia.   _Titus ad Liviam scrībēbat._

12. We were often happy.   _Saepe erāmus laetī._

Ex Scriptūrīs:

13. Scrībō vōbīs mandātum Dominī. (I Cor. 14:37, alt.; *mandātum, -ī, n.* – commandment)

   I write to you the commandment of the Lord.

F. Conjugate (1) *petō, petere* **and (2)** *gerō, gerere* **in imperfect tense.**

1. _petēbam_   _petēbāmus_   2. _gerēbam_   _gerēbāmus_

   petēbās   _petēbātis_   _gerēbās_   _gerēbātis_

   petēbat   _petēbant_   _gerēbat_   _gerēbant_

G. *Converte* these *verba* and phrases.

1. sexta decima   _sixteenth_   2. fifteenth   _quīntus decimus, -a, -um_

3. ad nauseam   _too long_   4. ante merīdiem   _before noon_

5. Tē Deum laudāmus.   _We praise you, O God._

6. Laws are silent among arms.   _Lēgēs inter arma silent._

7. Quota hōra est?   _What time is it?_

8. Ubi sunt calceī meī?   _Where are my shoes?_

9. Did you finish your assignment?   _Cōnfēcistīne dēlēgātum tuum?_

10. I came, I saw, I conquered.   _Vēnī, vīdī, vīcī._

H. Dērīvātī. Complete each sentence with an English *verbum* chosen from the following *verba*. The italicized *verbum* in the sentence should help you think of the Latin root.

   camisole   cinch   claustrophobia   petulant   Scripture

XVI – Sexta Decima   Nōmen: _____

1. He liked to _____cinch_____ up his *belt*. Latin root: __cingulum, -ī, n.__

2. _____Scripture_____ is God's *written* Word. Latin root: __scrībō, scrībere__

3. A _____camisole_____ is a woman's sleeveless *shirt*. Latin root: __camisia, -ae, f.__

4. The child's _____petulant_____ *begging* was very annoying. Latin root: __petō, petere__

5. _____Claustrophobia_____ is the fear of being *closed* in. Latin root: __claudō, claudere__

I. *Verbum* Search. Each of the *verba* listed below can be found in this grid, reading forward, backward, up, down, or diagonally. The verbs will be in the form given below or in the imperfect tense. All the unused letters, when read row by row from top to bottom, will tell three ways to translate the nonsense word *xēbam*:

Translation: _____I was x-ing, I kept x-ing, I used to x_____

```
B  M  U  L  U  G  N  I  C
C  R  S  M  I  T  T  O  S
A  I  A  I  W  A  H  U  S
M  X  I  C  T  N  M  G  I
I  K  E  P  A  A  A  T  X
S  C  R  I  B  E  B  A  S
I  I  T  E  E  L  E  A  N
A  P  R  O  D  A  U  O  D
G  E  A  G  U  D  D  D  I
G  T  D  E  A  E  N  E  C
I  O  O  L  L  P  I  R  O
U  S  U  E  C  L  A  C  S
E  E  R  A  M  D  T  O  X
```

WORD LIST

BRACAE
CALCEUS
CAMISIA
CINGULUM
CLAUDO
CREDO
DICO
DO (imperf. tense)
GERO
HOC
INDUO
LEGO
MITTO
PEDALE
PETO
SCRIBO
TRADO
SUM

J. Historia. Review the history and fill in the blanks.

1. What does Nero do while Rome burns? __Nero plays his harp and recites poetry.__

2. Whom does he blame for the fire? __Nero blames the Christians for the fire.__

3. In what year does Nero die? __Nero dies in 68 AD.__

XVII – Septima decima lectiō   TEMPORA ANNĪ
(17 – Seventeenth lesson)   (__seasons__ lit., __times of the year__)

I. Dictum

dramatis persōnae   __characters__   (lit., __masks of the drama__)

II. Colloquium
Latīnē   *Anglicē*

Flāvius:	Quotum tempus annī tibi maximē placet?	Which season do you like most?
Aurēlia:	Vēr mihi placet. Quotum tempus minimē placet?	I like spring. Which season do you like least?
Flāvius:	Autumnus mihi nōn placet.	I don't like fall.

III. Verba

Latīnē	Anglicē	Scrībe tōtum verbum Latīnum.	Dērīvātī
aestās, aestātis, f.	summer	aestās, aestātis, f.	aestival
autumnus, -ī, m.	autumn, fall	autumnus, -ī, n.	autumnal
hiems, hiemis, f.	winter	hiems, hiemis, f.	
vēr, vēris, n.	spring	vēr, vēris, n.	vernal
grātia, -ae, f.	grace	grātia, -ae, f.	grace

ningit, ningere, ninxit to snow

    ningit   *ningere*   *ninxit*

nix, nivis, f.   snow   nix, nivis, f.

pluit, pluere, pluit to rain

    pluit   *pluere*   *pluit*

pluvia, -ae, f.   rain   pluvia, -ae, f.

1. From which conjugation are the verbs above? ___ How can you tell? _____

2. Which nouns are from 1st declension? From 2nd? From 3rd?

N.B.: *Pluit* and *ningit* are <u>only</u> used in the 3rd-person singular and the infinitive forms.

XVII – Septima Decima Nōmen:

IV. Grammatica

Here is the <u>future tense of *3rd conjugation*</u>. It does not use the ordinary future tense endings. Instead, we change the stem vowel to an *a* (for 1st person singular) or to a long *ē* (for all others). When you learn 4th conjugation you will see that it works the same way. Memorize this silly rhyme about future tense: "*Bo, bi, bu* for one and two; *a* and *e* for four and three!"

This means that in the future tense of conjugations one and two, we see the endings *bō, bi* and *bu* (e.g.: *amābō, anābis, amābunt*). In conjugations four and three, however, we simply change the stem vowel to *a* and *ē* (e.g.: *crēdam, crēdēs*) and leave the usual personal endings in place.

		singular	plural	
1st person	*I will believe*	crēdam	crēdēmus	*We will believe*
2nd person	*You will believe*	crēdēs	crēdētis	*You all will believe*
3rd person	*He/she/it will believe*	crēdet	crēdent	*They will believe*

The <u>ablative case</u> has many uses besides being used for objects of prepositions. It is used with *dīgnus, -a, -um* to express the idea of being worthy <u>of</u> (something).

Deus est <u>laude</u> dīgnus.	God is worthy <u>of praise</u>.

And in <u>expressions of time</u>, the ablative case is used without any preposition: *in* is not needed.

<u>Hieme</u> ningit.	It snows <u>in winter</u>.

Conjugate (a) *dīcō, dīcere* and (b) *scrībō, scrībere* in future tense.

a.	*dīcam*	*dīcēmus*	b.	*scrībam*	*scrībēmus*
	dīcēs	*dīcētis*		*scrībēs*	*scrībētis*
	dīcet	*dīcent*		*scrībet*	*scrībent*

V. Historia (*Famous Men of Rome*, Chapter XXV)

After Nero dies, three generals—Galba, Otho, and Vitellius—become emperor, each for just a few months. Then in 69 AD, General Titus Flavius Vespasian, known as Vespasian, takes advantage of the turmoil and becomes emperor. In 70 AD, his son Titus destroys Jerusalem, and in 79 AD, he becomes emperor. Titus builds the Colosseum and the Baths of Titus. During his reign, Pompeii and Herculaneum are destroyed by the eruption of Mt. Vesuvius.

XVII – Septima Decima   Nōmen:

VI. Dēlēgāta

A. *Scrībe* the new Latin *verba* and their meanings.

Latīnē   *Anglicē*

1. aestās, aestātis, f.   1. summer
2. autumnus, -ī, m.   2. autumn, fall
3. hiems, hiemis, f.   3. winter
4. vēr, vēris, n.   4. spring
5. grātia, -ae, f.   5. grace
6. ningit, ningere, ninxit   6. to snow
7. nix, nivis, f.   7. snow
8. pluit, pluere, pluit   8. to rain
9. pluvia, -ae, f.   9. rain

B. *Variātiōnēs.* *Recitā* these sentence patterns several times. (N.B. Sentences 1-8 are idiomatic Latin, i.e., they are written as the Romans expressed these ideas, but they are not translated literally.)

1. Aestās mihi placet.   (I like summer. Lit., Summer is pleasing to me.)
2. Autumnus mihi placet.   (I like autumn.)
3. Hiems mihi placet.   (I like winter.)
4. Vēr mihi placet.   (I like spring.)
5. Placetne tibi aestās?   (Do you like summer?)
6. Placetne tibi autumnus?   (Do you like autumn?)
7. Placetne tibi hiems?   (Do you like winter?)
8. Placetne tibi vēr?   (Do you like spring?)
9. Hieme ningit.   (It snows in winter.)
10. Aestāte numquam ningit.   (It never snows in summer.)
11. Vēre saepe pluit.   (It often rains in spring.)
12. Autumnō non saepe pluit.   (It does not often rain in autumn.)

C. *Converte hās sententiās.*

1. Ningit super montēs.   It rains over the mountains.

2. Ningēbat ad flūmen.   It was raining toward/at the river.

XVII – Septima Decima   Nōmen: _____

3. Vēre multum pluit.   _In spring, it rains/rained a lot._

4. Autumnō parum pluēbat.   _In the fall, it was raining little._

5. Hiems erat bona.   _Winter was good._

6. Autumnus erit bonus.   _Fall will be good._

7. Vēr est bonum.   _Spring is good._

8. Lūcius brācās in cubiculō induēbat.
   Luke was putting on pants in his bedroom.

9. Cūr rēx hostibus nūntium mittit?
   Why does the king send a message to the enemies?

10. Amāsne natāre aestāte?   _Do you like to swim in summer?_

11. Ille rēx erat laude dīgnus.   _That king was worthy of praise._

D. *Converte hās sententiās aut scrībe illās Latīne.*

1. Hiems est tempus annī optimum.   _Winter is the best time of year._

2. Nix dē caelō dēscendēbat.   _Snow was coming down from the sky._

3. Nix et pluvia dē caelō dēscendent.   _Snow and rain will come down from the sky._

4. Haec nix est bella.   _This snow is beautiful._

5. Illa nix erat bella.   _That snow was beautiful._

6. Arcus illīus mīlitis valēbat.   _The bow of that soldier used to be strong._

7. Mendācia huius rēgis erant magna.   _The lies of this king were great._

8. Deus meus est glōriā dīgnus.   _My God is worthy of glory._

9. Brācae huius puellae flāvae erant.   _This girl's pants were yellow._

10. The flowers were blue.   _Flōrēs caeruleī erant._

11. The snow was white.   _Nix erat alba._

XVII – Septima Decima   Nōmen:

12. It was raining in the winter!   *Hieme pluēbat!*

Ex Scriptūrīs:

13. Grātia vōbīs et pax ab eō quī est, et quī erat, et quī ventūrus est. (Rev. 1:4; *ventūrus* – coming)

    Grace to you and peace from him who is, and who was, and who is coming.

14. In principiō erat Verbum, et Verbum erat apud Deum, et Deus erat Verbum. (John 1:1; *apud [+ Ac]* – with, in the presence of)

    In the beginning was the Word, and the Word was with God, and the Word was God.

15. Hoc erat in principiō apud Deum. (John 1:2)   He was in the beginning with God.

16. In eō vīta erat, et vīta erat lūx hominum. (John 1:4, alt.)

    In him was life, and the life was the light of men.

E. *Converte* these *verba* and phrases.

1. septima decima   **seventeenth**
2. sixteenth   **sextus decimus, -a, -um**
3. dramatis persōnae   **characters**
4. post merīdiem   **after noon (pm)**
5. Diēs Īrae   **Day of Wrath**
6. tempora annī   **seasons**
7. Quotum tempus annī tibi maximē placet?   **Which season do you like best?**

F. Conjugate (1) *placeō, -ēre*; and (2) *dīcō, dīcere* in future tense.

1.	placēbō	placēbimus	2.	dīcam	dīcēmus
	placēbis	placēbitis		dīcēs	dicētis
	placēbit	placēbunt		dīcet	dīcent

XVII – Septima Decima   Nōmen:

G. Conjugate (1) *mittō, mittere;* **and (2)** *sum, esse* **in the present tense.**

1.	mittō	mittimus	2.	sum	sumus
	mittis	mittitis		es	estis
	mittit	mittunt		est	sunt

H. Anagrams. Unscramble each *verbum*, and *scribe* it in the squares. When you finish, unscramble the letters in the shaded squares to finish *hanc sententiam Latīnam*:

Vēr est T E M P U S   A N N I .

Anagram	Solution
XNI	N I X
EVR	V E R
MHESI	H I E M S
TULIP	P L U I T
TGAARI	G R A T I A
TSAASE	A E S T A S
GTIINN	N I N G I T
UAVLIP	P L U V I A
USUTNUAM	A U T U M N U S

I. Historia. Review the history and fill in the blanks.

1. What three emperors have short reigns (68-69 AD)? _Galba, Otho, Vitelius_

2. Who becomes emperor after them? _Vespasian_

3. Although the ninth and tenth emperors have the same name, the son is known in history as _Titus_

4. What does Titus do in 70 AD? _Titus destroys the temple in Jerusalem._

5. What disaster happens during Titus's reign? _Mt. Vesuvius erupts._

XVIII – Duodēvīcēsima   Nōmen:

XVIII – Duodēvīcēsima lectiō   MENSĒS
(18 – Eighteenth lesson)   (Months)

I. Dictum

nōtā bene (___N.B.___)   ___Note well!___

II. Colloquium   *Latīnē*   *Anglicē*

Valeria:	Quō mense nātus es?	In what month were you born?
Quīntus:	Mense Augustō nātus sum.	I was born in the month of August.
	Quō mense nāta es tū?	In what month were you born?
Valeria:	Mense Februāriō nāta sum.	I was born in the month of February.

III. Verba

Latīnē	*Anglicē*	*Scrībe tōtum verbum Latīnum.*	*Dērīvātī*
mensis, mensis, m.	month	*mensis, mensis, m.*	*semester*
Iānuārius, -ī, m.	January	*Iānuārius, -ī, m.*	*January*
Februārius, -ī, m.	February	*Februārius, -ī, m.*	*February*
Martius, -ī, m.	March	*Martius, -ī, m.*	*March*
Aprīlis, Aprīlis, m.	April	*Aprīlis, Aprīlis, m.*	*April*
Māius, -ī, m.	May	*Māius, -ī, m.*	*May*
Iūnius, -ī, m.	June	*Iūnius, -ī, m.*	*June*
Iūlius, -ī, m.	July	*Iūlius, -ī, m.*	*July*
Augustus, -ī, m.	August	*Augustus, -ī, m.*	*August*
September, -bris, m.	September	*September, Septembris, m.*	*September*
Octōber, -bris, m.	October	*Octōber, Octōbris, m.*	*October*
November, -bris, m.	November	*November, Novembris, m.*	*November*
December, -bris, m.	December	*December, Decembris, m.*	*December*

XVIII – Duodēvīcēsima   Nōmen:

IV. Grammatica

You have probably noticed that the last four months are named after numbers: *septem, octō, novem,* and *decem.* But they aren't the seventh, eighth, ninth, and tenth months! The Roman calendar originally began in *Martius.* Thus, September *was* the seventh month, and the leap day (which is now in February every fourth year) was added at the end of the year. At some point, the Romans decided to start the year in *Iānuārius.* Plutarch, a first-century Greek writer, tells us that King Numa Pompilius made the decision because he thought it was more appropriate to begin the year honoring Janus, the god who looks backward and forward, than Mars, the god of war. We still use the new year as a time to think back on what has happened and to plan ahead and make resolutions for the coming year.

Plutarch also tells us about other months. *Māius* and *Iūnius*, he says, were either named for the goddesses Maia and Juno *or* to honor older people, *māiōrēs*, and younger people, *iūniōrēs*. According to the calendar, who do you think is greater: older people or younger people?

Julius Caesar named the seventh month after himself. Caesar Augustus followed suit and took the eighth month for himself. They each wanted a long month to reflect their greatness!

The seasons and the months can both be expressions of time, so, as with the seasons, the ablative case is used when one means *in___*, e.g., *Februāriō nāvigābit = He will sail in February.*

Conjugate (a) *possum, posse* and (b) *legō, legere* in imperfect tense.

a.	*poteram*	*poterāmus*	b.	*legēbam*	*legēbāmus*
	poterās	*poterātis*		*legēbās*	*legēbātis*
	poterat	*poterant*		*legēbat*	*legēbant*

Conjugate (a) *lūceō, lūcēre* and (b) *dīcō, dīcere* in future tense.

a.	*lūcēbō*	*lūcēbimus*	b.	*dīcam*	*dīcēmus*
	lūcēbis	*lūcēbitis*		*dīcēs*	*dīcētis*
	lūcēbit	*lūcēbunt*		*dīcet*	*dīcent*

V. Historia (*Famous Men of Rome,* Chapter XXVI)

Titus is followed by his brother Domitian, who amuses himself by killing flies, and Nerva. In 98 AD Nerva's adopted son, Trajan, becomes the thirteenth emperor of Rome. Trajan achieves great military victories in Dacia, Armenia, and Mesopotamia. He also promotes public works and literature. Plutarch and Tacitus live during his time.

XVIII – Duodēvīcēsima   Nōmen:

VI. Dēlēgata

A. *Scrībe* the new Latin *verba* and their meanings.

Latīnē   *Anglicē*

1. mensis, mensis, m.   1. month
2. Iānuārius, -ī, m.   2. January
3. Februārius, -ī, m.   3. February
4. Martius, -ī, m.   4. March
5. Aprīlis, Aprīlis, m.   5. April
6. Māius, -ī m.   6. May
7. Iūnius, -ī, m.   7. June
8. Iūlius, -ī, m.   8. July
9. Augustus, -ī m.   9. August
10. September, Septembris, m.   10. September
11. Octōber, Octōbris, m.   11. October
12. November, Novembris, m.   12. November
13. December, Decembris, m.   13. December

B. *Variātiōnēs*. *Recitā* these sentence patterns several times. (N.B.: *nātus* vs. *nāta*)

1. Mense Iānuāriō nātus / nāta sum.   (I was born in the month of January.)
2. Mense Februāriō nātus / nāta sum.   (I was born in the month of February.)
3. Mense Martiō nātus / nāta sum.   (I was born in the month of March.)
4. Mense Aprīle nātus / nāta sum.   (I was born in the month of April.)
5. Mense Māiō nātus / nāta sum.   (I was born in the month of May.)
6. Mense Iūniō nātus / nāta sum.   (I was born in the month of June.)
7. Mense Iūliō nātus / nāta sum.   (I was born in the month of July.)
8. Mense Augustō nātus / nāta sum.   (I was born in the month of August.)
9. Mense Septembre nātus / nāta sum.   (I was born in the month of September.)
10. Mense Octōbre nātus / nāta sum.   (I was born in the month of October.)
11. Mense Novembre nātus / nāta sum.   (I was born in the month of November.)
12. Mense Decembre nātus / nāta sum.   (I was born in the month of December.)

XVIII – Duodēvīcēsima　　　　　　Nōmen:

C. Converte hās sententiās.

1. Iānuārius est prīmus mensis. _January is the first month._
2. September est nōnus mensis. _September is the ninth month._
3. Iūniō multum natābimus. _In June, we will swim a lot._
4. Decembre multum cantābāmus. _In December we will sing a lot._
5. Iūliō natāre saepe poterāmus. _In July, we were able to swim often._
6. Aprīle natāre nōn poterāmus. _In April, we were not able to swim._
7. Augustō sine calceīs ambulāre poterās.
   In August we were able to walk without shoes.
8. Līvia semper pilleum Martiō gerit. _Livia always wears a hat in March._
9. Quotus mensis tibi maximē placet? _Which month do you like best?_
10. Quis natāre Februāriō amat? _Who likes to swim in February?_

D. Converte hās sententiās aut scrībe illās Latīne.

1. Annus duodecim mensēs habet. _The year has twelve months._
2. Māius est mensis vēris. _May is a month of spring._
3. November est mensis autumnī. _November is a month of autumn._
4. Nivēs Decembris semper bellae sunt.
   December's snows are always pretty.
5. Aprīle multum pluit. _It rains/rained a lot in April._
6. Augustō parum pluet. _In August, it will rain little._
7. Four gospels tell about the life of Christ.
   Quattuor evangelia dē vītā Christī dīcunt.
8. Rhea was born in April. _Rhea mense Aprīlis nāta est._

XVIII – Duodēvīcēsima   **Nōmen:** _____

9. We were able to swim in September.   _Septembre poterāmus natāre._

10. May is the fifth month.   _Māius est mēnsis quīntus._

11. The farmers were not able to plow in March.

   Martiō, agricolae arāre nōn poterant.

Ex Scriptūrīs:

12. "Ego sum Alpha et Omega, principium et fīnis," dīcit Dominus Deus quī est, et quī erat, et

   quī ventūrus est. (*ventūrus est – who is coming* Rev. 1:8)

   "I am the Alpha and the Omega, the beginning and the end," says the Lord God

   who is, and who was, and who is coming.

E. *Converte* these *verba* and phrases.

1. duodēvīcēsima _twelfth_   2. seventeenth _septimus decimus, -a, -um_

3. Nōtā bene. _Note well (N.B.)_   4. for example _exemplī grātiā (e.g.)_

5. Quō mēnse nātus / nāta es? _In which month were you born?_

F. Conjugate (1) *dō, dare* and (2) *dīcō, dīcere* in imperfect tense.

1.	dabam	dabāmus	2.	dīcēbam	dīcēbāmus
	dabās	dabātis		dīcēbās	dīcēbātis
	dabat	dabant		dīcēbat	dīcēbant

G. Conjugate (1) *possum, posse* in the present and (2) imperfect tenses.

1.	possum	possumus	2.	poteram	poterāmus
	potes	potestis		poterās	poterātis
	potest	possunt		poterat	poterant

H. Mixed-Up Calendar. The printer forgot to put the names of the months on this calendar and then got them all out of order. Can you figure out which month is which? (N.B. Two months in every year look exactly the same.)

XVIII – Duodēvīcēsima   Nōmen:

				Martius		
				1	2	3
4	5	6	7	8	9	10
11	12	13	14	15	16	17
18	19	20	21	22	23	24
25	26	27	28	29	30	31

				Augustus		
			1	2	3	4
5	6	7	8	9	10	11
12	13	14	15	16	17	18
19	20	21	22	23	24	25
26	27	28	29	30	31	

				Iūlius		
1	2	3	4	5	6	7
8	9	10	11	12	13	14
15	16	17	18	19	20	21
22	23	24	25	26	27	28
29	30	31				

				November		
				1	2	3
4	5	6	7	8	9	10
11	12	13	14	15	16	17
18	19	20	21	22	23	24
25	26	27	28	29	30	

				Iānuārius		
1	2	3	4	5	6	
7	8	9	10	11	12	13
14	15	16	17	18	19	20
21	22	23	24	25	26	27
28	29	30	31			

				Octōber		
1	2	3	4	5	6	
7	8	9	10	11	12	13
14	15	16	17	18	19	20
21	22	23	24	25	26	27
28	29	30	31			

				Aprīlis		
1	2	3	4	5	6	7
8	9	10	11	12	13	14
15	16	17	18	19	20	21
22	23	24	25	26	27	28
29	30					

				September		
						1
2	3	4	5	6	7	8
9	10	11	12	13	14	15
16	17	18	19	20	21	22
23	24	25	26	27	28	29
30						

				December		
						1
2	3	4	5	6	7	8
9	10	11	12	13	14	15
16	17	18	19	20	21	22
23	24	25	26	27	28	29
30	31					

				Iūnius		
					1	2
3	4	5	6	7	8	9
10	11	12	13	14	15	16
17	18	19	20	21	22	23
24	25	26	27	28	29	30

				Februārius		
				1	2	3
4	5	6	7	8	9	10
11	12	13	14	15	16	17
18	19	20	21	22	23	24
25	26	27	28			

				Māius		
		1	2	3	4	5
6	7	8	9	10	11	12
13	14	15	16	17	18	19
20	21	22	23	24	25	26
27	28	29	30	31		

I. Historia. Review the history and fill in the blanks.

1. What does Domitian do for fun? _____*Domitian tortures flies for fun.*_____

2. Who is the twelfth emperor of Rome? _____*Nerva is the twelfth emperor of Rome.*_____

3. In what year does Trajan's reign begin? _____*Trajan's reign begins in 98 AD.*_____

4. What two historians live during Trajan's reign? _____*Plutarch and Tacitus*_____

XIX – Ūndēvīcēsima   Nōmen:

XIX – Ūndēvīcēsima lectiō   QUID ERIT ERIT.
(19 – Nineteenth lesson)   (What will be will be.)

I. Dictum

    Ecce homō!   *Behold the man!*
      – Pilate

II. Colloquium   *Latīnē*   *Anglicē*

Publius:	Manē dum quaesō!	Wait a minute, please!
Līvia:	Minimē! Festīnā!	No! Hurry!

III. Verba

Latīnē	*Anglicē*	*Scrībe tōtum verbum Latīnum.*	*Dērīvātī*
fatuus, -a, -um	foolish, silly	*fatuus, -a, -um*	*infatuated*
labor, labōris, m.	work, labor, effort	*labor, labōris, m.*	*laborious*
nēmo, nēminis, m./f.	no one, nobody	*nēmō, nēminis, m./f.*	*Captain Nemo*
opus, operis, n.	(a) work	*opus, operis, n.*	*opera*
pauper, pauperis, m.	poor man	*pauper, pauperis, m.*	*pauper*
piscātor, piscātōris, m.	fisherman	*piscātor, piscātōris, m.*	
piscis, piscis, m.	fish	*piscis, piscis, m.*	*piscatology*
prophetia, -ae, f.	prophecy	*prophetia, -ae, f.*	*prophecy*
virgō, virginis, f.	young woman, maiden, virgin	*virgō, virginis, f.*	*virgin*

1. How many *verba* are nouns? Adjectives? Verbs?

2. How many *verba* are 1st-declension nouns? 2nd? 3rd?

3. How many nouns name people? Places? Things? Ideas?

4. What important detail distinguishes one declension from another?   *the gen. sing. ending*

XIX – Ūndēvīcēsima   Nōmen: _____

IV. Grammatica

The <u>future tense of</u> *sum, esse* is easy, but because it is an irregular verb you must memorize it.

Sum, esse also a _____linking verb_____ verb, and it means__ to be __.

	singular	plural	
1st person _I will be._	erō	erimus	_We will be._
2nd person _You will be._	eris	eritis	_Y'all will be._
3rd person _He/she/it will be._	erit	erunt	_They will be._

The <u>future tense of</u> *possum, posse* is also easy once you know the future tense of *sum, esse*.

	singular	plural	
1st person _I will be able._	poterō	poterimus	_We will be able._
2nd person _You will be able._	poteris	poteritis	_Y'all will be able._
3rd person _He/she/it will be able._	poterit	poterunt	_They will be able._

A. *Scrībe* the future tense conjugation of *sum, esse* two times.

1. _erō_   _erimus_   2. _erō_   _erimus_

   eris   _eritis_   _eris_   _eritis_

   erit   _erunt_   _erit_   _erunt_

B. *Scrībe* the future tense conjugation of *possum, posse* two times.

1. _poterō_ _poterimus_   2. _poterō_ _poterimus_

   poteris _poteritis_   _poteris_ _poteritis_

   poterit _poterunt_   _poterit_ _poterunt_

V. Historia (*Famous Men of Rome*, Chapter XXVII, Part I)

Beginning in 117, Trajan's cousin Hadrian governs well and builds a wall in Britain. He is followed by Antoninus Pius, who allows Christian worship. In 161, Marcus Aurelius, a Stoic philosopher, becomes emperor.

XIX – Ūndēvīcēsima   Nōmen:

VI. Dēlēgāta

A. *Scrībe* the new Latin *verba* and their meanings.

    Latīnē   *Anglicē*

1. fatuus, -a, -um   1. foolish, silly
2. labor, labōris, m.   2. work, labor, effort
3. nēmō, nēminis, m./f.   3. no one, nobody
4. opus, operis, n.   4. a work
5. pauper, pauperis, m.   5. poor man
6. piscātor, piscātōris, m. 6. fisherman
7. piscis, piscis, m.   7. fish
8. prophetia, -ae, f.   8. prophecy
9. virgō, virginis, f.   9. young woman, maiden, virgin

B. *Variātiōnēs.* *Recitā* these sentence patterns several times.

1. Pauper erat fatuus.   (The poor man was foolish.)
2. Pauper est fatuus.   (The poor man is foolish.)
3. Pauper erit fatuus.   (The poor man will be foolish.)
4. Virgō erat fatua.   (The young woman was foolish.)
5. Virgō est fatua.   (The young woman is foolish.)
6. Virgō erit fatua.   (The young woman will be foolish.)
7. Piscātōrēs erant fatuī.   (The fishermen were foolish.)
8. Piscātōrēs sunt fatuī.   (The fishermen are foolish.)
9. Piscātōrēs erunt fatuī.   (The fishermen will be foolish.)
10. Fatuae erāmus.   (We were foolish.)
11. Fatuae sumus.   (We are foolish.)
12. Fatuae erimus.   (We shall be foolish.)

C. *Converte hās sententiās.*

1. Virgō erit rēgīna.   The young woman will be queen.
2. Labōrēs meī erunt magnī.   My efforts will be great.
3. Hoc erit meum magnum opus.   This will be my great work.

XIX – Ūndēvīcēsima   Nōmen:

4. Prophetia dē Christō dīcit. — *The prophecy speaks about Christ.*

5. Nēmo portās claudēbat. — *No one was closing the gates.*

6. Nēmo portās claudere poterit. — *Nobody will be able to close the gates.*

7. Ursa piscem cēnābat. — *The bear was eating fish.*

8. Piscātor numquam labōrat. — *The fisherman never works.*

9. Ille piscātor fatuus est. — *That fisherman is foolish.*

10. Is erit pauper. — *He will be a poor man.*

11. Hominēs beātī in caelō erunt. — *People will be happy in heaven.*

12. Cum Christō ascendēmus. — *We will ascend with Christ.*

D. *Converte hās sententiās aut scrībe illās Latīnē.*

1. Christus erit rēx mundī huius. — *Christ will be king of this world.*

2. Piscātor aestāte erit dīves. — *The fisherman will be a rich man in summer.*

3. It will rain a lot in March. — *Martiō multum pluet.*

4. Virgō argentum nōn habet. — *The maiden does not have silver.*

5. Quandō rēx erit beātus? — *When will the king be happy?*

6. Cūr aleās tenēbās? — *Why were you holding dice?*

7. The fishermen are eager for work. — *Piscātōrēs labōrem student.*

8. No one will be happy in January. — *Nēmō Iānuāriō laetus erit.*

9. The fisherman used to have many fish. — *Piscātor multōs piscīs habēbat.*

10. The young women will be rich. — *Virginēs erunt dīvēs.*

Ex Scriptūrīs:

11. Simile erit rēgnum caelōrum decem virginibus. (Matt. 25:1)
    The kingdom of heaven will be like/similar to ten young women.

XIX – Ūndēvīcēsima   Nōmen:

12. Quīnque ex eīs erant fatuae. (Matt. 25:2, alt.) _Five of them were foolish._

13. Eritis piscātōrēs hominum. (Matt. 4:19, alt.) _You will be fishers of men._

E. Decline dīves fatuus. N.B.: These words are from different declensions!

dīves fatuus	dīvitēs fatuī
dīvitis fatuī	dīvitum fatuōrum
dīvitī fatuō	dīvitibus fatuīs
dīvitem fatuum	dīvitēs fatuōs
dīvite fatuō	dīvitibus fatuīs

F. Conjugate (1) *sum, esse* **and (2)** *possum, posse* **in future tense.**

1. erō / erimus   2. poterō / poterimus
   eris / eritis   poteris / poteritis
   erit / erunt   poterit / poterunt

G. *Converte* these *verba* and phrases.

1. ūndēvīcēsima _eleventh_   2. eighteenth _duodēvīcēsimus, -a, -um_
3. Ecce homō! _Behold the man!_   4. Festīnā! _Hurry!_
5. We praise You, O God. _Tē, Deum, laudāmus._
6. Manē dum quaesō. _Wait a minute, please._
7. Confēcistīne dēlēgātum tuum? _Did you finish your homework?_
8. Vēnī, vīdī, vīcī. _I came, I saw, I conquered._
9. In which month were you born? _Quō mense nātus/nāta es?_

H. Dērīvātī. Complete each sentence with an English *verbum* chosen from the following *verba*. The italicized *verbum* in the sentence should help you think of the Latin root.

pauper   virgin   fatuous   laboratory   magnum opus

1. A _laboratory_ is a place where *work* is done. Latin root: _labor, labōris, m._

XIX – Ūndēvīcēsima   **Nōmen:**

2. The _magnum opus_ of the spider Charlotte, in *Charlotte's Web*, was a *great work*.

   Latin roots: _opus, operis, m._ and _magnus, -a, -um_

3. A _pauper_ is a poor man. Latin root: _pauper, pauperis, m._

4. The _virgin_ Mary was a *young woman* when she became Jesus' mother.

   Latin root: _virgō, virginis, f._

5. The _fatuous_ child was so *foolish* and *silly*. Latin root: _fatuus, -a, um_

I. Crossword Puzzle. Be sure to use the endings for the grammar indicated. Unscramble the letters in the shaded squares to find out *when* what will be will be.

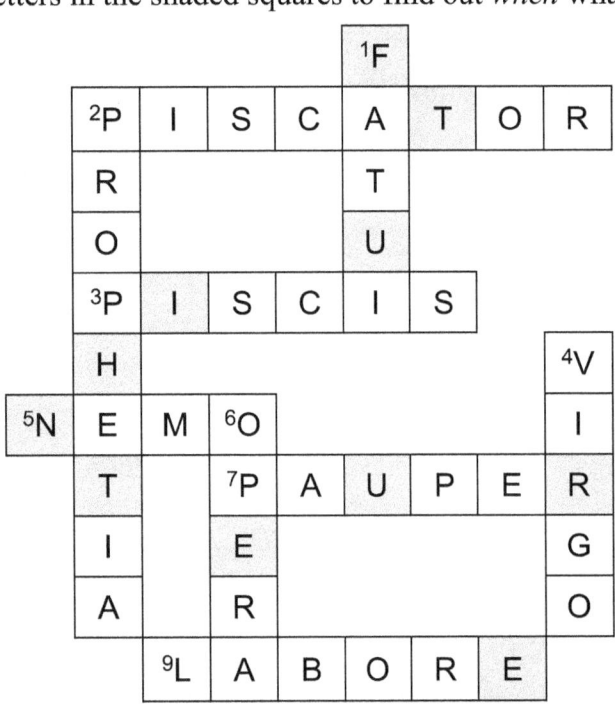

RĒCTĒ
2. fisherman (nom.)
3. of the fish (s.)
5. no one (s.)
7. poor man
9. effort (abl. s.)

DEORSUM
1. of a foolish man
2. prophecy
4. young woman (nom.)
6. works (nom. or acc.)

What will be, will be   I N   T H E   F U T U R E.

J. Historia. Review the history and fill in the blanks.

1. Who builds a defensive wall in Britain? _The emperor Hadrian builds a wall._

2. Who first allows Christian worship? _Antoninus Pius_

3. In what year does Marcus Aurelius become emperor? _117 AD_

4. What kind of philosopher is Marcus? _Marcus Aurelius is a stoic philospher._

XX – Vīcēsima   Nōmen:

XX – Vīcēsima lectiō   **PERFECT TENSE**
(20 – Twentieth lesson)

I. Dictum

      terra fīrma   <u> dry land </u> (lit.) <u> solid ground </u>

II. Colloquium   *Latīnē*   *Anglicē*

Iūlia:	Potesne venīre domum meam?	Can you come to my house?
Tiberius:	Certē! Quid possumus facere?	Sure! What can we do?

III. Verba

Latīnē	*Anglicēe*	*Scrībe tōtum verbum Latīnum.*	*Dērīvātī*
diēs, diēī, m. (Ab – diē)	day	*diēs, diēī, m.*	*day*
diēs Sōlis	Sunday	*diēs Sōlis*	
Dominica, -ae, f.	the Lord's Day	*Dominica, -ae, f.*	
diēs Lūnae	Monday	*diēs Lūnae*	
diēs Martis	Tuesday	*diēs Martis*	
diēs Mercuriī	Wednesday	*diēs Mercuriī*	
diēs Iovis	Thursday	*diēs Iovis*	
diēs Veneris	Friday	*diēs Veneris*	
diēs Sāturnī	Saturday	*diēs Sāturnī*	
epistula, -ae, f.	letter	*epistula, -ae, f.*	*epistle*
septimāna, -ae, f.	a week	*a week*	

N.B.: *Diēs* is from 5th declension. For now, just learn the nominative, genitive, and ablative.

1. There are no *verba Latīna* for <u> helping </u> <u> verbs </u> and <u> article </u> <u> adjectives </u>.

2. *sum, esse* is a <u> being </u> verb and a <u> linking </u> verb.

3. Adverbs cannot be <u> declined </u> or <u> conjugated </u>.

IV. Grammatica

In this *lectiō*, we begin the perfect tense. The word *perfect* is used in the sense of *complete*. An action (or state of being) described in the perfect tense happened in the past and is now completed. The perfect tense expresses action that happened in the past but was completed quickly or in a short period of time. Consider the different sense of *walk* in these two sentences:

1. When we lived at the other house, *I used to walk* to school.
2. On Tuesday, *I walked* to school.

The first sentence tells about a repeated action, one that wasn't completed all at one time. It would be written using the *imperfect* tense: *ambulābam*. The second sentence tells about a single, completed action. It would be written using the *perfect* tense: *ambulāvī*.

The perfect tense is most often translated using the *–ed* form of the English verb, e.g., *ambulāvī* = I walk*ed*. It can also be translated using the helping verb *did*, e.g., *I did walk*. N.B.: Many English verbs have irregular perfect-tense forms. Compare *I think* vs. *I thought*; *I sing* vs. *I sang*; *I write* vs. *I wrote*; *I lead* vs. *I led*. Latin, however, has no irregular perfect tense forms!

The perfect tense uses a new set of personal endings *and* a different stem. The stem for the perfect tense is the third principal part of the verb, minus the *–ī* ending. E.g., the third principal part of *ambulō, ambulāre, ambulāvī, ambulātum* is *ambulāvī*, so the perfect stem is *ambulāv-*. Here are the personal endings and a model verb.

	singular	plural
1st person	-ī	-imus
2nd person	-istī	-istis
3rd person	-it	-ērunt

		singular	plural	
1st person	*I walked.*	ambulāvī	ambulāvimus	*We walked.*
2nd person	*You walked.*	ambulāvistī	ambulāvistis	*You all walked.*
3rd person	*He, she, it walked.*	ambulāvit	ambulāvērunt	*They walked.*

V. Historia (*Famous Men of Rome,* Chapter XXVII, Parts II and III)

The reign of Marcus Aurelius is full of troubles, but he writes that God makes everything happen for the good of all existence and that we must keep sober by remembering that we are only a small part of everything. Marcus is very impressed with the Thundering Legion, some Christian soldiers whose prayer is apparently answered, but he remains a pagan.

XX – Vīcēsima   Nōmen: _____

VI. Dēlēgāta

A. *Scrībe* the new Latin *verba* and their meanings.

Latīnē   *Anglicē*

1. dīēs, diēī, m.   1. day
2. diēs Sōlis   2. Sunday
3. Dominica, -ae, f.   3. The Lord's day
4. diēs Lūnae   4. Monday
5. diēs Martis   5. Tuesday
6. diēs Mercuriī   6. Wednesday
7. diēs Iovis   7. Thursday
8. diēs Veneris   8. Friday
9. diēs Sāturnī   9. Saturday
10. epistula, -ae, f.   10. a letter
11. septimāna, septimānae, f. 11. a week.

B. *Variātiōnēs.* *Recitā* these sentence patterns several times. (Note the ablative of time.)

1. Diē Sōlis ad ecclēsiam ambulāvī.   (On Sunday I walked to church.)
2. Diē Lūnae in cubiculō meō labōrāvī.   (On Monday I worked in my bedroom.)
3. Diē Martis spectāculum spectāvī.   (On Tuesday I watched a show.)
4. Diē Mercuriī serpentem vīdī.   (On Wednesday I saw a snake.)
5. Diē Iovis gallīnam cēnāvī.   (On Thursday I ate chicken.)
6. Diē Veneris librum lēgī.   (On Friday I read a book.)
7. Diē Sāturnī epistulam scrīpsī.   (On Saturday I wrote a letter.)
8. Diē Sāturnī epistulam scrīpsistī.   (On Saturday you wrote a letter.)
9. Diē Sāturnī epistulam scrīpsit.   (On Saturday he wrote a letter.)

C. *Converte hās sententiās.*

1. Duo puerī pugnāvērunt.   Two boys fought.

2. Duae legiōnēs pugnāvērunt.   Two legions fought.

XX – Vīcēsima   Nōmen: _____

3. Mīlitēs lēgem novam lēgērunt.   *The soldiers read the new law.*

4. Soror et frāter ambulāvērunt.   *The brother and sister walked.*

5. Diē Lūnae nāvigāvimus.   *On Monday, we sailed.*

6. Diē Iovis dē grātiā dīximus.   *On Thursday, we spoke about grace.*

7. Dominicā ad ecclēsiam ambulāvimus.   *On Sunday, we walked to church.*

8. Fīlia huic puerō epistulam mīsit.   *The daughter sent a letter to this boy.*

9. Diē Mercuriī librōs bonōs lēgistis.   *On Wednesday, you read good books.*

10. Diē Sāturnī natāvimus.   *On Saturday, we swam.*

D. *Converte hās sententiās aut scrībe illās Latīnē.*

1. Māter mihi būtyrum trādidit.   *Mother passed the butter to me.*

2. Lydia tibi āleās trādidit.   *Lydia passed the butter to you.*

3. Prophetiae dē Christō dīxērunt.   *The prophecies spoke about Christ.*

4. Quandō natāre poteris?   *When will you be able to swim?*

5. Quandō trāns flūmen natāvistī?   *When did you swim across the river?*

6. Diē Veneris trāns flūmen natāvī.   *On Friday, I swam across the river.*

7. Why did you swim across the river?   *Cūr trāns flūmen natāvistī?*

8. On the Lord's Day we will write.   *Dominicā, scrībēmus.*

9. On Tuesday we worked in the kitchen.   *Diē Martis, in culīnā laborāvimus.*

10. On Friday my brothers wrote a letter.   *Diē Veneris, frātrēs meī epistulam scrīpsērunt.*

11. On Saturday Tullia read my letter.   *Diē Sāturnī, Tullia epistulam meam lēgit.*

Ex Scriptūrīs:

12. Deus nōs amāvit et Fīlium mīsit. (I Jn. 4:10) _____
   God loved us and sent his son.

XX – Vīcēsima   Nōmen:

E. Conjugate *natō, natāre, natāvī, natātum* **and** *dīcō, dīcere, dīxī, dictum* **in perfect tense.**

1. natāvī / natāvimus   2. dīxī / dīximus
   natāvistī / natāvistis   dīxistī / dīxistis
   natāvit / natāvērunt   dixit / dīxērunt

F. Conjugate (1) *sum, esse, fuī, futūrum* **and (2)** *possum, posse, potuī* **in perfect tense.**

1. fuī / fuimus   2. potuī / potuimus
   fuistī / fuistis   potuistī / potuistis
   fuit / fuērunt   potuit / potuērunt

G. Conjugate *doceō, docēre, docuī, doctum* **and** *legō, legere, lēgī, lectum* **in perfect tense.**

1. docuī / docuimus   2. lēgī / lēgimus
   docuistī / docuistis   lēgistis / lēgistis
   docuit / docuērunt   lēgit / lēgērunt

H. *Converte* these *verba* and phrases.

1. vīcēsima — twentieth
2. nineteenth — ūndēvīcēsimus, -a, -um
3. terra firma — solid ground
4. cast of characters — dramatis persōnae
5. Et tū, Brūte? — And you too, Brutus?
6. Wait a minute! — Manē dum!
7. Potesne venīre domum meam diē Martis? — Can you come to my house on Tuesday?
8. Potesne venīre domum meam diē Sōlis? — Can you come to my house on Sunday?
9. with great praise — magnā cum laude
10. ē plūribus ūnum — out of many, one
14. sine quā nōn — essential ingredient
11. after noon — post merīdiem
15. with praise — cum laude
12. too long — ad nauseam
16. Behold the man! — Ecce homo!
13. Pray and work. — Ōrā et labōrā.
17. Lamb of God — Agnus Deī

XX – Vīcēsima   Nōmen:

I. Crossword Puzzle. Use the grammar indicated. Letters in the shaded squares, when read from top to bottom and left to right, will make seven days: _____SEPTIMANA_____

RĒCTĒ
1. day (nom.)
6. away from
7. me (acc.)
8. in front of
11. *Dies* ___ (Wed.)
12. You (pl.) walked
14. in, into
15. you (acc.)
16. *Dies* ___ (Sun.)
19. She passed
20. this (f.)
21. He wrote
22. my (f. sing.)
23. They said
24. where?

DEORSUM
2. *Dies* ___ (Sat.)
3. *Dies* ___ (Fri.)
4. You (pl.) worked
5. They read (perf.)
9. this (n.)
10. letter
13. toward, near
17. I watched
18. We saw
23. You give

J. Historia. Review the history and fill in the blanks.

1. Marcus Aurelius believed everything happened for the good of _____the universe._____

2. What was the name of Marcus's Christian legion? _____the Thundering legion_____

XXI – Vīcēsima prīma lectiō — *-iō* VERBS
(21 – Twenty-first lesson)

I. Dictum

Dominus vōbīscum. — *The Lord be with you.*

Et tēcum. — *And also with you.*

II. Colloquium

Latīnē — *Anglicē*

Magister:	Quis respōnsum scit?	Who knows the answer?
Discipulī:	Ō! Ego! Sciō! Ego!	Oh! Me! I know! Me!
Magister:	Attollite manūs.	Raise your hands.

III. Verba

Latīnē — *Anglicē* — *Scrībe tōtum verbum Latīnum.* — *Dērīvātī*

accipiō, accipere, accēpī, acceptum to receive — *acceptable*

accipiō — accipere — accēpī — acceptum

capiō, capere, cēpī, captum to seize, to take — *capture*

capiō — capere — cēpī — captum

dēficiō, dēficere, dēfēcī, dēfectum to fail — *defect*

dēficiō — dēficere — dēfēcī — dēfectum

ēripiō, ēripere, ēripuī, ēreptum to rescue —

ēripiō — ēripere — ēripuī — ēreptum

faciō, facere, fēcī, factum to make, to do — *fashion*

faciō — facere — fēcī — factum

iaciō, iacere, iēcī, iactum to throw, to cast — *eject*

iaciō — iacere — iēcī — iactum

1. Most verbs have __4__ principal parts. Be sure to __memorize__ them!

N.B.: *faciō, facere, fēcī, factum* can mean *to play* when used with *lūdus, -ī, m.*

IV. Grammatica

The *–iō verbs of 3rd conjugation* end in *–iō* in the 1st-person singular present-tense form. Notice that present tense keeps the *i* in the 3rd-person plural.

	singular	plural	
1st person *I take.*	capiō	capimus	*We take.*
2nd person *You take.*	capis	capitis	*Y'all take.*
3rd person *He/she/it takes.*	capit	capiunt	*They take.*

The *imperfect tense of –iō verbs of 3rd conjugation* keeps the *i* in the stem in all forms, and like all 3rd conjugation verbs also has the usual long *ē* stem vowel. Pronounce *iē* like this: "Yay!"

1st person *I was taking.*	capiēbam	capiēbāmus	*We were taking.*
2nd person *You were taking.*	capiēbās	capiēbātis	*Y'all were taking.*
3rd person *He/she/it was taking.*	capiēbat	capiēbant	*They were taking.*

In *future tense of –iō verbs of 3rd conjugation* keep the *i* in the stem in all forms. Even though it looks funny, it still follows the rhyme: "*Bō, bi, bu* for one and two; *a* and *e* for four and three!"

1st person *I will take.*	capiam	capiēmus	*We will take.*
2nd person *You will take.*	capiēs	capiētis	*Y'all will take.*
3rd person *He/he/it will take.*	capiet	capient	*They will take.*

3rd conjugation *-iō* verbs are so much fun! The perfect tense is the same as for other verbs.

Conjugate *capiō, capere* in (a) present tense and (b) future tense.

a.	capiō	capimus	b.	capiam	capiēmus
	capis	capitis		capiēs	capiētis
	capit	capiunt		capiet	capient

V. Historia (*Famous Men of Rome*, Chapter XXVIII)

A period of many bad emperors is known as the Military Anarchy (180-285). The next emperor, Diocletian, decides the Empire is too large, and he divides it into the Eastern Roman Empire, ruled by himself at Nicomedia, and the Western Roman Empire, ruled by Maximian at Milan. Diocletian's attempts to reform the corrupt government fail, and within five years of his resignation, five men fight a civil war for the prize of the title of Emperor.

XXI – Vīcēsima Prīma   Nōmen: _____

VI. Dēlēgāta

A. *Scrībe* the new Latin *verba* and their meanings.

Latīnē   *Anglicē*

1. <u>accipiō, accipere, accēpī, acceptum</u>   1. <u>   to receive   </u>

2. <u>capiō, capere, cēpī, captum</u>   2. <u>   to take, to seize   </u>

3. <u>dēficiō, dēficere, dēfēcī, dēfectum</u>   3. <u>   to fail   </u>

4. <u>ēripiō, ēripere, ēripuī, ēreptum</u>   4. <u>   to rescue   </u>

5. <u>faciō, facere, fēcī, factum</u>   5. <u>   to make, to do   </u>

6. <u>iaciō, iacere, iēcī, iactum</u>   6. <u>   to throw, to cast   </u>

B. *Variātiōnēs*. *Recitā* these sentence patterns several times.

1. Āleās iaciō.   (I'm throwing the dice.)   7. Āleās iēcī.   (I threw the dice.)
2. Āleās iacis.   (You're throwing the dice.)   8. Āleās iēcistī.   (You threw the dice.)
3. Āleās iacit.   (She's throwing the dice.)   9. Āleās iēcit.   (He threw the dice.)
4. Āleās iacimus.   (We're throwing the dice.)   10. Āleās iēcimus.   (We threw the dice.)
5. Āleās iacitis.   (Y'all are throwing the dice.) 11. Āleās iēcistis. (Y'all threw the dice.)
6. Āleās iaciunt.   (They're throwing the dice.) 12. Āleās iēcērunt. (They threw the dice.)

C. *Converte hās sententiās.*

1. Soror mea epistulam accēpit.   <u>My sister received a letter.</u>

2. Epistulās accipere amō.   <u>I like to receive letters.</u>

3. Legiōnēs oppidum capiunt.   <u>The legions take the town.</u>

4. Diē Lūnae, legiōnēs signum hostium cēpērunt.

   <u>On Monday, the legions took the enemies' standard.</u>

5. Diē Veneris, legiōnēs oppidum capere dēfēcērunt.

   <u>On Friday, the legions failed to take the town.</u>

6. Portam facimus.   <u>We are making a gate.</u>

7. Quotum lūdum faciēbant?   <u>Which game were they playing? (see note p. 121)</u>

XXI – Vīcēsima Prīma Nōmen: _____

8. Diē Martis lūdum fēcimus. _We played a game on Tuesday._

9. Mīlitēs tēla iēcērunt. _The soldiers threw their weapons._

10. Mīlitēs tēla iaciēbant. _The soldiers were throwing their weapons._

11. Mīlitēs tēla iacient. _The soldiers will throw their weapons._

D. *Converte hās sententiās aut scrībe illās Latīnē.*

1. Rēx multās epistulās accipit. _The king receives many letters._

2. Agricola duās epistulās accēpit. _The farmer received two letters._

3. Mīlitēs tēla dē vallō iaciēbant. _The soldiers were casting weapons from the wall._

4. Claudius āleās cēpit et eās iacit. _Claudius took the dice and cast them._

5. My brothers are playing that game. _Frātrēs meī illud lūdum faciunt._

6. Christus nōs ē peccātō ēripuit. _Christ saved us from sin._

7. Servī portam facere nōn poterant. _The servants were not able to make the gate._

8. The slaves were able to close the windows. _Servī fenestrās claudere poterant._

9. Cato is throwing the dice. _Cato āleās iacit._

10. I received two letters on Thursday. _Diē Iovis, duās epistulās accēpī._

11. The farmer was making a bow. _Agricola arcum faciēbat._

Ex Scriptūrīs:

12. Petitis et nōn accipitis. (James 4:3) _You ask and you do not receive._

13. Dīgnus es, Domine, accipere glōriam. (Rev. 4:11)

You are worthy, Lord, to receive glory.

E. Conjugate *accipiō, accipere, accēpī, acceptum* **in present (1) and imperfect (2) tenses.**

1.	accipiō	accipimus	2.	accipiēbam	accipiēbāmus
	accipis	accipitis		accipiēbās	accipiēbātis
	accipit	accipiunt		accipiēbat	accipiēbant

XXI – Vīcēsima Prīma   Nōmen:

F. Conjugate *dēficiō, dēficere, dēfēcī, dēfectum* **in imperfect (1) and perfect (2) tenses.**

1. dēficiēbam   dēficiēbāmus   2. dēfēcī   dēfēcimus

   dēficiēbās   dēficiēbātis   dēfēcistī   dēfēcistis

   dēficiēbat   dēficiēbant   dēfēcit   dēfēcērunt

G. Conjugate *ēripiō, ēripere, ēripuī, ēreptum* **in present (1) and perfect (2) tenses.**

1. ēripiō   ēripimus   2. ēripuī   ēripuimus

   ēripis   ēripitis   ēripuistī   ēripuistis

   ēripit   ēripiunt   ēripuit   ēripuērunt

H. *Converte hās sententiās aut scrībe illās Latīnē.*

1. Your friends are preparing bread.   Amīcī tuī pānem parant.

2. Vallum urbis quattuor portās habet.   The wall of the city has four gates.

3. Trēs portae nigrae sunt.   Three gates are black.

4. The fourth gate is red.   Quarta porta est rufa.

5. Fenestrae trium portārum nigrārum sunt parvae.

   The windows of three of the gates are small.

6. The window of the fourth gate is large.

   Fenestra quartae portae est magna.

7. Geram ūnum pedāle album et ūnum pedāle flāvum.

   I will wear one white sock and one yellow sock.

I. Translate these words and phrases.

1. vīcēsima prīma   twenty-first   2. twentieth   vīcēsimus, -a, -um

3. Note well.   Nōtā bene.   4. Dominus vōbīscum.   The Lord be with you.

5. Attollite manūs.   Raise your hands.

XXI – Vīcēsima Prīma   Nōmen: _____

6. Quotum tempus annī tibi maximē placet? _Which season do you like best?_

7. Can you come to my house? _Potesne venīre domum meam?_

J. Dērīvātī. Complete each sentence with an English *verbum* chosen from the following *verba*. The italicized *verbum* in the sentence should help you think of the Latin root.

trajectory   deficient   accept   manufactured   captured

1. In earlier times, _manufactured_ products were *made* by *hand*.

   Latin roots: _manus, -ūs, f._ and _faciō, facere_

2. Wild animals are sometimes _captured_ by scientists so that they can study them more closely. Latin root: _capiō, capere_

3. A _deficient_ effort is in some way a *failure*. Latin root: _dēficiō, dēficere_

4. A _trajectory_ is the path of an object that is *thrown*. Latin root: _iaciō, iacere_

5. To _accept_ a gift is to *receive* it. Latin root: _accipiō, accipere_

K. *Verbum* Ladder. If you arrange five of this *lectiō*'s *verba* correctly in the horizontal spaces, the shaded spaces running vertically will spell the remaining *sextum verbum*.

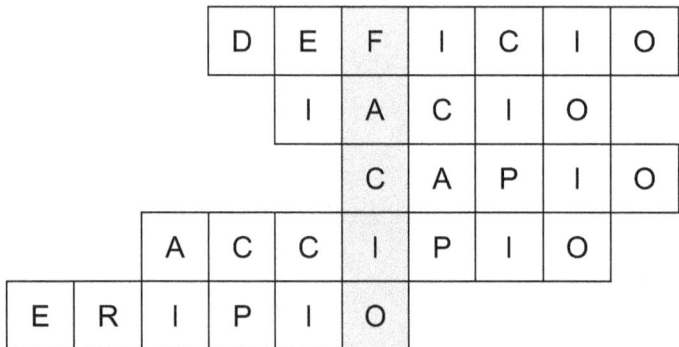

L. Historia. Review the history and fill in the blanks.

1. What are the dates of the Military Anarchy? _The Military Anarchy lasts from 180-215 AD._

2. Who divides the Empire into two parts? _Diocletian divides the empire._

3. What are the two capital cities of the divided Empire? _Milan (west) and Nicomedia (east)_

XXII – Vīcēsima Secunda   Nōmen: _____

XXII – Vīcēsima secunda lectiō   4th CONJUGATION
(22 – Twenty-second lesson)

I. Dictum

        In hōc signō vincēs.   *In this sign you will conquer.*

II. Colloquium   *Latīnē*   *Anglicē*

| **Iūlius:** | Scīsne natāre? | Do you know how to swim? |
| **Calpurnia:** | Ita, sciō natāre. | Yes, I know how to swim. |

III. Verba

Latīnē   *Anglicē*   *Scrībe tōtum verbum Latīnum.*   *Dērīvātī*

aperiō, aperīre, aperuī, apertum to open   *aperture*

   aperiō   *aperīre*   *aperuī*   *apertum*

audiō, audīre, audīvī, audītum to hear, to listen   *auditorium*

   audiō   *audīre*   *audīvī*   *audītum*

dormiō, dormīre, dormīvī, dormītum to sleep   *dormitory*

   dormiō   *dormīre*   *dormīvī*   *dormītum*

veniō, venīre, vēnī, ventum to come   *venture*

   veniō   *venīre*   *vēnī*   *ventum*

sciō, scīre, scīvī, scītum to know   *scientist*

   sciō   *scīre*   *scīvī*   *scītum*

inveniō, invenīre, invēnī, inventum to find   *invention*

   inveniō   *invenīre*   *invēnī*   *inventum*

1. How are these verbs different from verbs in other conjugations?
2. How do we know from what conjugation a verb comes?
3. The present, imperfect, and future tenses find their stem in the *infinitive*.

4. The 3rd principal part provides the stem for the *perfect* tense.

XXII – Vīcēsima Secunda   Nōmen:

IV. Grammatica

The new verbs are all from 4th conjugation. They are like -iō verbs of 3rd conjugation, except that in present tense, the *i* will be long when possible. 4th conjugation verbs are known by the infinitive ending *-īre* and the long stem vowel *ī*. Here's the form for the present tense of 4th conjugation.

	singular	plural	
1st person *I hear.*	audiō	audīmus	*We hear.*
2nd person *You hear.*	audīs	audītis	*Y'all hear.*
3rd person *He/she/it hears.*	audit	audiunt	*They hear.*

Here's the form for the imperfect tense of 4th conjugation. It's just like 3rd -iō!

1st person *I was hearing.*	audiēbam	audiēbāmus	*We were hearing.*
2nd person *You were hearing.*	audiēbās	audiēbātis	*Y'all were hearing.*
3rd person *He/she/it was hearing.*	audiēbat	audiēbant	*They were hearing.*

Just like *-io* verbs of 3rd conjugation, the Future tense of 4th conjugation keeps an *i* in the stem. Remember: "bō, bi, bu for one and two; a and ē for four and three."

1st person *I will hear.*	audiam	audiēmus	*We will hear.*
2nd person *You will hear.*	audiēs	audiētis	*Y'all will hear.*
3rd person *He/she/it will hear.*	audiet	audient	*They will hear.*

The perfect tense is the same as for other verbs.

N.B. *Sciō* with an infinitive can mean *I know how*. E.g., *Sciō natāre* = *I know how to swim*.

V. Historia (*Famous Men of Rome*, Chapter XXIX, Part I)

Although five men claim the title of Roman Emperor, Maxentius rules in Rome. Constantine decides to do battle with him. In 312, he sees a vision of a cross and hears a voice saying, "In this sign you will conquer." He has crosses painted on his soldiers' shields and banners, and he wins the Battle of Milvian Bridge. Constantine then becomes the first Christian emperor.

XXII – Vīcēsima Secunda   Nōmen: _____

VI. Dēlēgāta

A. *Scrībe* the new Latin *verba* and their meanings.

Latīnē	*Anglicē*
1. aperiō, aperīre, aperuī, apertum	1. to open
2. audiō, audīre, audīvī, audītum	2. to hear, to listen
3. dormiō, dormīre, dormīvī, dormītum	3. to sleep
4. veniō, venīre, vēnī, ventum	4. to come
5. sciō, scīre, scīvī, scītum	5. to know
6. inveniō, invenīre, invēnī, inventum	6. To find

B. *Variātiōnēs.* *Recitā* these sentence patterns several times.

1. Rēgīna legere scit.   (Regina knows how to read.)
2. Rēgīna scrībere scit.   (Regina knows how to write.)
3. Rēgīna lūdōs facere scit. (Regina knows how to play games.)
4. Rēgīna holera parāre scit. (Regina knows how to prepare vegetables.)

C. *Converte hās sententiās.*

1. Magistrum audīmus.   _We hear the teacher._
2. Quis avem audit?   _Who hears the bird._
3. Pastōrēs angelōs audīvērunt.   _The shepherds listened to angels._
4. Sextus iānuam claudit.   _Sextus shuts the door._
5. Iūlia iānuam aperiet.   _Julia will open the door._
6. Discipula fenestram aperiēbat.   _The student was opening the window._
7. Titus amīcum meum scit.   _Titus knows my friend._
8. Sorōrēs meae amīcam meam sciunt.   _My sisters know my friend._
9. Marcus natāre nōn scit.   _Marcus does not know how to swim._
10. Marcus natāre nōn potest.   _Marcus is not able to swim._

XXII – Vīcēsima Secunda Nōmen:

11. Puerī thēsaurum invēnērunt. _The boys found a treasure._

12. Sanctus Nicolaus ad oppidum venit. _Saint Nicholas is coming to town._

13. Grātia Dominī est magna. _The grace of the Lord is great._

14. Dormīvistisne bene? _Did you sleep well._

D. *Converte hās sententiās aut scrībe illās Latīnē.*

1. Tulia in cubiculō dormit. _Tulia is sleeping in the bedroom._

2. Eā diē Veneris in exedriō dormīvit. _On Friday, she slept in the living room._

3. Servus in focō dormiēbat. _The slave was sleeping on the hearth._

4. A soldier sent a letter to the king. _Mīles epistulam ad rēgem mīsit._

5. Nummōs antīquōs in agrō invēnī. _I found many ancient coins in the field._

6. The shepherd stood in front of the church. _Pastor ante ecclēsiam stetit._

7. Christus caelum nōbīs aperuit. _Christ opened heaven for us._

8. Lydia is opening the door. _Lydia iānuam aperit._

9. My friends came on Wednesday. _Diē Marcuriī, amīcī meī vēnērunt._

10. Titus does not know how to sing. _Titus cantāre nōn scit._

11. Iēsus nōs ēripiet ex infernō. _Jesus will rescue us from hell._

12. The keys of the gates are large. _Clāvēs portārum magnae sunt._

13. The farmer will plow the field. _Agricola agrum arābit._

14. Gaius is a poor man; Publius is a rich man. _Gaius pauper est; Publius dīvēs est._

15. Lampās agricolae oleum nōn habet. _The farmer's lamp has no oil._

16. Aurum in montibus vīdimus. _We saw gold in the mountains._

17. The girls were not sleeping well. _Puellae nōn bene dormiēbant._

18. Imperātor et mīlitēs hostīs vincent. _The general and soldiers will conquer the enemy._

XXII – Vīcēsima Secunda Nōmen: _____

Ex Scriptūrīs:

19. Veniet Fīlius hominis. (Matt. 25:31, alt.) _The son of man will come._

20. Beātus est homō quī invenit sapientiam. (Prov. 3:13)

   Blessed is the man who finds wisdom.

21. Sciō opera tua et labōrem et patientiam tuam. (Rev. 2:2)

   I know your works and labor and your patience.

22. Et nēmō poterat in caelō aut in terrā aut sub terrā aperīre librum. (Rev. 5:3 *aut* = or)

   And no one in heaven or in earth or under the earth was able to open the book.

E. Conjugate *audiō, audīre, audīvī, audītum* in present (1) and future (2) tenses.

1.	audiō	audīmus	2.	audiam	audiēmus
	audīs	audītis		audiēs	audiētis
	audit	audiunt		audiet	audient

F. Conjugate *sciō, scīre, scīvī, scītum* in imperfect (1) and perfect (2) tenses.

1.	sciēbam	sciēbāmus	2.	scīvī	scīvimus
	sciēbās	sciēbātis		scīvistī	scīvistis
	sciēbat	sciēbant		scīvit	scīvērunt

G. *Converte* these *verba* and phrases.

1. vīcēsima secunda _twenty-second_   2. twenty-first _vīcēsimus prīmus, -a, -um_

3. Behold the man! _Ecce homō!_   4. Diēs Īrae _Day of Wrath_

5. In hōc signō vincēs. _In this sign you will conquer._

6. Scīsne natāre? _Do you know how to swim?_

7. Raise your hands. _Attolite manūs._

8. Silent lēgēs inter arma. _Laws are silent among arms._

XXII – Vīcēsima Secunda Nōmen: _____

H. Dērīvātī. Complete each sentence with an English *verbum* chosen from the following *verba*. The italicized *verbum* in the sentence should help you think of the Latin root.

aperture   dormitories   dormant   invent   auditory

1. Creative people *find* new gadgets when they ___invent___ them.

   Latin root: ___inveniō, invenīre___

2. ___auditory___ learners learn best by *hearing*. Latin root: ___audiō, audīre___

3. A camera's ___aperture___ is a small *opening*. Latin root: ___aperiō, aperīre___

4. ___dormant___ plants *sleep* during the winter. Latin root: ___dormiō, dormīre___

5. College students *sleep* in ___dormitories___. Latin root: ___dormiō, dormīre___

I. *Verbum* Search. Each of the *verba* listed below can be found in this grid, reading forward, backward, up, down, or diagonally. All the unused letters, when read row by row from top to bottom, will tell you the best way to remember a verb's conjugation.

Secret message: ___YOU MUST MEMORIZE THE INFINITIVE___

A	U	D	I	O	Y	O	O	O
U	C	M	I	U	S	I	I	T
D	M	C	E	M	P	R	O	I
E	A	O	I	A	E	R	I	A
F	D	I	C	P	Z	E	P	C
I	S	O	A	O	I	T	I	I
C	H	C	R	E	I	O	R	O
I	I	N	I	M	F	N	E	I
O	N	I	T	O	I	I	E	V
I	N	V	E	N	I	O	E	V

WORD LIST

ACCIPIO
APERIO
AUDIO
CAPIO
DEFICIO
DORMIO
ERIPIO
FACIO
INVENIO
IACIO
SCIO
VENIO

J. Historia. Review the history and fill in the blanks.

1. Who is the first Christian emperor of Rome? ___Constantine___

2. What words does he hear in a vision? ___In this sign you will conquer.___

3. What is the year of the battle of Milvian Bridge? ___312 AD___

XXIII – Vīcēsima Tertia   Nōmen: _____

XXIII – Vīcēsima tertia lectiō   NEW ADJECTIVES
(23 – Twenty-third lesson)

I. Dictum

Fortīs fortūna adiuvat.   *Fortune favors the bold.*
— Terence

II. Colloquium   *Latīnē*   *Anglicē*

Catherīna: Est frīgidum! (Decembre)   It's cold!
Lūcius: Est calidum! (Augustō)   It's hot!

III. Verba

Latīnē	*Anglicē*	*Scrībe tōtum verbum Latīnum.*	*Dērīvātī*
brevis, breve (brevis, -e)	short	brevis, breve	abbrieviation
fortis, forte (fortis, -e)	strong, brave	fortis, forte	fortitude
longus, -a, -um	long	longus, -a, -um	longitude
omnis, omne (omnis, -e)	all, every	omnis, omne	omniscient
prūdēns, prūdentis	wise	prūdēns, prūdentis	imprudent
tristis, triste (tristis, -e)	sad	tristis, triste	
viridis, viride (viridis, -e)	green	viridis, viride	verdegris

1. What kind of *verba* are these? _____ *All of these words are adjectives.*

2. How are most of these *verba* different from other *verba* of this kind we have learned?

3. Adjectives must agree with the nouns they modify in _____ *case, number, and gender.*

4. Therefore, unlike adverbs, adjectives must be _____ *declined* _____ .

XXIII – Vīcēsima Tertia   **Nōmen:**

IV. Grammatica

Most of the adjectives in this *lectiō* are from 3rd declension. Before now, we used only 1st and 2nd declension adjectives, so called because all their endings fit into those declensions. You can tell a 1st and 2nd declension adjective by its nominative endings: *-us, -a, -um*.

The endings for 3rd declension adjectives are similar to those for 3rd declension i-stem nouns. Most show two endings in the dictionary entry: *-is* for masculine and feminine nominative singular, and *-e* for neuter nominative singular. Adjectives of any declension may be used with any noun of any declension. Their endings do not need to *look* the same, but they *must* agree with the nouns they modify in gender, number, and case.

Here are the forms for the 3rd-declension adjectives.

		masculine	feminine	neuter
Singular	nominative	omnis	omnis	omne
	genitive	omnis	omnis	omnis
	dative	omnī	omnī	omnī
	accusative	omnem	omnem	omne
	ablative	omnī	omnī	omnī
Plural	nominative	omnēs	omnēs	omnia
	genitive	omnium	omnium	omnium
	dative	omnibus	omnibus	omnibus
	accusative	omnīs	omnīs	omnia
	ablative	omnibus	omnibus	omnibus

Which case endings are different from those for 3rd-declension i-stem nouns? _m./f. abl. sing._

V. Historia (*Famous Men of Rome,* Chapter XXIX, Part II)

Constantine improves Roman laws and government. In 324, the last remaining claimant to the title, Licinius, dies, leaving Constantine sole ruler and the first Christian emperor of the whole Roman Empire. Constantine then moves the capital to Byzantium and renames it Constantinople.

XXIII – Vīcēsima Tertia   Nōmen:

VI. Dēlēgāta

A. *Scrībe* the new Latin *verba* and their meanings.

Latīnē	*Anglicē*
1. brevis, breve	1. short
2. fortis, forte	2. strong, brave
3. longus, -a, -um	3. long
4. omnis, omne	4. all, every
5. prūdēns, prudentis	5. wise
6. tristis, triste	6. sad
7. viridis, viride	7. green

B. *Variātiōnēs.* *Recitā* these sentence patterns several times.

1. Via est longa.   (The road is long.)
2. Arcus est longus.   (The bow is long.)
3. Vallum est longum.   (The wall is long.)
4. Via est brevis.   (The way is short.)
5. Arcus est brevis.   (The bow is short.)
6. Vallum est breve.   (The wall is short.)
7. Lectus est viridis. (The couch is green.)
8. Herba est viridis.   (The plant is green.)
9. Pōculum est viride. (The cup is green.)
10. Iānua est viridis. (The door is green.)

C. *Converte hās sententiās.*

1. Cāritās Deī est longa.   The love of God is long.
2. Cāritās Deī est alta.   The love of God is deep.
3. Cāritās Deī est fortis.   The love of God is strong.
4. Pauper erat beātus.   The poor man was happy.
5. Dīves erit tristis.   The rich man will be sad.
6. Omnia māla nōn sunt rūfa.   All the apples are not red.
7. Hoc mālum viride est.   This apple is green.
8. Illud mālum est flāvum.   That apple is yellow.

XXIII – Vīcēsima Tertia   Nōmen: _____

9. Hic nauta est fatuus. _This sailor is foolish._

10. Ille nauta est prūdēns. _That sailor is wise._

11. Fēmina prūdēns Deum laudat. _A wise woman praises God._

12. Homō prūdēns sapientiam studet. _A wise man is eager for wisdom._

13. Omnis flōs est bellus. _Every flower is pretty._

14. Hic liber brevis est. _This book is short._

D. *Converte hās sententiās aut scrībe illās Latīnē.*

1. Fēles sub sellā dormiēbat. _The cat was sleeping under the chair._

2. Canis sub sellam ambulāvit. _The dog walked under the chair._

3. Fēles nunc nōn dormit! _The cat is not sleeping now!_

4. Spectāculum triste spectāvimus. _We saw a sad show._

5. Vīdistisne gemmam viridem? _Did you see the green gem?_

6. Quomodō gemmam viridem invēnistis? _How did you find the green jewel?_

7. Homō fortis mē ex igne ēripuit. _A brave man saved me from the fire._

8. Avus omnibus puellīs dōna dābat. _Grandfather was giving all the girls gifts._

9. Puerī Iūniō in flūmine natāvērunt. _The boys swam in the river in June._

10. The sailors will see the land on Sunday. _Diē Sōlis, nautae terram vidēbunt._

11. The strong farmer is carrying a table. _Agricola fortis mēnsam portat._

12. The sad man works without patience. _Vir fatuus sine patientiā labōrat._

13. Every lamp has oil. _Omnis lampās ōleum habet._

14. The green apple is large. _Mālum viride est magnum._

Ex Scriptūrīs:

15. Omnēs scientiam habēmus. (I Cor. 8:1). _We all have knowledge._

XXIII – Vīcēsima Tertia   **Nōmen:**

16. Deus dedit Illī nōmen super omne nōmen. (Phil. 2:9, alt.; *illī* – to that one – to Him)

    God gave to Him the name above every name.

17. Deus, quī fēcit mundum et omnia in eō, caelī et terrae Dominus est. (Ac. 17:24 alt.;)

    God, who made the world and everything in it, is the Lord of heaven and earth.

E. Decline *fortis, -e* in masculine (1), feminine (2), and neuter (3), singular (S) and plural (P).

(S) 1. *fortis*   2. *fortis*   3. *forte*

     fortis   *fortis*   *fortis*

     fortī   *fortī*   *fortī*

     fortem   *fortem*   *forte*

     fortī   *fortī*   *fortī*

(P) 1. *fortēs*   2. *fortēs*   3. *fortia*

     fortium   *fortium*   *fortium*

     fortibus   *fortibus*   *fortibus*

     fortīs   *fortīs*   *fortia*

     fortibus   *fortibus*   *fortibus*

F. *Converte* these *verba* and phrases.

1. vīcēsima tertia *twenty-third*   2. twenty-second *vīcēsimus secundus, -a, -um*

3. dry land *terra firma*   4. exemplī grātiā *for example*

5. Est frīgidum. *It's cold.*   6. Manē dum! *Wait a minute!*

G. Derivati. Complete each sentence with an English *verbum* chosen from the following *verba*. The italicized *verbum* in the sentence should help you think of the Latin root.

     verdant   fortitude   prudent   omnipotent   brief

1. God is *omnipotent* ; i.e., He is *all-powerful*. Latin root: *omnis, -e*

XXIII – Vīcēsima Tertia Nōmen: _____

2. ___prudent___ students *wisely* take responsibility for their homework.

   Latin root: _____prūdēns, prūdentis_____

3. The *green* of spring provides beautiful ___verdant___ scenery.

   Latin root: _____viridis, viride_____

4. ___brief___ reports are *short*. Latin root: _____brevis, -e_____

5. The ___fortitude___ of *brave* soldiers is admirable. Latin root: ___fortis, -e___

H. Alphabet Code. Unscramble the letters given to write the *feminine singular* form of the *verba* in this *lectiō*. Use the code letters under each blank to find the secret message.

Scrambled	Unscrambled		Scrambled	Unscrambled
AOLNG	L O N G A q k p o v		IVRSDII	V I R I D I S r b g b a b c
MSOIN	O M N I S k d p b c		TTISRSI	T R I S T I S h g b c h b c
ITFSRO	F O R T I S u k g h b c		PSNRUED	P R U D E N S t g n a w p c
VESBRI	B R E V I S x g w r b c			

> The difference between the 3rd declension adjective forms and the 3rd declension noun forms is mostly in the…
>
> A B L A T I V E   S I N G U L A R
> v x q v h b r w   c b p o n q v g

I. Historia. Review the history and fill in the blanks.

1. When does Constantine become sole ruler of Rome? _____324 AD_____

2. To which place does he move the capitol? ___He moved the capitol to Byzantium.___

3. What does he rename the capital? ___He renames it Constantinople.___

XXIV – Vīcēsima Quarta   Nōmen:

XXIV – Vīcēsima quarta lectiō   COMMANDS
(24 – Twenty-fourth lesson)

I. Dictum

Tempus fugit.   *Time flies.*

II. Colloquium   *Latīnē*   *Anglicē*

| **Aemilia:** | Quotus diēs mēnsis est? | What's the date? |
| **Lūcius:** | Vīcēsimus quartus diēs Iānuāriī est. | It's the 24th of January. |

III. Verba

Latīnē	*Anglicē*	*Scrībe tōtum verbum Latīnum.*	*Dērīvātī*
canticum, -ī, n.	song	canticum, -ī, n.	canticle
cārissimus, -a, -um	dear, beloved	cārissimus, -a, -um	Carissa
honor, honōris, m.	honor	honor, honōris, m.	honorable

1. Which *verba* are nouns? *canticum, honor*

2. *Scrībe* the declension of each noun to its left.

3. What kind of *verbum* is *cārissimus, -a, -um*? *It is an adjective.*

4. How does one find the stem of a Latin noun? *Drop the ending from the gen. sing.*

5. What is the genitive singular case ending for 1st declension? *-ae* 2nd? *-ī* 3rd? *-is*

6. Which declension has no neuter nouns? *The 1st decl. has no neuter nouns.*

7. What are two ways to ask a question *Latīnē*? a. *add the suffix -ne to the first word*

   b. *use an interrogative adjective or adverb (e.g. quid, quotus, cūr, etc.)*

8. What detail differentiates one conjugation from another? *the infinitive ending*

9. There are *4* conjugations of Latin verbs.

10. What vowel identifies 1st conjugation? *ā* 2nd? *ē* 3rd? *e* 4th? *ī*

XXIV – Vīcēsima Quarta   Nōmen:

IV. Grammatica

Commands are very easy in Latin. In general, to use a verb in the *imperative mood* (command form) when commanding *one* person, just use the stem. To make a negative command, use the irregular verb *nōlō* (which looks like it belongs in the 4th conjugation) with an infinitive. Here are some examples:

Labōrā!	**Work!**
Manē!	**Stay!**
Sedē!	**Sit!**
Lege!	**Read!**
Venī!	**Come!**
Nōlī cantāre	**Don't sing!**

To command more than one person, add *–te* to the stem. In 3rd conjugation, the stem vowel changes to an *–i* in the plural. Here are some examples of plural imperatives:

Labōrāte!	**Work!**
Manēte!	**Stay!**
Sedēte!	**Sit!**
Legite!	**Read!**
Venīte!	**Come!**
Nōlīte cantāre	**Don't sing!**

Now you can train your dog in a foreign language!

A. *Scrībe* these commands to one person *Latīnē*.

1. Write!   *Scrībe!*
2. Sing!   *Cantā!*
3. Rejoice!   *Gaudē!*
4. Don't talk! *Nōlī dīcere*

B. *Scrībe* these commands to more than one person *Latīnē*.

1. Believe!   *Crēdite!*
2. Hurry!   *Festināte!*
3. Be silent! *Silēte!*
4. Don't fight! *Nōlīte pugnāre!*

V. Historia (*Famous Men of Rome*, Chapter XXX)

In 364, Emperor Valentinian again divides the Empire into eastern and western sections. Then Bishop Ambrose of Milan makes Emperor Theodosius do penance. Barbarian tribes pour into western Europe, and in 476, the last Emperor, Romulus Augustus, is taken prisoner, and the Roman Empire in the west falls. The Byzantine Empire survives until 1453.

XXIV – Vīcēsima Quarta   Nōmen:

VI. Dēlēgāta

A. *Scrībe* the new Latin *verba* and their meanings.

Latīnē	*Anglicē*
1. canticum, -ī, n.	1. song
2. cārissimus, -a, -um	2. dear, beloved
3. honor, honōris, m.	3. Honor

B. *Variātiōnēs.* *Recitā* these sentence patterns several times.

1. Tertius diēs Iānuāriī est. (It's the 3rd of January.)
2. Quārtus diēs Februāriī est. (It's the 4th of February.)
3. Octāvus diēs Martiī est. (It's the 8th of March.)
4. Nōnus diēs Aprīlis est. (It's the 9th of April.)
5. Duodecimus dies Maiī est. (It's the 12th of May.)
6. Quīntus decimus diēs Iūniī est. (It's the 15th of June.)
7. Ūndēvīcēsimus diēs Iūliī est. (It's the 19th of July.)
8. Vīcēsimus prīmus diēs Augustī est. (It's the 21st of August.)
9. Duodētrīcēsimus diēs Septembris est. (It's the 28th of September.)
10. Ūndetrīcēsimus diēs Octōbris est. (It's the 29th of October.)
11. Trīcēsimus diēs Novembris est. (It's the 30th of November.)
12. Trīcēsimus prīmus diēs Decembris est. (It's the 31st of December.)

C. *Converte hās sententiās.*

1. Cantāte canticum bellum. Sing a beautiful song.
2. Cārissimō meō canticum cantābō. I will sing a song to my beloved.
3. Cārissimae meae canticum cantābō. I will sing a song to my beloved.
4. Laudā Deum! Praise God!
5. Laudāte Dominum! Praise God!
6. Dīves sine honōre est pauper. The rich man without honor is a poor man.
7. Dā mihi pānem quaesō. Give me bread, please.
8. Trāde mihi mālum quaesō. Pass me an apple, please.
9. Tenē equōs tuōs! Hold your horses!

XXIV – Vīcēsima Quarta Nōmen: _____

10. Salūtā aviam tuam, Maria. _Greet your grandmother, Maria._

11. Salūtā avum, Secunde. _Greet your grandfather, Secundus._

12. Parāte viam Dominī. (Matt. 3:3) _Prepare the way of the Lord._

13. Patellās in culīnam portā, quaesō. _Please carry the plates into the kitchen._

D. *Converte hās sententiās aut scrībe illās Latīnē.*

1. Dominus super omnem terram regnat. _The Lord reigns over all the earth._

2. Spectāte porcum meum. _Look at my pig._

3. Cēnāte omnia holera vestra. _Eat all your vegetables._

4. Cēnā omnīs fābās tuās. _Eat all your beans._

5. Epistulam mihi mitte. _Send me a letter._

6. Claudite ōra et aperīte librōs. _Close your mouths and open your books._

7. Marcus calculum sub lectō invēnit. _Marcus found a pebble under his bed._

8. Tarquinia librum bonum leget. _Tarquinia will read a good book._

9. Rēx et rēgīna ad oppidum meum vēnient. _The king and queen will come to the town._

10. Mīles cum duōbus arcīs est fortis. _The soldier with two bows is strong._

11. We were listening to a song. _Canticum audiēbāmus._

12. Now I hear a sad song. _Canticum trīste nunc audiō._

13. My beloved is happy. _Cārissimus meus est beātus._

14. The good soldier fights with honor. _Mīles bonus cum honōre pugnat._

15. I know how to sing a song. _Canticum sciō cantāre._

16. Rejoice (P) in the Lord! _Gaudēte in Dominō!_

17. Carry (S) the books to the table, please. _Librōs ad mēnsam portā, quaesō._

XXIV – Vīcēsima Quarta   Nōmen:

Ex Scriptūrīs:

18. Hic est Fīlius meus cārissiumus; audīte illum! (Mark 9:7; *illum* – to him).

    This is my beloved son, hear him!

19. Quod vidēs, scrībe in librō et mitte septem ecclesiīs. (Rev. 1:11; *quod* – *that which*)

    What you see, write in a book and send to the seven churches.

20. Timēte Deum et dāte illī honōrem. (Rev. 14:7; *illī* – to him)

    Fear God and give him honor.

21. Iēsus dīxit, "Dāte quae sunt Caesāris Caesārī, et quae sunt Deī Deō." (Mark 12:17, alt.; *quae* – the things which)

    Jesus said, "Give the things which are Caesar's to Caesar,

    and the things which are God's, to God.

E. Decline canticum triste. Be careful!

canticum triste	cantica tristia
canticī tristis	canticōrum tristium
canticō tristī	canticīs tristibus
canticum triste	cantica tristia
canticō tristī	canticīs tristibus

F. *Converte* these *verba* and phrases.

1. vīcēsima quarta *twenty-fourth*   2. twenty-third *vīcēsimus tertius, -a, -um*

3. Tempus fugit. *Time flies.*   4. too long *ad nauseam*

5. dramatis persōnae *characters*   6. It's cold. *Est frīgidum*

7. Fortune favors the bold. *Fortīs fortūna adiūvat.*

8. Quotus diēs mensis est? *What is the date?*

9. Manē dum quaesō! *Wait a moment!*

XXIV – Vīcēsima Quarta   Nōmen: _____

10. Vēnī, vīdī, vīcī. _____ *I came, I saw, I conquered.* _____

11. Tē Deum laudāmus. _____ *We praise you, O God.* _____

G. Dērīvātī. Complete each sentence with an English *verbum* chosen from the following *verba*. The italicized *verba* in the sentence should help you think of the Latin root.

cantor   canticle

1. A ____*canticle*____ is a *song*. Latin root: _____canticum, -ī, n._____

2. A ____*cantor*____ *sings* during a Jewish worship service. Latin root: __*cantō, cantāre*__

H. Crossword Puzzle. All nouns and adjectives are in the nominative case.

	¹C	A	R	I	²S	S	I	M	A	³F		
	U				E					L		
	M				L			⁴H	O	N	O	R
					L					S		
	⁵C	E	R	A	S	U	M	R	U	F	U	M
	A			V						L		
	⁶N	I	V	I	S			⁷T	R	A	N	S
	T			R			⁸A			V		
⁹P	I	S	C	I	S	F	U	S	C	U	S	
	C			D			D			S		
	U			I			I					
¹⁰O	M	N	I	S		¹¹F	O	R	T	I	S	

RĒCTĒ
1. beloved (f.)
4. honor
5. red cherry
6. of the snow
7. across
9. brown fish (sing.)
10. every (f. sing.)
11. brave (m. sing.)

DEORSUM
1. with
2. green chair
3. yellow flower
5. song
8. I hear

I. Historia. Review the history and fill in the blanks.

1. Who divides the Empire in 364? _____*Diocletian divided the empire.*_____

2. Who is the last western emperor? _*The last western emperor is Romulus Augustulus.*_

3. In what year does the Roman Empire end? _____*The empire in the est falls in 476 AD.*_____

Glossary – Latin to English

Roman numeral indicates lesson number.
Vocabulary from *Schola Latina Book I* are marked (BI)

<u>Nōtā bene</u>: Noun dictionary entries are often shortened by listing only the genitive singular *ending* rather than the full genitive singular *form*. So **lectus, lectī, m.** would become **lectus, -ī, m.** and **vallum, vallī, n.** would become **vallum, -ī, n.** This seems confusing at first, but you can still see the stem of these nouns in the nominative singular forms <u>lectus</u> and <u>vallum</u>. However, nouns like **culter, cultrī, m.** and **māter, mātris, f.** will *not* be abbreviated, because their stems are not visible in the nominative singular form.

A

ā / ab (+Abl)	from, away from (X)
abacus, -ī, m.	gameboard (IV)
accipiō, accipere, accēpī, acceptum	to receive (XXI)
ad (+Acc)	to, toward, at (VIII)
aestās, aestātis, f.	summer (XVII)
aeternus, -a, -um	eternal (BI)
ager, agrī, m.	farm field (XI)
agnus, -ī, m.	lamb (BI)
agricola, -ae, m.	farmer (BI)
albus, -a, -um	white (XIV)
ālea, -ae, f.	(game) die (IV)
altus, -a, -um	high, deep (BI)
ambulō, ambulāre, ambulāvī, ambulātum	to walk (BI)
amīcus, -ī, m.	friend (BI)
amō, amāre, amāvī, amātum	to love, to like (BI)
angelus, -ī, m.	angel (II)
angustus, -a, -um	narrow (BI)
annus, -ī, m.	year (BI)
ante (+Acc)	before, in front of (VIII)
antīquus, -a, -um	old, ancient (BI)
aperiō, aperīre, aperuī, apertum	to open (XXII)
Aprīlis, -is, m.	April (XVIII)
aqua, -ae, f.	water (BI)
aquila, -ae, f.	eagle (BI)
arcus, -ī, m.	bow, rainbow (XV)
argentum, -ī, n.	silver (III)
arō, arāre, arāvī, arātum	to plow (BI)
ascendō, ascendere, ascendī, ascensum	to ascend (XIII)
audiō, audīre, audīvī, audītum	to hear (XXII)
Augustus, -ī, m.	August (XVIII)
aurantius, -a, -um	orange (XV)
auris, auris, f.	ear (BI)
aurum, -ī, n.	gold (III)
autumnus, -ī, m.	autumn (XVII)
avia, -ae, f.	grandmother (XIV)
avis, avis, f.	bird (BI)
avus, -ī, m.	grandfather (XV)

B

beātus, -a, -um	happy, blessed (IX)
bellus, -a, -um	pretty (BI)
bellum, -ī, n.	war (BI)
bene	well (BI)
bonus, -a, -um	good (BI)
bōs, bovis, m./f.	ox, cow (BI)
brācae, -ārum, f.	pants (XVI)
bracchium, -ī, n.	arm (BI)
brevis, -e	short (XXIII)
būtyrum, -ī, n.	butter (X)

C

caelum, ī, n.	sky, heaven (BI)
Caesar, Caesaris, m.	Caesar (BI)
caeruleus, -a, -um	blue (BI)
calamus, -ī, m.	pen (BI)
calceus, -ī, m.	shoe (XVI)
calculus, -ī, m.	stone, gamepiece (IV)

Glossary — Latin to English

Latin	English
camisia, -ae, f.	shirt (XVI)
canis, canis, m./f.	dog (BI)
canticum, -ī, n.	song (XXIV)
cantō, cantāre, cantāvī, cantātum	to sing (BI)
capillus, -ī, m.	(a) hair (BI)
capiō, capere, cēpī, captum	to seize (XXI)
caput, capitis, n.	head (BI)
cārissimus, -a, -um	beloved (XXIV)
cāritās, cāritātis, f.	love (V)
cāseus, -ī, m.	cheese (IX)
cēnō, cēnare, cēnāvī, cēnātum	to dine, to eat (BI)
cerasum, -ī, n.	cherry (VII)
charta, -ae, f.	paper (BI)
Christus, -ī, m.	Christ (BI)
cingulum, -ī, n.	belt (XVI)
circum (+ Acc)	around, about (VIII)
cīvitās, cīvitātis, f.	state (XI)
claudō, claudere, clausī, clausum	to close (XVI)
clāvis, clāvis, f.	key (VII)
cochleāre, cochleāris, n.	spoon (BI)
cōgitō, cōgitāre, cōgitāvī, cōgitātum	to think (BI)
collis, collis, m.	hill (BI)
corōna, -ae, f.	crown (BI)
corpus, corporis, n.	body (BI)
crēdō, crēdere, crēdidī, crēditum	to believe (XIII)
crūs, crūris, n.	leg (BI)
crux, crucis, f.	cross (BI)
cubiculum, -ī, n.	bedroom (BI)
cubīle, cubīlis, n.	bed (BI)
culīna, -ae, f.	kitchen (BI)
culpa, -ae, f.	fault (BI)
culter, cultrī, m.	knife (BI)
cum (+ Ab)	with (X)
cūr	why (XII)

D

Latin	English
dē (+Abl)	about, concerning down from (X)
December, Decembris, m.	December (XVIII)
dēficiō, dēficere, dēfēcī, dēfectum	to fail (XXI)
dēns, dentis, m.	tooth (BI)
dēscendō, -ere, dēscendī, dēscensum	to descend (XIII)
Deus, -ī, m.	God (BI)
dextera, -ae, f.	right hand (IV)
dīcō, dīcere, dīxī, dictum	to say, to tell (XIII)
diēs, diēī, m.	day (XX)
diēs Iovis	Thursday (XX)
diēs Lūnae	Monday (XX)
diēs Martis	Tuesday (XX)
diēs Mercuriī	Wednesday (XX)
diēs Sāturnī	Saturday (XX)
diēs Sōlis	Sunday (XX)
diēs Veneris	Friday (XX)
dīgnus, -a, -um	worthy (VI)
digitus, -ī, m.	finger, toe (BI)
discipula, -ae, f.	student (BI)
discipulus, -ī, m.	student (BI)
dīves, dīvitis, m./f.	rich person (V)
dō, dare, dedī, datum	to give (III)
doceō, docēre, docuī, doctum	to teach (BI)
doleō, dolēre, doluī, dolitūrum	to ache (BI)
Dominica, -ae, f.	Lord's Day (XX)
dominus, -ī, m.	lord, master (BI)
domus, domūs, f.	house (BI)
dōnum, -ī, n.	gift (BI)
dormiō, dormīre, dormīvī, dormītum	to sleep (XXII)
dubitō, dubitāre, dubitāvī, dubitātum	to doubt (BI)
dūrō, dūrāre, dūrāvī, dūrātum	to endure (BI)

E

Latin	English
ē / ex (+Abl)	out of, out from, from (X)
ecce	behold! (XV)
ecclēsia, -ae, f.	church (BI)
ego	I, me (II)
epistula, -ae, f.	letter (XX)
equus, -ī, m.	horse (BI)
ēripiō, ēripere,	to rescue (XXI)

Latin	English
ēripuī, ēreptum	
errō, errāre, errāvī, errātum	to err, to wander, be mistaken (BI)
et	and (BI)
evangelium, -ī, n.	gospel (VII)
exedrium, -ī, n.	living room (BI)

F

Latin	English
fāba, -ae, f.	bean (VI)
faciō, facere, fēcī, factum	to make, to do (XXI)
fatuus, -a, -um	foolish (XIX)
Februārius, -ī, m.	February (XVIII)
fēles, fēlis, f.	cat (BI)
fēmina, -ae, f.	woman (BI)
fenestra, -ae, f.	window (BI)
festīnō, festīnāre, festīnāvī, festīnātum	to hurry (BI)
fīlia, -ae, f.	daughter (BI)
fīlius, -ī, m.	son (BI)
fīnis, fīnis, m.	end, border (VII)
flāvus, -a, -um	yellow (XIV)
fleō, flēre, flēvī, flētum	to weep, to cry (BI)
flōs, flōris, m.	flower (IX)
flūmen, flūminis, n.	river (BI)
focus, -ī, m.	fireplace (BI)
fortis, -e	strong, brave (XXIII)
frāter, frātris, m.	brother (BI)
fulvus, -a, -um	brown (XV)
furca, -ae, f.	fork (BI)

G

Latin	English
Gallia, -ae, f.	Gaul (France) (BI)
gallīna, -ae, f.	chicken (BI)
gaudeō, gaudēre, gāvīsus sum	to rejoice (BI)
gaudium, -ī, n.	joy (BI)
gemma, -ae, f.	gem, jewel (XI)
gerō, gerere, gessī, gestum	to wear, to manage (XVI)
gladius, -ī, m.	sword (BI)
glōria, -ae, f.	glory (BI)
grātia, -ae, f.	grace (XVII)

H

Latin	English
habeō, habēre, habuī, habitum	to have, to possess (III)
septimāna, septimānae, f.	week
herba, -ae, f.	plant, herb (BI)
hīc	here (BI)
hic, haec, hoc	this (X)
hiems, hiemis, f.	winter (XVII)
Hispania, -ae, f.	Spain (BI)
holus, holeris, n.	vegetable (VI)
homō, hominis, m.	person, man, human (BI)
honor, honōris, m.	honor (XXIV)
hōra, -ae, f.	hour (BI)
hostis, hostis, m./f.	enemy (BI)
humilitās, humilitātis, f.	humility (V)

I

Latin	English
iaciō, iacere, iēcī, iactum	to throw, to cast (XXI)
iānua, -ae, f.	door (BI)
Iānuārius, -ī, m.	January (XVIII)
ibi	there (BI)
ignis, ignis, m.	fire (BI)
ille, illa, illud	that (XI)
imperātor, imperātōris, m.	commander (BI)
imperō, imperāre, imperāvī, imperātum	to rule, to order (BI)
in (+Abl)	in, on (XI)
in (+Acc)	into, onto (XI)
indō, induere, induī, indūtum	to put on (XVI)
infernus, -ī, m.	underworld, hell (VII)
īnsula, -ae, f.	island (BI)
intrō, intrāre, intrāvī, intrātum	to enter (III)
inveniō, invenīre, invēnī, inventum	to find (XXII)
is, ea, id	he, she, it; they
Ītalia, -ae, f.	Italy (IV)
iūdicō, iūdicāre, iūdicāvī, iūdicātum	to judge (II)

L

labor, labōris, m.	labor, effort (XIX)
labōrō, labōrāre, labōrāvī, labōrātum	to work (BI)
lacūnar, lacūnāris, n.	ceiling (BI)
lampas, lampadis, f.	lamp, torch (VII)
lātus, -a, -um	wide (BI)
laudō, laudāre, laudāvī, laudātum	to praise (III)
laus, laudis, f.	praise (X)
lectus, -ī, m.	couch, bed (BI)
legiō, legiōnis, f.	legion (BI)
legō, legere, lēgī, lectum	to read (XIII)
lēx, lēgis, f.	law (BI)
liber, librī, m.	book (BI)
līberō, līberāre, līberāvī, līberātum	to free (XIV)
lingua, -ae, f.	language, tongue (BI)
longus, -a, -um	long (XXIII)
lūceō, lucēre, lūxī	to shine (BI)
lūdus, -ī, m.	game, school (IV)
lūna, -ae, f.	moon (BI)
lūx, lūcis, f.	light (BI)

M

magister, magistrī, m.	teacher (BI)
magistra, -ae, f.	teacher (BI)
magnus, -a, -um	large, great (BI)
Māius, -ī, m.	May (XVIII)
male	badly (BI)
mālum, -ī, n.	apple (III)
mālum aurantium	orange (XV)
malus, -a, -um	bad, evil (BI)
maneō, manēre, mānsī, mānsum	to stay, to remain (BI)
manus, manūs, f.	hand (BI)
margarīta, -ae, f.	pearl (XI)
Maria, -ae, f.	Mary (BI)
Martius, -ī, m.	March (XVIII)
māter, mātris, f.	mother (BI)
mendācium, -ī, n.	lie, falsehood (BI)
mēnsa, -ae, f.	table (BI)
mensis, mensis, m.	month (XVIII)
meus, -a, -um	my (BI)
mīles, mīlitis, m.	soldier (BI)
misereō, miserēre,	to be sorry (BI)
mittō, mittere, mīsī, missum	to send (XIII)
mōns, montis, m.	mountain (BI)
mors, mortis, f.	death (BI)
moveō, movēre, mōvī, mōtum	to move (BI)
multum	a lot (BI)
multus, -a, -um	much, many (BI)
mundus, -ī, m.	world (BI)
mūrus, -ī, m.	wall (BI)

N

nāsus, -ī, m.	nose (BI)
natō, natāre, natāvī, natātum	to swim (VIII)
nauta, -ae, m.	sailor (BI)
nāvigō, nāvigāre, nāvigāvī, nāvigātum	to sail (BI)
nāvis, nāvis, f.	ship (BI)
nēmō, nēminis, m./f.	no one, nobody (XIX)
niger, nigra, nigrum	black (XIV)
nimbus, -ī, m.	cloud (BI)
ningit, ningere	to snow (XVII)
nix, nivis, f.	snow (XVII)
nōmen, nōminis, n.	name (BI)
nōn	not (BI)
nōs	us (II)
November, Novembris, m.	November (XVIII)
novus, -a, -um	new (BI)
nox, noctis, f.	night (BI)
nummus, -ī, m.	coin (VI)
numquam	never (BI)
nunc	now (BI)
nūntius, -ī, m.	messenger, message (BI)

O

Octōber, Octōbris, m.	October (XVIII)
oculus, -ī, m.	eye (BI)
oleum, -ī, n.	oil (X)

omnis, -e	all, every (XXIII)	portō, portāre,	to carry (IX)
oppidum, -ī, n.	town (BI)	portāvī, portātum	
optimus, -a, -um	best (BI)	possum, posse, potuī	to be able, can (BI)
opus, operis, n.	work (XIX)	praemium, -ī, n.	reward (BI)
ōrō, ōrāre,	to pray,	prīmus, -a, -um	first (BI)
ōrāvī, ōrātum	to speak (BI)	principium, -ī, n.	beginning (VII)
ōs, ōris, n.	mouth (BI)	prophetia, -ae, f.	prophecy (XIX)
		prūdēns, prūdentis	wise (XXIII)

P

		puella, -ae, f.	girl (BI)
pānis, pānis, m.	bread (IX)	puer, puerī, m.	boy (BI)
parō, parāre,	to prepare (XIV)	pugnō, pugnāre,	to fight (BI)
parāvī, parātum		pugnāvī, pugnātum	
pars, partis, f.	part (BI)	purpureus, -a, -um	purple (XV)
parum	a little (BI)	puteus, -ī, m.	a well (BI)
parvus, -a, -um	small (BI)		

Q

pastor, pastōris, m.	shepherd (BI)	quandō	when (XII)
patella, -ae, f.	plate (BI)	quantus, -a, um	how much (XII)
pateō, patēre, patuī	to be open (BI)	quī	who; (he) who (XIV)
pater, patris, m.	father (BI)	quid	what? (XII)
patientia, -ae, f.	patience (X)	quis	who? (XII)
patria, -ae, f.	fatherland country (BI)	quōmodo	how? (XII)
pauper, pauperis, m.	poor man (XIX)	quot	how many? (XII)
pax, pācis, f.	peace (BI)	quotus, -a, -um	which? (XII)

R

peccātum, -ī, n.	sin (BI)		
peccō, peccāre,	to sin (BI)	recitō, recitāre,	to recite,
peccāvī, peccātum		recitāvī, recitātum	to read aloud (BI)
pecūnia, -ae, f.	money (BI)	rēgīna, -ae, f.	queen (BI)
pedāle, pedālis, n.	sock (V)	rēgnō, rēgnāre,	to reign (BI)
per (+ Acc)	through (VII)	rēgnāvī, rēgnātum	
pēs, pedis, m.	foot (BI)	rēgnum, -ī, n.	kingdom (BI)
petō, petere,	to seek, to beg,	resurrectiō,	resurrection (V)
petīvī, petitum	to ask for (XVI)	resurrectiōnis, f.	
pilleus, -ī, m.	hat (IX)	rēx, rēgis, m.	king (BI)
piscātor, piscātōris, m.	fisherman (XIX)	rīdeō, rīdēre, rīsī, rīsum	to laugh (VII)
piscis, piscis, m.	fish (XIX)	Rōma, -ae, f.	Rome (BI)
placeō, placēre, placuī, placitum	to please (BI)	rūfus, -a, -um	red (XIV)

S

pluit, pluere	to rain (XVII)		
pluvia, -ae, f.	rain (XVII)	saepe	often (XV)
pōculum, -ī, n.	cup (BI)	salūtō, salūtāre,	to greet (XIV)
pōmum, -ī, n.	fruit (VI)	salūtāvī, salūtātum	
porcus, -ī, m.	pig (BI)		
porta, -ae, f.	gate (XI)	salveō, salvēre	to be well (BI)
portiō, portiōnis, f.	portion, snack (V)	sanctus, -a, -um	holy (BI)

sapientia, -ae, f.	wisdom (III)		
scientia, -ae, f.	knowledge (VII)	**T**	
sciō, scīre, scīvī, scītum	to know (XXII)	tardō, tardāre, tardāvī, tardātum	to be slow (BI)
scrībō, scrībere, scrīpsī, scrīptum	to write (XVI)	taurus, -ī, m.	bull (BI)
		tēlum, -ī, n.	weapon (BI)
secundum (+ Acc)	beside, according to (VIII)	tempus, tempōris, n.	time (BI)
secundus, -a, -um	second (BI)	teneō, tenēre, tenuī, tentum	to hold (IV)
sedeō, sedēre, sēdī, sessum	to sit (BI)	terra, -ae, f.	land, earth (BI)
sella, -ae, f.	chair (BI)	terreō, terrēre, terruī, territum	to frighten (VI)
semper	always (BI)		
September, Septembris, m.	September (XVIII)	thēsaurus, -ī, m.	treasure (XI)
		thronus, -ī, m.	throne (II)
serpens, serpentis, m./f.	snake (BI)	timeō, timēre, timuī	to fear, to be afraid (BI)
servō, servāre, servāvī, servātum	to save, to keep, to guard (XIII)	timor, timōris, m.	fear (VII)
		tōtus, -a, -um	whole (BI)
servus, -ī, m.	slave, servant (BI)	trādō, trādere, trādidī, trāditum	to pass, to hand over (XIII)
signum, -ī, n.	sign (BI)		
sileō, silēre, siluī	to be silent (BI)	trāns (+Acc)	across (VII)
silva, -ae, f.	forest (BI)	tristis, -e	sad (XXIII)
similis, -e (+ Dat)	similar to (XI)	tū	you (sing.) (III)
sine (+ Abl)	without (X)	tūtus, -a, -um	safe (BI)
solum, -ī, n.	floor (BI)	tuus, -a, -um	your (sing.) (BI)
soror, sorōris, f.	sister (BI)		
spatium, -ī, n.	space (IV)	**U**	
spectāculum, -ī, n.	sight, show (VI)	ubi	where? (XII)
spectō, spectāre, spectāvī, spectātum	to look at, to observe (VI)	urbs, urbis, f.	city (BI)
		ursa, -ae, f.	bear (BI)
speculum, -ī, n.	mirror (BI)		
spīritus, spīritūs, m.	spirit (BI)		
stella, -ae, f.	star (BI)	**V**	
stīlus, -ī, m.	pencil (BI)	valeō, valēre, valuī, valitūrum	to be strong, to have power (BI)
stō, stāre, stetī, statum	to stand (BI)		
stomachus, -ī, m.	stomach (BI)	vallum, -ī, n.	wall, rampart (BI)
studeō, -ēre, studuī	to be eager for, to study (XIII)	velim	I would like (III)
		velīsne	Would you like? (IV)
sub (+ Acc/Abl)	under, up to, up under (XI)	veniō, venīre, vēnī, ventum	to come (XXII)
sum, esse, fuī, futūrum	to be (BI)	vēr, vēris, n.	spring (XVII)
super (+ Acc)	above, over (VII)	verbum, -ī, n.	word (BI)
superō, superāre, superāvī, superātum	to overcome, to conquer (III)	vēritās, vēritātis, f.	truth (BI)
		vērus, -a, -um	true (IX)

via, -ae, f.	road, way (BI)
victōria, -ae, f.	victory (BI)
videō, vidēre, vīdī, vīsum	to see (III)
vīnum, -ī, n.	wine (BI)
virgō, virginis, f.	young woman, maiden (XIX)
viridis, -e	green (XXIII)
virtūs, virtūtis, f.	courage, virtue, manliness (BI)
vīta, -ae, f.	life (BI)
volō, volāre, volāvī, volātum	to fly (BI)
vōs	you (pl.) (III)
vōx, vōcis, f.	voice (BI)

Glossary – English to Latin

Roman numeral indicates lesson number.
Vocabulary from *Schola Latina Book I* are marked (BI)

Nōtā bene: Noun dictionary entries are often shortened by listing only the genitive singular *ending* rather than the full genitive singular *form*. So **lectus, lectī, m.** would become **lectus, -ī, m.** and **vallum, vallī, n.** would become **vallum, -ī, n.** This seems confusing at first, but you can still see the stem of these nouns in the nominative singular forms **lectus** and **vallum**. However, nouns like **culter, cultrī, m.** and **māter, mātris, f.** will *not* be abbreviated, because their stems are not visible in the nominative singular form.

A

able, to be	possum, posse, potuī (XVII)
about	circum (+ Acc) (VII)
	dē (+ Abl) (X)
above	super (+ Acc) (VIII)
according to	secundum (+ Acc) (VIII)
ache, to	doleō, dolēre, doluī, dolitūrum (BI)
across	trāns (+ Acc) (VIII)
all	omnis, -e (XXIII)
a lot	multum (BI)
always	semper (BI)
ancient	antīquus, -a, -um (BI)
and	et (BI)
angel	angelus, -ī, m. (II)
apple	mālum, -ī, n. (III)
April	Aprīlis, -is, m. (XVIII)
arm	bracchium, -ī, n. (BI)
around	circum (+ Acc) (VII)
ascend, to	ascendō, ascendere, ascendī, ascensum (XIII)
ask for, to	petō, petere, petīvī, petitum (XVI)
at	ad (+ Acc) (VIII)
August	Augustus, -ī, m. (XVIII)
autumn	autumnus, -ī, m. (XVII)

B

bad	malus, -a, -um (BI)
be, to	sum, esse, fuī, futūrum (BI)
bean	fāba, -ae, f. (VI)
badly	male (BI)
bear	ursa, -ae, f. (BI)
bed	cubīle, cubīlis, n. (BI)
	lectus, -ī, m. (BI)
bedroom	cubiculum, -ī, n. (BI)
before	ante (+ Ac) (VIII)
beg for, to	petō, petere, petīvī, petitum (XVI)
beginning	principium, -ī, n. (VII)
behold!	ecce (XV)
believe, to	crēdō, crēdere, crēdidī, crēditum (XIII)
beloved	cārissimus, -a, -um (XXIV)
belt	cingulum, -ī, n. (XVI)
beside	secundum (+ Acc) (VIII)
best	optimus, -a, -um (BI)
bird	avis, avis, f. (BI)
black	niger, nigra, nigrum (XIV)
blessed	beātus, -a, -um (IX)
blue	caeruleus, -a, -um (XV)
body	corpus, corporis, n. (BI)
book	liber, librī, m. (BI)
border	fīnis, fīnis, m. (VII)
bow	arcus, -ī, m. (XV)
boy	puer, puerī, m. (BI)
brave	fortis, -e (XXIII)
bread	pānis, pānis, m. (IX)
breath	spīritus, spīritūs, m. (BI)
brother	frāter, frātris, m. (BI)
brown	fulvus, -a, -um (XV)
bull	taurus, -ī, m. (BI)
butter	būtyrum, -ī, n. (X)

Glossary			**English to Latin**
C			(BI)
Caesar	Caesar, Caesaris, m. (BI)	dog	canis, canis, m./f. (BI)
carry, to	portō, portāre, portāvī, portātum (IX)	door	iānua, -ae, f. (BI)
cat	fēles, fēlis, f. (BI)	doubt, to	dubitō, dubitāre, dubitāvī, dubitātum (BI)
ceiling	lacūnar, lacūnāris, n. (BI)	down from	dē (+ Abl) (X)
chair	sella, -ae, f. (BI)		
cheese	cāseus, -ī, m. (IX)	**E**	
cherry	cerasum, -ī, n. (VII)	eager, to be	studeō, studēre, studuī (XIII)
chicken	gallīna, -ae, f. (BI)	eagle	aquila, -ae, f. (BI)
Christ	Christus, -ī, m. (BI)	ear	auris, auris, f. (BI)
church	ecclesia, -ae, f. (BI)	earth	terra, -ae, f. (BI)
city	urbs, urbis, f. (BI)	eat, to	cēnō, cēnāre, -āvī, -ātum (BI)
close, to	claudō, claudere, clausī, clausum (XVI)	effort	labor, labōris, m. (XIX)
cloud	nimbus, -ī, m. (BI)	end	fīnis, fīnis, m. (VII)
coin	nummus, -ī, m. (VI)	endure, to	dūrō, dūrāre, -āvī, -ātum (BI)
come, to	veniō, venīre, vēnī, ventūrum (XXII)	enemy	hostis, hostis, m./f. (BI)
commander	imperātor, imperātōris, m. (BI)	enter, to	intrō, intrāre, -āvī, -ātum (BI)
		eternal	aeternus, -a, -um (BI)
concerning	dē (+ Abl) (X)	every	omnis, -e (XXIII)
conquer, to	superō, superāre, superāvī, superātum (BI)	evil	malus, -a, -um (XIII)
		eye	oculus, -ī, m. (BI)
couch	lectus, -ī, m. (BI)	**F**	
country	patria, -ae, f. (BI)	fail, to	dēficiō, dēficere, dēfēcī, dēfectum (XXI)
courage	virtūs, virtūtis, f. (BI)	farmer	agricola, -ae, m. (BI)
cow	bōs, bovis, m./f. (BI)	father	pater, patris, m. (BI)
cross	crux, crucis, f. (BI)	fatherland	patria, -ae, f. (BI)
crown	corōna, -ae, f. (BI)	fault	culpa, -ae, f. (BI)
cup	pōculum, -ī, n. (BI)	fear	timor, timōris, m. (VII)
cry, to	fleō, flēre, flēvī, flētum (BI)	fear, to	timeō, timēre, timuī (BI)
		February	Februārius, -ī, m. (XVIII)
		field	ager, agrī, m. (XI)
D		fight, to	pugnō, pugnāre, pugnāvī, pugnātum (BI)
daughter	fīlia, -ae, f. (BI)		
day	diēs, diēī, m. (XX)	find, to	inveniō, invenīre, invēnī, inventum (XXII)
death	mors, mortis, f. (BI)		
December	December, Decembris (XVIII)	finger	digitus, -ī, m. (BI)
		fire	ignis, ignis, m. (BI)
deep	altus, -a, -um (BI)	fireplace	focus, -ī, m. (BI)
descend, to	dēscendō, dēscendere, dēscendī, dēscēnsum (XIII)	first	prīmus, -a, -um (BI)
		fish	piscis, piscis, m. (XIX)
		fisherman	piscātor, piscātōris, m. (XIX)
die (game)	ālea, -ae, f. (IV)	floor	solum, -ī, n. (BI)
dine, to	cēnō, cēnāre, -āvī, -ātum	flower	flōs, flōris, m. (IX)

English	Latin
fly, to	volō, volāre, -āvī, -ātum (BI)
foolish	fatuus, -a, -um (XIX)
foot	pēs, pedis, m. (BI)
forest	silva, -ae, f. (BI)
fork	furca, -ae, f. (BI)
free, to	līberō, līberāre, līberāvī, līberātum (XIV)
friend	amīcus, -ī, m. (BI) amīca, -ae, f.
frighten, to	terreō, terrēre, terruī, territum (VI)
from	ā / ab (+ Abl) (X)
in front of	ante (+ Acc) (VIII)
fruit	pōmum, -ī, n. (VI)

G

English	Latin
game	lūdus, -ī, m. (IV)
gameboard	abacus, -ī, m. (IV)
game piece	calculus, -ī, m. (IV)
gate	porta, -ae, f. (XI)
Gaul	Gallia, -ae, f. (BI)
gift	dōnum, -ī, n. (BI)
girl	puella, -ae, f. (BI)
give, to	dō, dare, dedī, datum (III)
glory	glōria, -ae, f. (BI)
God	Deus, -ī, m. (BI)
gold	aurum, -ī, n. (III)
good	bonus, -a, -um (BI)
gospel	evangelium, -ī, n. (VIII)
grace	grātia, -ae, f. (XVII)
grandfather	avus, -ī, m. (XV)
grandmother	avia, -ae, f. (XIV)
great	magnus, -a, -um (BI)
green	viridis, -e (XXIII)
greet, to	salūtō, salūtāre, salūtāvī, salūtātum (XIV)
guard, to	servō, servāre, servāvī, servātum (XIII)

H

English	Latin
hair (a)	capillus, -ī, m. (BI)
hand	manus, manus, f. (4th d., BI)
hand over, to	trādō, trādere, trādidī, trāditum (XIII)
happy	beātus, -a, -um (IX)
hat	pilleus, -ī, m. (IX)
have, to	habeō, habēre, habuī, habitum (III)
he	is (see is, ea, id)
he who	quī (XIV)
head	caput, capitis, n. (BI)
hear, to	audiō, audīre, audīvī, audītum (XXII)
heaven	caelum, -ī, n. (BI)
hell	infernus, -ī, m. (VII)
here	hīc (BI)
high	altus, -a, -um (BI)
hill	collis, collis, m. (BI)
hold, to	teneō, tenēre, tenuī, tentum (IV)
holy	sanctus, -a, -um (BI)
honor	honor, honōris, m. (XXIV)
horse	equus, -ī, m. (BI)
hour	hōra, -ae, f. (BI)
house	domus, domūs, f. (BI)
how	quōmodo (XII)
how many	quot (XII)
how much	quantus, -a, -um (XII)
humility	humilitās, humilitātis, f. (V)
hurry, to	festīnō, festināre, festīnāvī, festīnātum (BI)

I

English	Latin
I	ego
in	in (+ Abl) (XI)
into	in (+ Acc) (XI)
island	īnsula, -ae, f. (BI)
it	id (see is, ea, id)
Italy	Ītalia, -ae, f. (BI)

J

English	Latin
January	Iānuārius, -ī, m. (XVIII)
jewel	gemma, -ae, f. (XI)
joy	gaudium, -ī, n. (BI)
judge, to	iūdicō, iūdicāre, iūdicāvī, iūdicātum (BI)
July	Iūlius, -ī, m. (XVIII)
June	Iūnius, -ī, m. (XVIII)

K

keep, to	servō, servāre, servāvī, servātum (XIII)
key	clāvis, clāvis f. (VII)
king	rēx, rēgis, m. (BI)
kingdom	rēgnum, -ī, n. (BI)
kitchen	culīna, -ae, f. (BI)
knife	culter, cultrī, m. (BI)
know, to	sciō, scīre, scīvī, scītum (XXII)
knowledge	scientia, -ae, f. (VII)

L

labor	labor, labōris, m. (XIX)
lamb	agnus, -ī, m. (BI)
lamp	lampas, lampadis, f. (VII)
land	terra, -ae, f. (BI)
language	lingua, -ae, f. (BI)
large	magnus, -a, -um (BI)
laugh, to	rideō, ridēre, rīsī, rīsum (BI)
law	lēx, lēgis, f. (BI)
leg	crūs, crūris, n. (BI)
legion	legiō, legiōnis, f. (BI)
letter	epistula, -ae, f. (XX)
lie	mendācium, -ī, n. (BI)
life	vīta, -ae, f. (BI)
light	lūx, lūcis, f. (BI)
like	similis, -e (XI)
like, to	amō, amāre, -āvī, -ātum (BI)
little, a	parum (BI)
living room	exedrium, -ī, n. (BI)
long	longus, -a, -um (BI)
look at, to	spectō, spectāre, spectāvī, specātum (VI)
lord	dominus, -ī, m. (BI)
Lord's Day	Dominica, -ae, f. (XX)
lot, a	multum (BI)
love, to	amō, amāre, -āvī, -ātum (BI)
love	cāritās, cāritātis, f. (V)

M

maiden	virgō, virginis, f. (XIX)
make, to	faciō, facere, fēcī, factum (XXI)
man	homō, hominis, m. (BI)
manage, to	gerō, gerere, gessī, gestum (XVI)
March	Martius, -ī, m. (XVIII)
manliness	virtūs, virtūtis, f. (BI)
many	multus, -a, -um (BI)
Mary	Maria, -ae, f. (BI)
master	dominus, -ī, m. (BI)
me	ego (II)
message	nūntius, -ī, m. (BI)
messenger	nūntius, -ī, m. (BI)
mirror	speculum, -ī, n. (BI)
Monday	diēs Lūnae (XX)
money	pecūnia, -ae, f. (BI)
month	mensis, mensis, m. (XVIII)
moon	lūna, -ae, f. (BI)
mother	māter, mātris, f. (BI)
mountain	mōns, montis, m. (BI)
mouth	ōs, ōris, n. (BI)
move, to	moveō, movēre, mōvī, mōtum (BI)
much	multus, -a, -um (BI)
my	meus, -a, -um (BI)

N

name	nōmen, nōminis, n. (BI)
narrow	angustus, -a, -um (BI)
never	numquam (BI)
new	novus, -a, -um (BI)
night	nox, noctis, f. (BI)
nobody	nēmo, nēminis, m./f. (XIX)
no one	nēmō, nēminis, m./f. (XIX)
nose	nāsus, -ī, m. (BI)
not	nōn (BI)
November	November, Novembris, m. (XVIII)
now	nunc (BI)

O

October	Octōber, Octōbris, m. (XVIII)
often	saepe (BI)
oil	oleum, -ī, n. (X)
old	antīquus, -a, -um (BI)
on	in (+ Abl) (XI)

open, to	aperiō, aperīre, aperuī, apertum (XXII)	purple	purpureus, -a, -um (XV)
open, to be	pateō, patēre, patuī (BI)	put on, to	induō, induere, induī, indūtum (XVI)
orange	aurantius, -a, -um (XV)		
orange	mālum aurantium, -ī, n. (XV)	**Q**	
		queen	rēgīna, -ae, f. (BI)
order, to	imperō, imperāre, imperāvī, imperātum (BI)	**R**	
		rain	pluvia, -ae, f. (XVII)
out from	ē / ex (+ Abl) (X)	rainbow	arcus, -ī, m. (XV)
out of	ē / ex (+ Abl) (X)	rain, to	pluit, pluere (XVII)
over	super (+ Ac) (VIII)	rampart	vallum, -ī, n. (BI)
overcome, to	superō, superāre, -āvī, superātum (BI)	read, to	legō, legere, lēgī, lectum (XIII)
ox	bōs, bovis, m./f. (BI)	read aloud, to	recitō, recitāre, -āvī, -ātum (BI)
P		receive, to	accipiō, accipere, accēpī, acceptum (XXI)
pants	brācae, -ārum, f. (XVI)		
paper	charta, -ae, f. (BI)	recite, to	recitō, recitāre, recitāvī, recitātum (BI)
part	pars, partis, f. (BI)		
pass, to	tradō, trādere, trādidī, trāditum (XIII)	red	rūfus, -a, -um (XIV)
		reign, to	rēgnō, rēgnāre, rēgnāvī, rēgnātum (BI)
patience	patientia, -ae, f. (X)		
peace	pax, pācis, f. (BI)	rejoice, to	gaudeō, gaudēre, gāvīsus sum (BI)
pearl	margarīta, -ae, f. (XI)		
pen	calamus, -ī, m. (BI)	remain, to	maneō, manēre, mansī, mansum (BI)
pencil	stīlus, -ī, m. (BI)		
pig	porcus, -ī, m. (BI)	rescue, to	ēripiō, ēripere, ēripuī, ēreptum (XXI)
plant	herba, -ae, f. (BI)		
plate	patella, -ae, f. (BI)	resurrection	resurrectiō, resurrectiōnis, f. (V)
please, to	placeō, placēre, placuī (BI)		
		reward	praemium, -ī, n. (BI)
plow, to	arō, arāre, arāvī, arātum (BI)	rich person	dīves, dīvitis, m./f. (V)
		right hand	dextera, -ae, f. (IV)
poor man	pauper, pauperis, m. (XIX)	river	flūmen, flūminis, n. (BI)
		road	via, -ae, f. (BI)
portion	portiō, portiōnis, f. (V)	Rome	Rōma, -ae, f. (BI)
praise, to	laudō, laudāre, -āvī, laudātum (X)	rule, to	imperō, imperāre, imperāvī, imperātum (BI)
praise	laus, laudis, f. (X)		
pray, to	ōrō, ōrāre, -āvī, -ātum (BI)	**S**	
		sad	tristis, -e (XXIII)
prepare, to	parō, parāre, -āvī, -ātum (XIV)	safe	tūtus, -a, -um (BI)
		sail, to	nāvīgō, nāvigāre, nāvigāvī, nāvigātum (BI)
pretty	bellus, -a, -um (BI)		
prophecy	prophetia, -ae, f. (XIX)	sailor	nauta, -ae, m. (BI)

Glossary			English to Latin
Saturday	diēs Sāturnī (XX)	snack	portiō, portiōnis, f. (V)
save, to	servō, servāre, servāvī, servātum (XIII)	snake	serpens, serpentis, m./f. (BI)
		snow	nix, nivis, f. (XVII)
say, to	dīcō, dīcere, dīxī, dictum (XIII)	snow, to	ningit, ningere (XVII)
		sock	pedāle, pedālis, n. (V)
school	lūdus, -ī, m. (IV)	soldier	mīles, mīlitis, m. (BI)
second	secundus, -a, -um (BI)	son	fīlius, -ī, m. (BI)
see, to	videō, vidēre, vīdī, vīsum (III)	song	canticum, -ī, n. (XXIV)
		sorry, to be	misereō, miserēre (BI)
seize, to	capiō, capere, cēpī, ceptum (XXI)	space	spatium, -ī, n. (IV)
		Spain	Hispania, -ae, f. (BI)
send, to	mittō, mittere, mīsī, missum (XIII)	speak, to	ōrō, ōrāre, -āvī, -ātum (BI)
			dīcō, dīcere, dīxī, dictum (XIII)
September	September, Septembris, m. (XVIII)	spirit	spīritus, spīritūs, m. (XXIV)
		spoon	cochleāre, cochleāris, n. (BI)
servant	servus, -ī, m. (BI)	spring	vēr, vēris, n. (XVII)
she	ea (see is, ea, id)	stand, to	stō, stāre, stetī, statum (BI)
shepherd	pastor, pastōris, m. (BI)	star	stella, -ae, f. (BI)
shine, to	luceō, lucēre, lūxī (BI)	state	cīvitās, cīvitātis, f. (XI)
ship	nāvis, nāvis, f. (BI)	stay, to	maneō, manēre, mansī, mansum (BI)
shirt	camisia, -ae, f. (XVI)		
shoe	calceus, -ī, m. (XVI)	stomach	stomachus, -ī, m. (BI)
short	brevis, -e (XXIII)	stone	calculus, -ī, m. (IV)
show	spectāculum, -ī, n. (VI)	strong	fortis, -e (XXIII)
sight	spectāculum, -ī, n. (VI)	strong, to be	valēre, valuī, valitūrum (BI)
sign	signum, -ī, n. (BI)	student	discipulus, -ī, m. discipula, -ae, f. (BI)
silent, to be	sileō, silēre, siluī (BI)		
silver	argentum, -ī, n. (III)	study, to	studeō, studēre, studuī (XIII)
similar	similis, -e (+ Dat) (XI)	summer	aestās, aestātis, f. (XVII)
sin	peccātum, -ī, n. (BI)	Sunday	diēs Sōlis (XX)
sin, to	peccō, peccāre, peccāvī, peccātum (BI)	swim, to	natō, natāre, natāvī, natātum (VIII)
sing, to	cantō, cantāre, cantāvī, cantātum (BI)	sword	gladius, -ī, m. (BI)
sister	soror, sorōris, f. (BI)	**T**	
sit, to	sedeō, sedēre, sēdī, sessum (BI)	table	mēnsa, -ae, f. (BI)
		teach, to	doceō, docēre, docuī, doctum (BI)
sky	caelum, -ī, n. (BI)		
slave	servus, -ī, m. (BI)	teacher	magister, magistrī, m. magistra, -ae, f. (BI)
sleep, to	dormiō, dormīre, dormīvī, dormītum (XXII)		
		tell, to	dīcere, dīxī, dictum (XIII)
		that	ille, illa, illlud (XI)
slow, to be	tardō, tardāre, tardāvī, tardātum (BI)	there	ibi (BI)
		they	(see: is, ea, id)
small	parvus, -a, -um (BI)	think, to	cogitō, cogitāre, cōgitāvī, cōgitātum (BI)

this	hic, haec, hoc (X)		spectāvī, spectātum (VI)
throne	thronus, -ī, m. (II)	**water**	aqua, -ae, f. (BI)
through	per (+ Acc) (VII)	**way**	via, -ae, f. (BI)
throw, to	iaciō, iacere,	**we**	nōs (III)
	iēcī, iactum (XXI)	**weapon**	tēlum, -ī, n. (BI)
Thursday	diēs Iovis (XX)	**wear, to**	gerō, gerere,
time	tempus, temporis, n. (BI)		gessī, gestum (XVI)
to	ad (+ Acc) (VIII)	**Wednesday**	diēs Mercuriī (XX)
toe	digitus, -ī, m. (BI)	**week**	septimāna, septimānae, f. (XX)
tongue	lingua, -ae, f. (BI)	**weep, to**	fleō, flēre, flēvī, flētum (BI)
tooth	dēns, dentis, m. (BI)	**well, to be**	salveō, salvēre (BI)
torch	lampas, lampadis, f. (VII)	**well**	puteus, -ī, m. (BI)
toward	ad (+ Ac) (VIII)	**well**	bene (BI)
town	oppidum, -ī, n. (BI)	**what**	quid (XII)
treasure	thēsaurus, -ī, m. (XI)	**when**	quandō (XII)
true	vērus, -a, -um (IX)	**where**	ubi (XII)
truth	vēritās, vēritātis, f. (BI)	**which**	quotus, -a, -um (XII)
Tuesday	diēs Martis (XX)	**white**	albus, -a, -um (XIV)
		who	quis (XII)
U		**whole**	tōtus, -a, -um (BI)
uncertain,	dubitō, dubitāre, dubitāvī,	**why**	cūr (XII)
to be	dubitātum (BI)	**wide**	lātus, -a, -um (BI)
under	sub (+ Acc / Abl) (XI)	**window**	fenestra, -ae, f. (BI)
underworld	infernus, -ī, m. (VII)	**wine**	vīnum, -ī, n. (BI)
us	nōs (II)	**winter**	hiems, hiemis, f. (XVII)
		wisdom	sapientia, -ae, f. (III)
V		**wise**	prūdens, prūdentis (XXIII)
vegetable	holus, holeris, n. (VI)	**with**	cum (+ Abl) (X)
victory	victōria, -ae, f. (BI)	**without**	sine (+ Abl) (X)
virgin	virgō, virginis, f. (XIX)	**woman**	fēmina, -ae, f. (BI)
virtue	virtūs, virtūtis, f. (BI)	**word**	verbum, -ī, n. (BI)
voice	vōx, vōcis, f. (BI)	**work**	labor, labōris, m. (XIX)
		work, to	labōrō, labōrāre,
W			labōrāvī, labōrātum (BI)
walk, to	ambulō, ambulāre,	**world**	mundus, -ī, m. (BI)
	ambulāvī, ambulātum	**worthy**	dīgnus, -a, -um (VI)
	(BI)	**write, to**	scrībō, scrībere,
wall	vallum, -ī, n. (BI)		scrīpsī, scriptum (XVI)
	(of a fortress)		
wall	mūrus, -ī, m. (BI)	**Y**	
	(of a building or room)	**year**	annus, -ī, m. (BI)
wander, to	errō, errāre, -āvī, -ātum	**yellow**	flāvus, -a, -um (XIV)
	(BI)	**you**	tū (sing.), vōs (pl.) (III)
war	bellum, -ī, n. (BI)	**young woman**	virgō, virginis, f. (XIX)
watch, to	spectō, spectāre,	**your** (sing.)	tuus, -a, -um (BI)

Numbers

	Cardinals	Ordinals	Roman Numerals
1	ūnus, -a, -um	prīmus, -a, -um	I
2	duo, duae, duo	secundus, -a, -um	II
3	trēs, trēs, tria	tertius, -a, -um	III
4	quattuor	quartus, -a, -um	IV
5	quīnque	quīntus, -a, -um	V
6	sex	sextus, -a, -um	VI
7	septem	septimus, -a, -um	VII
8	octō	octāvus, -a, -um	VIII
9	novem	nōnus, -a, -um	IX
10	decem	decimus, -a, -um	X
11	ūndecim	ūndecimus, -a, -um	XI
12	duodecim	duodecimus, -a, -um	XII
13	tredecim	tertius decimus, -a, -um	XIII
14	quattuordecim	quartus decimus, -a, -um	XIV
15	quīndecim	quīntus decimus, -a, -um	XV
16	sēdecim	sextus decimus, -a, -um	XVI
17	septendecim	septimus decimus, -a, -um	XVII
18	duodēvīgintī	duodēvīcēsimus, -a, -um	XVIII
19	ūndēvīgintī	ūndēvīcēsimus, -a, -um	XIX
20	vīgintī	vīcēsimus, -a, -um	XX
21	vīgintī ūnus, -a, -um	vīcēsimus prīmus, -a, -um	XXI
22	vīgintī duo, duae, duo	vīcēsimus secundus, -a, -um	XXII
23	vīgintī trēs, trēs, tria	vīcēsimus tertius, -a, -um	XXIII
24	vīgintī quattuor	vīcēsimus quartus, -a, -um	XXIV
25	vīgintī quīnque	vīcēsimus quīntus, -a, -um	XXV
26	vīgintī sex	vīcēsimus sextus, -a, -um	XXVI
27	vīgintī septem	vīcēsimus septimus, -um	XXVII
28	duodētrīginta	duodētrīcēsimus, -a, -um	XXVIII
29	undētrīginta	undētrīcēsimus, -a, -um	XXIX
30	trīginta	trīcēsimus, -a, -um	XXX
40	quadrāgintā	quadrāgēsimus, -a, -um	XL
50	quīnquāgintā	quīnquāgēsimus, -a, -um	L
60	sexāgintā	sexāgēsimus, -a, -um	LX
70	septuāgintā	septuāgēsimus, -a, -um	LXX
80	octōgintā	octōgēsimus, -a, -um	LXXX
90	nōnāgintā	nōnāgēsimus, -a, -um	XC
100	centum	centēsimus, -a, -um	C
1000	mīlle	mīlēsimus, -a, -um	M

Vocabulary by Lectio

<u>Nōtā bene</u>: Noun dictionary entries are often shortened by listing only the genitive singular *ending* rather than the full genitive singular *form*. So **lectus, lectī, m.** would become **lectus, -ī, m.** and **vallum, vallī, n.** would become **vallum, -ī, n.** This seems confusing at first, but you can still see the stem of these nouns in the nominative singular forms **lectus** and **vallum**.

However, nouns like **culter, cultrī, m.** and **māter, mātris, f.** will *not* be abbreviated, because their stems are not visible in the nominative singular form.

II – Secunda lectiō

angelus, -ī, m.	angel
thronus, -ī, m.	throne
ego	I, me; us, we

III – Tertia lectiō

argentum, -ī, n.	silver
aurum, -ī, n.	gold
mālum, -ī, n.	apple
dō, dare, dedī, datum	to give
laudō, laudāre, laudāvī, laudātum	to praise
habeō, habēre, habuī, habitum	to have, to possess
videō, vidēre, vīdī, vīsum	to see
tū	you

IV – Quarta lectiō

abacus, -ī, m.	gameboard
ālea, -ae, f.	(game) die
calculus, -ī, m.	stone, game piece
dextera, -ae, f.	right hand
lūdus, -ī, m.	game, school
spatium, -ī, n.	space
teneō, tenēre, tenuī, tentum	to hold

V – Quīnta lectiō

cāritās, cāritātis, f.	(Christian) love
dīves, dīvitis, m./f.	rich person
humilitās, humilitātis, f.	humility
pedāle, pedālis, n.	sock (pl. – pedālia)
portiō, portiōnis, f.	portion, snack
resurrectiō, resurrectiōnis, f.	resurrection

VI – Sexta lectiō

dignus, -a, um	worthy
faba, -ae, f.	bean
holus, holeris, n.	vegetable
nummus, -ī, m.	coin
pōmum, -ī, n.	fruit
spectāculum, -ī, n.	sight, show
spectō, spectāre, spectāvī, spectātum	to look at, to watch
terreō, terrēre, terruī, territum	to frighten

VII – Septima lectiō

cerasum, -ī, n.	cherry
clāvis, clāvis, f.	key
fīnis, fīnis, m.	end, border
infernus, -ī, m.	hell, underworld
lampās, lampadis, f.	lamp, torch
principium, -ī, n.	beginning
scientia, -ae, f.	knowledge
timor, timōris, m.	fear

VIII – Octava lectiō

ad (+ Acc)	to, toward, near, at
ante (+ Acc)	before, in front of
circum (+ Acc)	around, about

Vocabulary by Lectio

per (+ Acc)	through	sub (+ Acc /Abl)	under
secundum (+ Acc)	beside, according to	thēsaurus, -ī, m.	treasure

XII – Duodecima lectiō

super (+ Acc)	above, over
trāns (+ Acc)	across
evangelium, -ī, n.	gospel
natō, natāre, natāvī, natātum	to swim

IX – Nōna lectiō

beātus, -a, -um	happy, blessed
cāseus, -ī, m.	cheese
flōs, flōris, m.	flower
pānis, pānis, m.	bread
pilleus, -ī, m.	hat
portō, portāre, portāvī, portātum	to carry
sapientia, -ae, f.	wisdom
studeō, studēre, studuī	to be eager for, to study
vērus, -a, -um	true

X – Decima lectiō

ā / ab (+ Abl)	from, away from
būtyrum, -ī, n.	butter
cum (+ Abl)	with
dē (+ Abl)	about, concerning, down from
ē / ex (+ Abl)	out of, out from
laus, laudis, f.	praise
oleum, -ī, n.	oil
patientia, -ae, f.	patience
sine (+ Abl)	without

XI – Ūndecima lectiō

ager, agrī, m.	field (on farm)
cīvitās, cīvitātis, f.	state
gemma, -ae, f.	gem, jewel
in (+ Acc)	into, onto
in (+ Abl)	in, on
margarīta, -ae, f.	pearl
porta, -ae, f.	gate
similis, simile (+Dat)	similar to, like

XII – Duodecima lectiō

cūr	why
quandō	when
quantus, -a, -um	how much
quid	what
quis	who
quōmodō	how
quot	how many
quotus, -a, -um	which
ubi	where, when
servō, servāre, servāvī, servātum	to save, keep, guard

XIII – Tertia decima lectiō

ascendō, ascendere, ascendī, ascensum	to ascend
crēdō, crēdere, crēdidī, crēditum	to believe
dēscendō, dēscendere, dēscendī, dēscensum	to descend
dīcō, dīcere, dīxī, dictum	to say, to tell, to speak
legō, legere, lēgī, lectum	to read
mittō, mittere, mīsī, mīssum	to send
servō, servāre, servāvī, servātum	to save, to keep, to guard
studeō, studēre, studuī, ---	to be eager for, to study
trādō, trādere, trādidī, trāditum	to pass, to hand over

XIV – Quarta decima lectiō

albus, -a, -um	white
avia, -ae, f.	grandmother
flāvus, -a, -um	yellow
līberō, līberāre, līberāvī, līberātum	to free
niger, nigra, nigrum	black

Vocabulary by Lectio

parō, parāre, parāvī, parātum	to prepare
quī	who; (he) who
rūfus, -a, -um	red
salūtō, salūtāre, salūtāvī, salūtātum	to greet

XV – Quīnta decima lectiō

arcus, -ī, m.	bow, rainbow
aurantius, -a, -um	orange
avus, -ī, m.	grandfather
caeruleus, -a, -um	blue
ecce	behold! (a command)
fulvus, -a, -um	brown
mālum aurantium, -ī, n.	(an) orange
purpureus, -a, -um	purple

XVI – Sexta decima lectiō

brācae, brācārum, f.	pants
calceus, -ī, m.	shoe
camisia, -ae, f.	shirt
cingulum, -ī, n.	belt
claudō, claudere, clausī, clausum	to close
gerō, gerere, gessī, gestum	to wear, to manage
induō, induere, induī, indūtum	to put on
petō, petere, petīvī, petītum	to seek, to beg, to ask for
scrībō, scrībere, scrīpsī, scrīptum	to write

XVII – Septima decima lectiō

aestās, aestātis, f.	summer
autumnus, -ī, m.	autumn, fall
hiems, hiemis, f.	winter
vēr, vēris, n.	spring
grātia, -ae, f.	grace
ningit, ningere	to snow
nix, nivis, f.	snow
pluit, pluere, pluit	to rain
pluvia, -ae, f.	rain

XVIII – Duodēvīcēsima lectiō

mensis, mensis, m.	month
Iānuārius, -ī, m.	January
Februārius, -ī, m.	February
Martius, -ī, m.	March
Aprīlis, Aprīlis, m.	April
Māius, -ī, m.	May
Iūnius, -ī, m.	June
Iūlius, -ī, m.	July
Augustus, -ī, m.	August
September, -bris, m.	September
Octōber, -bris, m.	October
November, -bris, m.	November
December, -bris, m.	December

XIX – Ūndēvīcēsima lectiō

fatuus, -a, -um	foolish, silly
labor, lābōris, m.	work, labor, effort
nēmō, nēminis, m./f.	no one, nobody
opus, operis, n.	(a) work
pauper, pauperis, m.	poor man
piscātor, -is, m.	fisherman
piscis, piscis, m./f.	fish
prophetia, -ae, f.	prophecy
virgō, virginis, f.	young woman, maiden, virgin

XX – Vīcēsima lectiō

diēs, diēī, m.	day (Abl – diē)
diēs Sōlis	Sunday
Dominica, -ae, f.	Lord's Day
diēs Lūnae	Monday
diēs Martis	Tuesday
diēs Mercuriī	Wednesday
diēs Iovis	Thursday
diēs Veneris	Friday
diēs Sāturnī	Saturday
epistula, -ae, f.	letter
septimāna, septimānae, f.	a week

Vocabulary by Lectio

XXI – Vīcēsima prīma lectiō

accipiō, accipere, accēpī, acceptum	to receive
capiō, capere, cēpī, captum	to seize
dēficiō, dēficere, dēfēcī, dēfectum	to fail
ēripiō, ēripere, ēripuī, ēreptum	to rescue
faciō, facere, fēcī, factum	to make, to do
iaciō, iacere, iēcī, iactum	to throw, to cast

XXII – Vīcēsima secunda lectiō

aperiō, aperīre, aperuī, apertum	to open
audiō, audīre, audīvī, audītum	to hear, to listen
dormiō, dormīre, dormīvī, dormītum	to sleep
veniō, venīre, vēnī, ventum	to come
sciō, scīre, scīvī, scītum	to know
inveniō, invenīre, invēnī, inventum	to find

XXIII – Vīcēsima tertia lectiō

brevis, breve (brevis, -e)	short
fortis, forte (fortis, -e)	strong, brave
longus, -a, -um	long
omnis, omne (omnis, -e)	all, every
prūdēns, prūdentis	wise
tristis, triste (tristis, -e)	sad
viridis, viride (viridis, -e)	green

XXIV – Vīcēsima quarta lectiō

canticum, -ī, n.	song
cārissimus, -a, um	beloved
honor, honōris, m.	honor

Paradigms

I: amō, amāre – 1st conjugation
present tense

	SINGULAR	PLURAL
1st PERSON	amō	amāmus
2nd PERSON	amās	amātis
3rd PERSON	amat	amant

present tense personal endings

1st PERSON	-ō	-mus
2nd PERSON	-s	-tis
3rd PERSON	-t	-nt

ursa, -ae, f. – 1st declension m./f.

NOM.	ursa	ursae
GEN.	ursae	ursārum
DAT.	ursae	ursīs
ACC.	ursam	ursās
ABL.	ursā	ursīs

1st-declension m./f. case endings

NOM.	-a	-ae
GEN.	-ae	-ārum
DAT.	-ae	-īs
ACC.	-am	-ās
ABL.	-ā	-īs

II: sum, esse
present tense

	SINGULAR	PLURAL
1st PERSON	sum	sumus
2nd PERSON	es	estis
3rd PERSON	est	sunt

nimbus, -ī, m. – 2nd declension m./f.

NOM.	nimbus	nimbī
GEN.	nimbī	nimbōrum
DAT.	nimbō	nimbīs
ACC.	nimbus	nimbōs
ABL.	nimbō	nimbīs

2nd-declension m./f. case endings

NOM.	-us	-ī
GEN.	-ī	-ōrum
DAT.	-ō	-īs
ACC.	-um	-ōs
ABL.	-ō	-īs

dōnum, -ī, n. – 2nd declension N

NOM.	dōnum	dōna
GEN.	dōnī	dōnōrum
DAT.	dōnō	dōnīs
ACC.	dōnum	dōna
ABL.	dōnō	dōnīs

2nd declension n. case endings

NOM.	-um	-a
GEN.	-ī	-ōrum
DAT.	-ō	-īs
ACC.	-um	-a
ABL.	-ō	-īs

ego

NOM.	ego	nōs
GEN.	meī	nostrī
DAT.	mihi	nōbīs
ACC.	mē	nōs
ABL.	mē	nōbīs

Paradigms

III: maneō, manēre – 2nd conjugation
present tense

	SINGULAR	PLURAL
1st PERSON	maneō	manēmus
2nd PERSON	manēs	manētis
3rd PERSON	manet	manent

tū

NOM.	tū	vōs
GEN.	tuī	vestrī
DAT.	tibi	vōbīs
ACC.	tē	vōs
ABL.	tē	vōbīs

IV: amō, amāre – 1st conjugation
future tense

1st PERSON	amābō	amābimus
2nd PERSON	amābis	amābitis
3rd PERSON	amābit	amābunt

maneō, manēre – 2nd conjugation
future tense

1st PERSON	manēbō	manēbimus
2nd PERSON	manēbis	manēbitis
3rd PERSON	manēbit	manēbunt

future tense personal endings

1st PERSON	-bō	-bimus
2nd PERSON	-bis	-bitis
3rd PERSON	-bit	-bunt

possum, posse
present tense

1st PERSON	possum	possumus
2nd PERSON	potes	potestis
3rd PERSON	potest	possunt

V: pater, patris, m. – 3rd decl. M/F

	SINGULAR	PLURAL
NOM.	pater	patrēs
GEN.	patris	patrum
DAT.	patrī	patribus
ACC.	patrem	patrēs
ABL.	patre	patribus

3rd declension m./f. case endings

NOM.	(varies)	-ēs
GEN.	-is	-um
DAT.	-ī	-ibus
ACC.	-em	-ēs
ABL.	-e	-ibus

flumen, fluminis, n. – 3rd decl. N

NOM.	flūmen	flūmina
GEN.	flūminis	flūminum
DAT.	flūminī	flūminibus
ACC.	flūmen	flūmina
ABL.	flūmine	flūminibus

3rd-declension n. case endings

NOM.	(varies)	-a
GEN.	-is	-um
DAT.	-ī	-ibus
ACC.	(varies)	-a
ABL.	-e	-ibus

feles, felis, f. 3rd decl. M/F i-stem

NOM.	fēles	fēlēs
GEN.	fēlis	fēlium
DAT.	fēlī	fēlibus
ACC.	fēlem	fēlīs
ABL.	fēle	fēlibus

3rd decl. m./f. i-stem case endings

NOM.	(varies)	-ēs
GEN.	-is	-ium
DAT.	-ī	-ibus
ACC.	-em	-īs
ABL.	-e	-ibus

Paradigms

VI: is, ea, id

SINGULAR

	M.	F.	N.
NOM.	is	ea	id
GEN.	eius	eius	eius
DAT.	eī	eī	eī
ACC.	eum	eam	id
ABL.	eō	eā	eō

PLURAL

	M.	F.	N.
NOM.	eī	eae	ea
GEN.	eōrum	eārum	eōrum
DAT.	eīs	eīs	eīs
ACC.	eōs	eās	ea
ABL.	eīs	eīs	eīs

VII: ūnus, -a, -um (singular only)

	M.	F.	N.
NOM.	ūnus	ūna	ūnum
GEN.	ūnīus	ūnīus	ūnīus
DAT.	ūnī	ūnī	ūnī
ACC.	ūnum	ūnam	ūnum
ABL.	ūnō	ūnā	ūnō

VIII: duo, duae, duo (plural only)

	M.	F.	N.
NOM.	duo	duae	duo
GEN.	dōrum	duārum	duōrum
DAT.	duōbus	duābus	duōbus
ACC.	duōs	duās	duo
ABL.	duōbus	duābus	duōbus

IX: trēs, trēs, tria (plural only)

	M.	F.	N.
NOM.	trēs	trēs	tria
GEN.	trium	trium	trium
DAT.	tribus	tribus	tribus
ACC.	trīs	trīs	tria
ABL.	tribus	tribus	tribus

X: hic, haec, hoc

SINGULAR

	M.	F.	N.
NOM.	hic	haec	hoc
GEN.	huius	huius	huius
DAT.	huic	huic	huic
ACC.	hunc	hanc	hoc
ABL.	hōc	hāc	hōc

PLURAL

	M.	F.	N.
NOM.	hī	hae	haec
GEN.	hōrum	hārum	hōrum
DAT.	hīs	hīs	hīs
ACC.	hōs	hās	haec
ABL.	hīs	hīs	hīs

XI: ille, illa, illud

SINGULAR

	M.	F.	N.
NOM.	ille	illa	illud
GEN.	illīus	illīus	illīus
DAT.	illī	illī	illī
ACC.	illum	illam	illud
ABL.	illō	illā	illō

PLURAL

	M.	F.	N.
NOM.	illī	illae	illa
GEN.	illōrum	illārum	illōrum
DAT.	illīs	illīs	illīs
ACC.	illōs	illās	illa
ABL.	illīs	illīs	illīs

XIII: crēdō, crēdere – 3rd conjugation present tense

1ST PERSON	crēdō	crēdimus
2ND PERSON	crēdis	crēditis
3RD PERSON	crēdit	crēdunt

Paradigms

XIV: amō, amāre – 1ˢᵗ conjugation
imperfect tense

	SINGULAR	PLURAL
1ˢᵀ PERSON	amābam	amābāmus
2ᴺᴰ PERSON	amābās	amābātis
3ᴿᴰ PERSON	amābat	amābant

maneō, manēre – 2ⁿᵈ conjugation
imperfect tense

	SINGULAR	PLURAL
1ˢᵀ PERSON	monēbam	monēbāmus
2ᴺᴰ PERSON	monēbās	monēbātis
3ᴿᴰ PERSON	monēbat	monēbant

imperfect tense personal endings

1ˢᵗ PERSON	-bam	-bāmus
2ⁿᵈ PERSON	-bās	-bātis
3ʳᵈ PERSON	-bat	-bant

XV: sum esse
imperfect tense

1ˢᵀ PERSON	eram	erāmus
2ᴺᴰ PERSON	erās	erātis
3ᴿᴰ PERSON	erat	errant

possum, posse
imperfect tense

1ˢᵀ PERSON	poteram	poterāmus
2ᴺᴰ PERSON	poterās	poterātis
3ᴿᴰ PERSON	poterat	poterant

XVI: crēdō credere – 3ʳᵈ conjugation
imperfect tense

1ˢᵀ PERSON	crēdēbam	crēdēbāmus
2ᴺᴰ PERSON	crēdēbās	crēdēbātis
3ᴿᴰ PERSON	crēdēbat	crēdēbant

XVII: crēdō credere – 3ʳᵈ conjugation
future tense

1ˢᵀ PERSON	crēdam	crēdēmus
2ᴺᴰ PERSON	crēdēs	crēdētis
3ᴿᴰ PERSON	crēdet	crēdent

XIX: sum, esse
future tense

	SINGULAR	PLURAL
1ˢᵀ PERSON	erō	erimus
2ᴺᴰ PERSON	eris	eritis
3ᴿᴰ PERSON	erit	erunt

possum, posse
future tense

1ˢᵗ PERSON	poterō	poterimus
2ᴺᴰ PERSON	poteris	poteritis
3ᴿᴰ PERSON	poterit	poterunt

XX: amō, amāre, amāvī, amātum –
1ˢᵗ conjugation, perfect tense

1ˢᵀ PERSON	amāvī	amāvimus
2ᴺᴰ PERSON	amāvistī	amāvistis
3ᴿᴰ PERSON	amāvit	amāvērunt

perfect tense personal endings

1ˢᵀ PERSON	-ī	-imus
2ᴺᴰ PERSON	-istī	-istis
3ᴿᴰ PERSON	-it	-ērunt

XXI: capiō, capere – 3ʳᵈ conj.- iō verbs
present tense

1ˢᵀ PERSON	capiō	capimus
2ᴺᴰ PERSON	capis	capitis
3ᴿᴰ PERSON	capit	capiunt

capiō, capere
imperfect tense

1ˢᵀ PERSON	capiēbam	capiēbāmus
2ᴺᴰ PERSON	capiēbās	capiēbātis
3ᴿᴰ PERSON	capiēbat	capiēbant

capiō, capere
imperfect tense

1ˢᵀ PERSON	capiam	capiēmus
2ᴺᴰ PERSON	capiēs	capiētis
3ᴿᴰ PERSON	capiet	capient

Paradigms

XXII: audiō, audīre – 4th conjugation
present tense

	SINGULAR	PLURAL
1ST PERSON	audiō	audīmus
2ND PERSON	audīs	audītis
3RD PERSON	audit	audiunt

audiō, audīre
imperfect tense

	SINGULAR	PLURAL
1ST PERSON	audiēbam	audiēbāmus
2ND PERSON	audiēbās	audiēbātis
3RD PERSON	audiēbat	audiēbant

audio, audīre
future tense

	SINGULAR	PLURAL
1ST PERSON	audiam	audiēmus
2ND PERSON	audiēs	audiētis
3RD PERSON	audiet	audient

XXIII: omnis, omne (3rd-decl. adjectives)

	SINGULAR	
	M./F.	N.
NOM.	omnis	omne
GEN.	omnis	omnis
DAT.	omnī	omnī
ACC.	omnem	omne
ABL.	omnī	omnī

	PLURAL	
NOM.	omnēs	omnia
GEN.	omnium	omnium
DAT.	omnibus	omnibus
ACC.	omnīs	omnia
ABL.	omnibus	omnibus

Dicta
Roman numeral indicates lesson number.

I	Audēmus iūra nostra dēfendere.	We dare to defend our rights.
II	Hannibal ad portās!	Hannibal [is] at the gates!
III	Ē plūribus ūnum.	Out of many, one.
IV	Carthagō dēlenda est! - Cato the Censor	Carthage must be destroyed!
V	Senātus Populusque Rōmānus (SPQR)	The Roman Senate and People
VI	sine quā nōn	essential ingredient (lit., "without which not)
VII	id est (i.e.)	that is
VIII	ad nauseam	too long (lit., to the point of seasickness)
IX	ante merīdiem (a.m.) post merīdiem (p.m.)	before noon after noon
X	cum laude magnā cum laude summā cum laude	with praise with great praise with the highest praise
XI	Vēnī, vīdī, vīcī - Julius Caesar	I came, I saw, I conquered.
XII	Et tū, Brūte? -*Julius Caesar*, Shakespeare	You too, Brutus? (lit., and you, Brutus?)
XIII	Silent lēgēs inter arma. -Marcus Tullius Cicero	Laws are silent among arms.
XIV	Diēs Īrae	Day of Wrath
XV	exemplī grātiā	for the sake of example
XVI	Tē Deum laudāmus.	We praise you, O God.
XVII	dramatis persōnae	cast of characters (lit., masks of the drama)
XVIII	nōtā bene (N.B.)	note well (*or* pay attention!)

Dicta

XIX Ecce Homō!
        -Pontius Pilate

Behold the Man!

XX terra fīrma

dry land (lit., stable/firm land)

XXI Dominus vōbīscum.
Et tēcum.

The Lord be with you.
And with you.

XXII In hōc signō vincēs.

In this sign you will conquer.

XXIII Fortēs Fortūna adiuvat.

Fortune favors the bold.

XXIV Tempus fugit.

Time flies.

Colloquia
Roman numeral indicates lesson number.

I	Salvē! Quomodō aestās erat?	Hi! How was the summer?
	Optimē! Et quōmodō tē habēs?	Great! And how are you?
	Bene mē habeō.	I'm well.
	Optimē mē habeō.	I'm great.
	Pessimē mē habeō.	I'm feeling terrible.
	Male mē habeō.	I'm not well.
	Satis bene mē habeō.	I'm well enough.
II	Ubi habitās?	Where do you live?
	In Alabāmā.	In Alabama.

N.B.: the preposition *in* takes the Ablative case. Here are the names of all the states:

Alabāma, -ae, f.	AL	Illinoesia, -ae, f.	IL	Novum Eborācum, -ī, n.	NY
Alaska, -ae, f.	AK	Indiāna, -ae, f.	IN	Ohiōa, -ae, f.	OH
Arizōna, -ae, f.	AZ	Īnsula Rhodēnsia, -ae, f.	RI	Ōklahōma, -ae, f.	OK
Arkānsia, -ae, f.	AR	Īova, -ae, f.	IA	Oregōnia, -ae, f.	OR
California, -ae, f.	CA	Kānsia, -ae, f.	KS	Pennsilvānia, -ae, f.	PA
Carolīna, -ae Merīdiōnālis, -is, f	SC	Kentukia, -ae, f.	KY	Tennessia, -ae, f.	TN
Carolīna, -ae Septentriōnālis, -is, f.	NC	Ludovīciāna, -ae, f.	LA	Terra, -ae, f. Mariae	MD
Cenomanica, -ae, f.	ME	Massachuseta, -ae, f.	MA	Texia, -ae, f.	TX
Nivāta, -ae, f.	NV	Michigānia, -ae, f.	MI	Ūta, -ae, f.	UT
Colorāta, -ae, f.	CO	Minnesōta, -ae, f.	MN	Vasingtōnia, -ae, f.	WA
Connecticūta, -ae, f.	CT	Mississippia, -ae, f.	MS	Viominga, -ae, f.	WY
Dakōta, -ae Merīdiōnālis, -is, f.	SD	Missūria, -ae, f.	MO	Virginia Occidentālis f.	WV
Dakōta, -ae Septentriōnālis, -is, f.	ND	Mons Viridis, -is, m.	VT	Virginia, -ae, f.	VA
Delevāria, -ae, f.	DE	Montāna, -ae, f.	MT	Viscōnsinia, -ae, f.	WI
Flōrida, -ae, f.	FL	Nebraska, -ae, f.	NE		
Georgia, -ae, f.	GA	Nova Caesarēa, -ae, f.	NJ		
Havaiī, -ōrum, m.	HI	Nova Hantōnia, -ae, f.	NH		
Idahōa, -ae, f.	ID	Nova Mexica, -ae, f.	NM		

III	Salvē, bone vir. Possumne tibi ministrāre?	Hello, good sir. Can I help you?
	Velim mālum.	I'd like an apple.
IV	Velīsne lūdum facere?	Would you like to play a game?
	Certē volō lūdum facere!	Sure, I want to play a game!
V	Silentium quaesō.	Silence, please.
	Aperīte librōs ad lectiōnem quīntam.	Open your books to the 5th lesson.
VI	Quid amās facere?	What do you like to do?
	Lūdōs facere amō.	I like to play games.

Colloquia

VII Salvē, Claudia. — Hello, Claudia.
Quid est tibi? — What's wrong with you?
Mē male habeō. — I feel poorly.

N.B.: Here are the names from book I and II, in both m. and f. forms (where possible):

Aemilius / Aemilia	Fābius / Fābia	Nicolaus, -ī, m.
Anna, -ae, f.	Flāvius / Flāvia	Petrus, -ī, m.
Antōnius / Antōnia	Gāius / Gāia	Porcius / Porcia
Aurēlius / Aurēlia	Horātius / Horātia	Publius / Publia
Brūtus / Brūta	Iēsus, Iēsū, m.	Quīntus / Quīnta
Caesar, Caesaris, m.	Iūlius / Iūlia	Scipiō, Scipiōnins, m.
Cāius / Cāia	Iūnius / Iūnia	Septimus / Septima
Cassius / Cassia	Livius / Livia	Sextus / Sexta
Catherīna, -ae, f.	Lūcius / Lūcia	Tarquinius / Tarquinia
Cato, Catōnis, m.	Lydia, -ae, f.	Tiberius / Tiberia
Cicero, Ciceronis, m.	Marcus / Marcia	Titus
Claudius / Claudia	Marius / Maria	Tullius / Tullia
Cornēlius / Cornēlia	Monica, -ae, f.	Valerius / Valeria

VIII Multum sternuō — I am sneezing a lot
et caput mihi dolet. — and my head hurts.
Gravedine labōrās! — You have a cold!
Vīse mēdicum. — Go see a doctor.

N.B.: Here are some other words for illnesses:

allergia, -ae, f	an allergy		pestilentiae, -ae, f.	plague
dēfectiō, -nis animī	a faint		vertigo, vertīginis, f.	dizziness
dolor, dolōris, m.	an ache		vulnus, vulneris, n.	a wound, a cut
eczēma, -ae, f.	a rash		tussis, tussis, f.	a cough
februs, febris, f.	a fever		umentēs narēs f. pl.	runny nose
fractūra, -ae, f.	broken bone			
gravedō, gravedinis, f.	a cold		sternuō, sternuere	to sneeze
horror, horrōris, m.	chills		tussiō, tussīre	to cough
luxatiō, luxātiōnis, f.	a sprain		vomitō, vomitāre	to vomit
nausea, -ae, f.	nausea		doleō, dolēre	to ache

IX Salvē, mēdice. — Hello, doctor.
Salvē. Quid est? — Hello. What's up?
Ego sum aeger! — I am sick!
Manē in lectō trīs diēs. — Stay in bed for three days.

X Quid velīs? — What would you like?
Trāde mihi būtyrum, quaesō. — Please pass me the butter.
Ecce. — Here it is. (lit., Behold!)

XI Claudite librōs. Hōra est quaestiunculae. — Close your books. It's time for a quiz.
Oieī! — Ouch!

Colloquia

XII	Quota hōra est?	What time is it?
	Octāva hōra est.	It's eight o'clock.
XIII	Bla, bla, bla.	Blah, blah, blah.
	Silēte. Nunc attendite.	Be quiet. Now pay attention.
XIV	Converte hanc sententiam ex Anglicam in Latīnam: I prepare. Latīnē dīcimus: Parō.	Translate this sentence from English into Latin: I prepare In Latin we say: I prepare.
XV	Confēcistisne dēlāgātum vestrum?	Did you finish your assignment?
	Certē confēcimus!	Of course we finished!
XVI	Ubi sunt calceī meī?	Where are my shoes?
	Hīc sunt!	Here they are!
XVII	Quotum tempus annī tibi maximē placet? Vēr mihi placet. Quotum tempus annī minimē placet? Autumnus mihi nōn placet.	Which season do you like most? I like spring. Which season do you like least? I don't like fall.
XVIII	Quō mense nātus es? Mense Augustō nātus sum. Quō mense nāta es tū? Mense Februāriō nāta sum.	In which month were you born? I was born in the month of August. In which month were you born? I was born in the month of February
XIX	Manē dum, quaesō!	Wait a minute, please!
	Minimē! Festīnā!	No! Hurry up!
XX	Potesne venīre domum meam?	Can you come to my house?
	Certē! Quid possumus facere?	Sure! What can we do?
XXI	Quis rēsponsum scit? Ō! Ego! Sciō! Ego! Attolite manūs.	Who knows the answer? Oh! Me! I know! Me! Raise your hands.
XXII	Scīsne natāre?	Do you know how to swim?
	Ita, sciō natāre.	Yes, I know how to swim.
XXIII	Est frīgidum! (Decembre)	It's cold! (in December)
	Est calidum! (Augustō)	It's hot! (in August)
XXIV	Quotus diēs mensis est?	What day of the month is it?
	Vīcēsimus quartus diēs Iānuāriī est	It's the 24th of January.

Timeline

264-241 BC	**1st Punic War between Rome and Carthage**
218-201 BC	**2nd Punic War between Rome and Carthage**
149-146 BC	**3rd Punic War between Rome and Carthage**
133-121 BC	Land Reforms and the Gracchi
102-101 BC	Teutones and Cimbri invade Italy.
90-88 BC	The Social War between Rome and Italian allies
88 BC	Sulla elected consul; Marius exiled
83-82 BC	**Civil War between Marius and Sulla**
70 BC	Pompey elected consul
67 BC	Pompey defeats the pirates.
63 BC	Cicero consul; Cataline Conspiracy
63 BC	Pompey defeats Mithridates.
60 BC	**1st triumvirate between Caesar, Pompey, and Crassus**
58-51 BC	Caesar conquers Gaul and invades Britain.
49-48 BC	**Civil War between Caesar and Pompey**
47-44 BC	Caesar elected dictator; assassinated on the Ides of March
43 BC	**2nd triumvirate between Mark Antony, Lepidus, and Octavian**
31 BC	**End of the Republic; Battle of Actium**
23 BC	**Roman Empire: Julio-Claudian emperors**
	• Octavian, Rome's 1st emperor (23 BC-14 AD) "Augustus"
	• Tiberius (14-37 AD)
	• Caligula (37-41 AD)
	• Claudius (41-54 AD)
	• Nero (54-68 AD)
	• Military emperors Galba, Otho, Vitellius (68-69 AD)
69 AD	**Flavian and Antonine emperors**
	• Vespasian (69-79 AD); eruption of Vesuvius (79 AD)
	• Titus (79-81 AD); Jerusalem destroyed (70 AD)
	• Domitian (81-96 AD)
	• Nerva (96-98 AD)
	• Trajan (98-117 AD)
	• Hadrian (117-138 AD)
	• Antoninus Pius (138-161 AD)
	• Marcus Aurelius (161-180 AD) and Lucius Verus (to 169 AD)
180 AD	**Decline of the empire**
285 AD	**Reorganization of the empire**
	• Diocletian (285-305 AD) reforms the government.
	• Constantine (310-337 AD); Christianity sanctioned (313 AD)
	• Valentinian I (364-375 AD)
476 AD	**Barbarian invasions; fall of the Western Roman Empire**
1453 AD	**Ottoman invasion; fall of the Eastern (Byzantine) Empire**

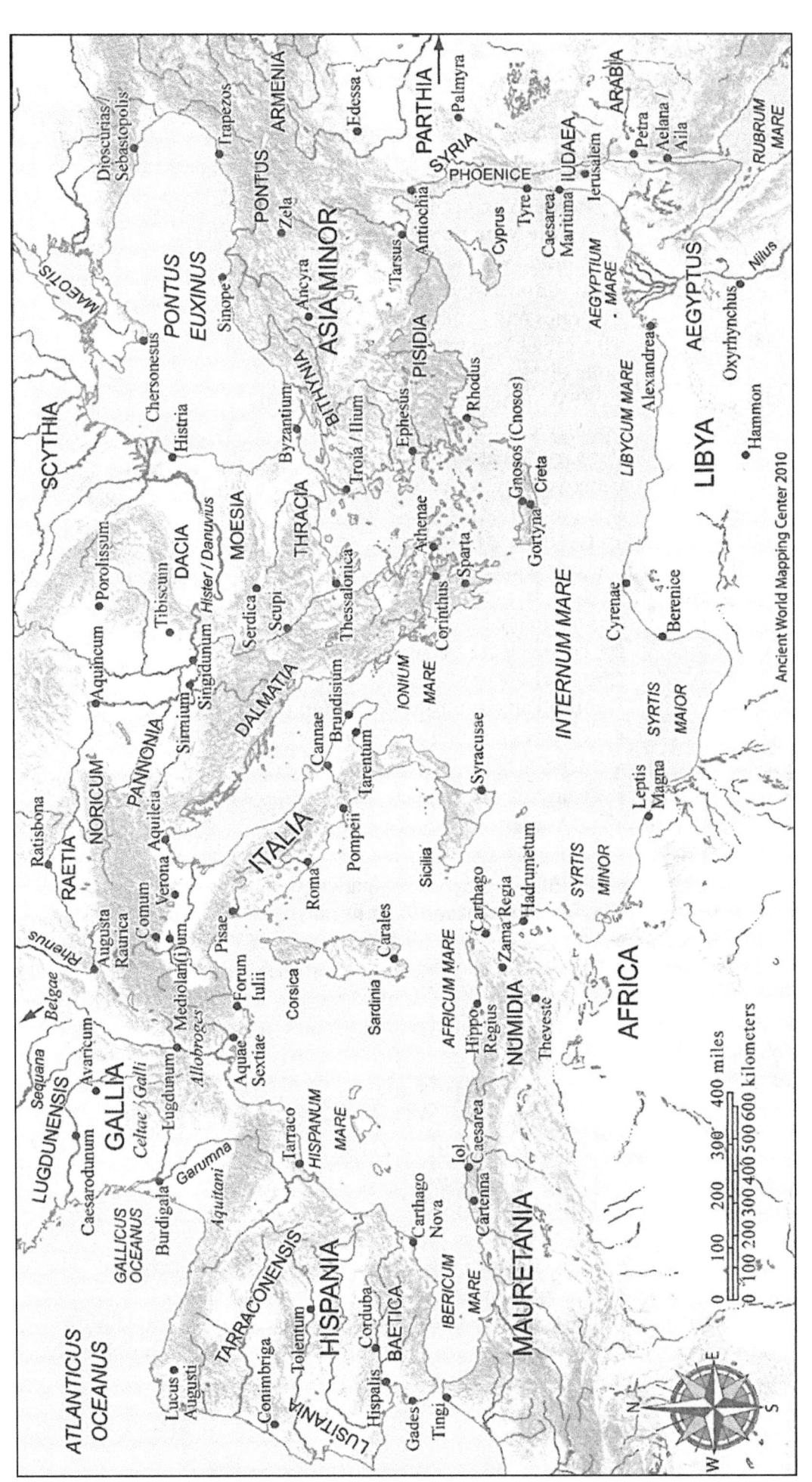

THE ROMAN EMPIRE

Used by permission of the Ancient World Mapping Center

Famous Men of Rome
by John H. Haaren and A. B. Poland
Revised by Thomas Caucutt and Ruth Baldwin

I – Prīma Lectiō: Regulus (*Famous Men of Rome* XIV.1-2)

The next great war the Romans engaged in was with Carthage. It was about the possession of the island of Sicily, in the Mediterranean Sea. It began not long after Pyrrhus left Italy and was the first of three wars called the Pu´nic Wars. Punic means Phoe-ni´ci-an, and the people who founded Carthage came from Phoe-ni´ci-a, so Carthage was called a Punic or Phoenician colony.

When the First Punic War began, both Rome and Carthage were very rich and powerful. Rome had great armies and great generals. Its common soldiers, too, were remarkably brave and patriotic. It was very successful in its wars. Before it began to fight Carthage, it had conquered nearly all Italy. *(264-241 BC The First Punic War)*

Carthage also had fine armies, but its greatest strength was in its navy. No other country in the world at that time had so many ships of war and trading ships. The ships of the Carthaginians went everywhere in the Mediterranean. Some of them even went past the Pillars of Hercules, as the rocky capes at the Strait of Gibraltar were then called, and sailed for some distance on the Atlantic Ocean.

The Carthaginian ships were small, but they were very strong. The warships were built to carry a good many soldiers, as well as sailors and oarsmen. They had great rounded iron prows, which could do much damage to an enemy's ships when run up against them. Each ship had a mast and large sail, but it was also rowed with oars by many oarsmen who sat on long benches, placed one above the other. With the sail and the oars, the ship could be made to go very fast through the water.

Carthage was in North Africa, in the country now called Tunis. It stood at the head of a beautiful bay of the Mediterranean. It was a large and handsome city and had a great commerce.

Many years before the beginning of the First Punic War, Carthage conquered a great part of Sicily and made it a Carthaginian colony. But the Romans wanted the island, and so under the pretense of protecting an Italian tribe that had settled there, they sent an army into Sicily. This was how the First Punic War began.

Both Rome and Carthage fought fiercely, and for a long time neither had much advantage over the other. At first the Romans had no warships. Up to that time they did not need any, for all their fighting was on land. But when they began war with the Carthaginians, they found that they must have ships to carry their soldiers to Sicily and to fight the Carthaginians at sea. So the Romans set to work to build ships and to train men to row them, and in a short time they had a great navy.

In the ninth year of the war the armies and fleets of Rome were put under the command of a general named Marcus A-ti´li-us Reg´u-lus. He was a great hero and patriot. He had been a general before the Punic War and had often led the Romans to victory. After years of good service, fighting, and winning battles for his country, he went to live on his little farm and, like Cincinnatus, he cultivated it with his own hands. A story is told of him which well illustrates ancient Roman honor and patriotism.

Until Regulus took command, the Punic War was carried on only in Sicily and on the Mediterranean. But he thought that Rome should fight the Carthaginians in their own country, and so he organized an immense army and navy to invade Carthage. He had 330 warships of the largest size and about 60,000 soldiers.

In those times, in fights at sea, they had an engine called a boarding bridge. One end of it was fixed to the deck of the ship. The other end, which was free, could be swung round and on to an enemy's ship, and it had a heavy iron spike underneath, so that when it fell on the deck, it would sink into it and thus hold the enemy's vessel for the attacking party to board it.

When everything was ready, Regulus set sail for Africa. Soon after starting, he met a large Carthaginian fleet, and in a short battle he destroyed it. Then he sailed on and, after landing in Africa, began a march toward Carthage. On his way he captured several towns, and he met and defeated a Carthaginian army. He then continued his march until he met another army of Carthaginians. This army was commanded by Xan-thip´pus, a famous general of Sparta in Greece, who happened to be in Carthage at that time. In the battle that followed, the Romans were defeated, and Regulus was made prisoner and taken off to Carthage.

But the Romans had other generals and other armies, and they carried on the war and defeated the Carthaginians in many battles.

At last the Carthaginians thought it better to try to make peace, and so they send ambassadors to Rome to propose that the war should be stopped on certain terms, which they were ready to offer. They sent Regulus with the ambassadors, but they made him swear that he would return to Carthage if the Roman Senate should refuse to agree to their terms. They thought that in order to gain his own freedom Regulus would try to get the Senate to accept their proposals. Regulus agreed to go and made the promise required.

"I give you my word of honor," said he, "that I will return if your terms are not accepted."

Then he set out for Rome with the ambassadors. As he approached the gates of the city, thousands of people came forth to welcome him and to escort him through the streets. But he refused to enter.

"I cannot enter Rome," said he. "I am no longer a Roman officer, but a prisoner of Carthage. Do not urge me to enter the gates. I am not even worth exchanging for a Carthaginian prisoner."

The people, however, insisted that he should enter the city, and so amid shouts and cheers, he was escorted to the Senate house.

In a little while the Carthaginian ambassadors presented their proposals, and the Senate began to consider them. After some discussions, Regulus was asked to give his opinion whether the terms ought to be accepted or not.

Regulus at first was unwilling to speak in the Senate. He said that by becoming a prisoner he had lost the honor of being a senator.

"I am no longer a Roman senator," said he. "I am a prisoner of Carthage."

The Senate, however, insisted that he should speak. Then Regulus said that the Senate ought not to accept the terms of peace offered by Carthage. He thought that they were not good terms for Rome, and he advised the Senate not to agree to them.

But the Senate was inclined to accept the terms for the sake of Regulus himself. If peace were not made, he would have to go back and remain a prisoner in Carthage or perhaps he would be put to death. Therefore the Senate was for agreeing to the Carthaginian terms. But Regulus again spoke strongly against them, and at last the Senate decided to reject the Carthaginian proposals.

Regulus now prepared to return to Carthage, but his family and friends clung to him saying: "You must not go! You must not go!"

To all their appeals he made but one answer: "I have given my word of honor to return, and I cannot break it."

So Regulus returned to Carthage with the ambassadors. When the people of that city heard that by his advice the terms had been rejected, they were very angry. They had wished very much to make peace with Rome, for the long war had cost them a great many lives and a great deal of money, and they wanted to stop it. Therefore, they were enraged against Regulus, and they put him to death in a very cruel way.

It is said that Regulus was shut into a chest into which nails had been driven so that, try as he might, he could never avoid their sharp points. Never able to rest or sleep, he finally died from exhaustion.

The war between Rome and Carthage continued for some years more, but at last the Carthaginians were defeated in a great sea battle near the coast of Sicily. They were then obliged to give up Sicily and pay a large sum of money to the Romans as a fine. This was the end of the First Punic War, in 241 BC.

II – Secunda Lectiō: Scipio Africanus (*Famous Men of Rome* XV.1-2)

218-201 BC
The Second Punic War

But peace did not last long between Rome and Carthage. Some years after the end of the First Punic War, the Carthaginians attacked and took possession of a town in Spain, the people of which were friends and allies of Rome. This caused the Second Punic War, which began in 218 BC.

One of the great soldiers of this war was Pu´bli-us Cornelius Sci´pi-o. In the latter part of his life he was called Scipio Af-ri-ca´nus, on account of the great victories which he won in Africa.

Scipio was a brave soldier from his youth. When only seventeen years old, he fought in a battle and saved his father's life. He was always gallant and heroic in war, so he soon became noted in the Roman army and rose to high rank. And although he was a member of a noble family, he was well liked by the plebeians, and they elected him ae´dile.

The aediles were magistrates, or judges. They were also superintendents of public buildings and of the games and shows of which the Roman people were so fond.

When Scipio was about 27 years of age, he was appointed to command the Roman army that was fighting the Carthaginians in Spain. Carthage had conquered some parts of Spain, and Rome had conquered other parts, and the two nations were often at war about places in that country.

When Scipio went to Spain, many of the people there were against him, but they soon became his friends. Whenever he took a city, he allowed the chiefs who were captured to go free, and he gave great presents to many of them. He always showed great respect to women and children who were taken prisoners. In those times it was the cruel custom to make slaves of women who were found in towns that had been taken in war. But Scipio never did this in Spain. He always let the women go free.

One day a beautiful Spanish girl who had been taken prisoner was brought before him. She seemed very much frightened, but Scipio spoke kindly to here and told her that no one should harm her. While speaking with her, he learned that a young man who was her lover had also been taken prisoner by the Roman soldiers. He sent for the young man and said to him: "Take your sweetheart and go. I set you both free. Go and be happy, and in future, be friends of Rome."

And so by many acts of kindness Scipio gained the friendship of the Spaniards. After a while they began to join the Romans and gave them great help in their war against the Carthaginians.

When his services were no longer needed in Spain, Scipio returned to Rome. He got a great reception in the city. There was a grand parade in his honor. He brought home an immense quantity of silver, which he obtained from the rich Spanish mines and from the cities he had taken. The silver was put into the Roman treasury to pay the expenses of the war.

Soon after he returned from Spain, Scipio was elected consul. The Carthaginian general, Han´ni-bal, was then in Italy with a large army. This Hannibal was one of the greatest generals of ancient times. When he was but nine years old, his father, who was also a great general, made him take an oath that he would hate Rome and the Romans forever. Then he took the boy with him to Spain and gave him a thorough training as a soldier.

When his father died, Hannibal became commander of the Carthaginian army in Spain. He was then little more that 21 years old. He fought well in Spain for some time and was well liked by his soldiers. Suddenly he resolved to make war on the Romans in their own country and to go by land to Italy. So he got ready an immense army and set out on his march. In passing through France he had to cross the broad River Rhone. This was not easy to do, for there was no bridge. He got his men over in boats, but he had a number of elephants in his army, and they were too big and heavy to be taken across in that way. The boats were small, and the elephants were afraid to go into them. Hannibal therefore got rafts or floats, made of trunks of trees tied together, and in these the elephants were carried over.

After crossing the Rhone, Hannibal marched over the Alps into Italy. He and his army suffered many hardships in making their way over those snow-covered mountains. He had often to fight fierce tribes that came to oppose him, but he defeated them all, and after being defeated, many of them joined his army and brought him provisions for his soldiers.

Very soon Roman armies were sent against Hannibal, but he defeated them in many battles. His army got into place near high hills where he could not march farther except through one narrow pass between the hills. The Roman general, Quintus Fabius, sent 4,000 of his troops to take possession of the pass, and he posted the rest of his army on hills close by.

Quintus Fabius

Hannibal saw that he was in a trap, but he found a way of escaping. He caused vine branches to be tied to the horns of a large number of the oxen that were with his army. Then he ordered his men to set the branches on fire in the middle of the night and to drive the oxen up the hills.

As soon as the animals felt the pain, they rushed madly about and set fire to the shrubs and bushes they met on the way. The Romans at the pass thought that the Carthaginians were escaping by torchlight. So they hastily quit their posts and hurried toward the hills to help their comrades. Then Hannibal, seeing the pass free, marched his army out and so escaped from the trap.

Quintus Fabius was very slow and cautious in his movements. The Romans had been defeated so often that he thought the best plan was to harass Hannibal in every possible way but not to venture to fight him in a great battle until he should be sure of winning. For this reason the Romans gave Fabius the name of *Cunc-ta'tor*, which means *delayer*, and so the plan of extreme delay or caution in any undertaking is often called a *Fabian* policy.

In spite of the caution of Fabius, Hannibal gained many great victories. His greatest victory was at the battle of Can'nae, in the south of Italy. Here he defeated and destroyed a Roman army of 70,000 men. And for several years after this battle, Hannibal remained in Italy doing the Romans all the harm he could.

At last Scipio thought it was time to follow the plan of Regulus. So he said to the Senate:

"We have acted too long as if we were afraid of Hannibal and Carthage. We defend ourselves bravely when we are attacked, and so far we have saved Rome from destruction; but we do not make any attacks on our enemies. We certainly ought to do this, for our armies are strong and fully ready to meet the Carthaginians."

Scipio then proposed that an army led by himself should go to Africa and carry on war there. He believed that if this were done, Hannibal would have to got to Africa to defend Carthage.

Perhaps on account of what had happened to Regulus, the Senate did not like Scipio's plan. Nevertheless, it gave him permission to go to Africa but would not give him an army. Scipio then raised a splendid army of volunteers and sailed across the Mediterranean Sea to Africa.

III – Tertia Lectiō: Scipio Africanus (*Famous Men of Rome* XV.3-4)

Scipio then tried for some time to obtain the aid of Sy´phax, a powerful king of Nu-mid´i-a, in Africa. But Syphax decided to join the Carthaginians. So Scipio found two great armies ready to fight him. One was the army of Carthage, with 33,000 men, commanded by Has´dru-bal Gis´co, and the other was the army of Numidia, with 60,000 men, commanded by King Syphax.

But Scipio found in Africa one strong friend, and that was a Numidian prince named Mas´i-nis´sa. This prince had a host of supporters among his countrymen and was therefore able to bring a large force of good soldiers to the aid of the Romans. He was of great service to Scipio in many ways.

When everything was ready, the Roman army, with Masinissa's force, encamped about six miles from the camps of the enemy. Scipio sent spies among the Carthaginians and the soldiers of King Syphax, and from them he learned that both armies were lodged in huts made of stakes and covered with reeds and dried leaves. He resolved to set those huts on fire.

So one very dark night the Roman army left its camp and marched silently to the plain occupied by the enemy. Then a division of the Romans went to the encampments of the Numidians, and a soldier crept cautiously from the Roman lines and set one of the huts on fire. The fire spread rapidly, and in a few minutes the whole camp was in flames.

The Numidian soldiers, suddenly awakened by the fire, fled from the burning huts without their weapons and made frantic efforts to escape from the camp. Hundreds of them were knocked down and trampled to death in the rush and confusion; hundreds more lost their lives in the fire. Those who got to the open country were attacked by the Romans and killed. The ground was covered with the bodies of the slain. King Syphax and a few horsemen managed to escape, but the rest of the vast Numidian army was destroyed.

In the meantime the Carthaginians had been aroused by the noise in the camp of the Numidians. They thought that the fire had been caused by an accident, and some of them ran forward to assist the Numidians. But the greater number stood in a confused throng, without their arms, outside their camp, looking at the fire with terror.

While they were in this helpless state, the Carthaginians were suddenly attacked by the Romans with Scipio at their head. Many were killed, and the others were driven back into their camp, which was immediately set on fire in a number of places. Then there was a frightful scene. Thousands of Carthaginians, struggling to escape the fire, were slain by the Romans while thousands more perished in the flames. Hasdrubal Gisco, the commander, and some of his officers escaped but only a few of the others. In less than an hour there was little left of the Carthaginian army.

Scipio now began to march toward the great, rich city of Carthage. He captured a number of towns and a great deal of treasure. In a few weeks, however, the Carthaginians were able to form another army of 30,000 men, and then they came boldly forth to meet Scipio.

A fierce battle followed. The Romans were driven back for a time, but with wonderful courage they charged the Carthaginians again and again and at last totally defeated them.

The Carthaginians now sent a message to Italy requesting Hannibal to come to the relief of his country. The renowned general did not want to leave Italy, for he hoped to be able to take Rome; but he thought it best to obey the call of Carthage, so he sailed for Africa with his army.

After arriving in Africa, Hannibal led his army to a wide plain near Za´ma, a town not far from Carthage. Here he awaited the Romans.

Hannibal had great admiration for Scipio, and he desired to see him before engaging in battle. So he sent a messenger to Scipio requesting an interview. The request was granted, and the two generals met.

They greeted each other cordially, and each complemented the other on his victories and greatness as a soldier. Then Hannibal proposed terms of peace to Scipio.

"We will give Spain and the islands of Sicily and Sardinia to Rome. Then we will divide the sea with you. What more would you have? Rome and Carthage would then be the two great nations of the world."

Scipio thought it was too late to make terms. "We must fight it out," said he, "until one side or the other is vanquished."

The generals then parted, and the next day the two armies were drawn up in battle array. On each side there were about 30,000 men, but Hannibal had a herd of fighting elephants.

The battle was long and severe. Both armies fought heroically, and there was terrible slaughter. But Hannibal's elephants were of little use to him, as the Romans frightened them by blowing trumpets and hurling balls of fire at them. At a moment when the lines of the Carthaginians were breaking, a strong force of Roman horsemen came up suddenly in the rear and overpowered all before it. This won the battle for the Romans. When Hannibal saw that the battle was lost, he fled from the field with a few friends (202 BC).

Scipio was now master of Carthage. He compelled the Carthaginians to pay him a vast amount in gold and silver and to give up some of their towns and lands. He also compelled them to destroy their great fleet of warships and to promise not to make war in future upon any people without the permission of the Romans.

When Scipio returned to Rome, he entered the city at the head of a grand procession. The greatest honors were paid to him, and he was called Scipio Africanus.

Some years afterward Scipio met Hannibal at the court of the king in Syria. The two generals had a friendly conversation and Scipio asked Hannibal who he thought was the greatest general who ever lived. Hannibal answered:

"Alexander the Great."

"Who was the second?" asked Scipio.

"Pyrrhus," replied Hannibal.

"Who was the third?"

"Myself," answered Hannibal.

"But what would you have said," asked Scipio, "if you had conquered me?"

"I should then have said," replied Hannibal, "that I was greater than Alexander, greater than Pyrrhus, and greater than all other generals."

IV – Quarta Lectiō: Cato the Censor (*Famous Men of Rome* XVI)

On a farm near Tusculum, a little town about 15 miles from Rome, there once lived a boy named Marcus Por´ci-us Ca´to. His father and his grandfather before him had been farmers, and he, too, expected to be one.

When he was about 17, Hannibal's army crossed the Alps into Italy, and young Cato became a Roman soldier. When the war ended, the country boy had become a man, stern and forceful. He attracted the attention of a neighbor, a rich man, who persuaded him to go to Rome and practice law.

In time he was elected to office, and he did his duty so well that he rose higher and higher, until he became one of the consuls. That same year a rebellion arose in Spain and Cato led an army against the Spaniards. It is said that in 400 days he captured 400 villages. On his return to Rome, he was honored with a triumph.

Shortly after this he was sent to Greece, where An-ti´o-chus was attacking Greek cities that were friendly to Rome. He defeated Antiochus in the Pass of Ther-mo´py-lae and won great fame as a soldier.

Cato was a very hard man: hard on himself; hard on his friends. And although he was rich and held office in a great city, he lived a hard life, taking no pleasures and saving his money. He ate the plainest food and drank the same cheap wine that he bought for his slaves.

Cato thought that the luxury and extravagance of the rich were taking away the strength of Rome. In order to put a stop to these things, Cato asked the people of Rome to elect him censor. The patricians opposed him bitterly, but he was elected by a large majority. One of the first things he did was to expel from the senate several senators who were leading improper lives. He had a heavy tax put on carriages so as to compel people to walk. He also placed a tax on jewels, handsome dresses, carpets, and fine furniture. So well did he do his work that he is always known in history as Cato the Censor, just as if he were the only man who ever held the office. A statue erected in his honor says nothing about his victories in Spain or at Thermopylae, but only that "When the Roman Republic was degenerating, Cato restored it by strict discipline."

In the later years of his life Cato was sent to Carthage to look into a certain matter for Rome. The trouble was this: you will remember that Carthage had agreed to make war upon no nation without the consent of the Roman Senate. A few years later, Masinissa, who was a friend of Rome, attacked the Carthaginians, and they appealed to Rome for protection. This was refused, and the people of Carthage took up arms to defend themselves against Masinissa.

Cato was sent to Carthage to find out who was to blame. When he arrived in the city, he was surprised to find it large and strong and flourishing. Only 26 years had passed since Scipio Africanus had conquered Carthage, and yet Cato saw crowds of young men on the street, stacks of arms in the arsenals, and a forest of masts in the harbor. The city itself was rich and prosperous.

Cato returned to Rome and warned his countrymen that Carthage must be destroyed. From that time forward, whenever he made a speech in the senate, no matter upon what subject, he always ended it by saying, "And my opinion is that Carthage must be destroyed." In time, the words of Cato had their effect, and war was declared against Carthage.

Cato's words were: Carthāgō dēlenda est!

The troops had already embarked when envoys from Carthage reached Rome and offered to do whatever might be asked. The Roman Senate promised that the laws and liberties of Carthage should not be touched, but demanded hostages. So 300 children of the leading families of Carthage were sent to Rome. When the Roman army reached Carthage, the consuls insisted that the Carthaginians should give up their arms. This was done, and the Carthaginians asked if the Romans required anything more.

149-146 BC
The Third Punic War

Then one of the consuls said, "Your city must be destroyed, and you must move ten miles inland from the sea." The Carthaginians now saw that they had been deceived. They closed their gates and determined to defend themselves to the last. They asked an armistice of 30 days, so that an embassy might go to Rome. It was granted, and thus a month of time was gained. During this time, men, women, and children went to work to make arms to defend their homes. The women even cut off their hair to furnish strings for the bows of the war machines with which stones were hurled at the enemy.

The embassy failed in its mission to Rome and the siege of Carthage began. It lasted three years.

The son of Paulus Ae-mil'i-us had been adopted by the son of Scipio Africanus and had taken the name Scipio. He was sent to Carthage and about a year after his arrival, forced an entrance into the city and captured it (146 BC). The walls were torn down and the buildings set on fire. Cato,

Historia

Scipio Africanus Minor (i.e., the younger) was the adopted grandson of Scipio Africanus Maior (i.e., the older). The grandfather had defeated Hannibal and had won the second Punic War for Rome. The grandson destroyed Carthage and won the third and final war with Carthage.

who was so largely responsible for the war, did not live to see its end. He died almost two years before the city was destroyed.

The Senate honored Scipio with the title of Africanus, which the older conqueror of Carthage had borne.

The young Scipio won fame not only in Africa but also in Spain, where he was sent against the Nu-man′ti-ans. These brave people had defeated two Roman armies, but Scipio soon succeeded in shutting them within the walls of Numantia. Around its walls he built walls of his own behind which his soldiers were safe from attack. Food soon became scarce in Nu-man′ti-a. At the end of 15 months the citizens were starving. They were willing to lose their lives, but Scipio stayed behind his own walls and refused to fight. Rather than trust to the mercy of Rome, the Numantians killed themselves.

In time all Spain was forced to submit and become a Roman province.

IV – Quīnta Lectiō: The Gracchi (*Famous Men of Rome* XVII)

The Gracchi brothers

Between the Second and Third Punic Wars there lived in Rome two brothers named Ti-be′ri-us and Caius Grac′chus, commonly called the Gracchi. They were very good men and great friends of the common people.

The mother of the Gracci was Cor-ne′li-a, a daughter of Scipio Africanus. She was an excellent woman, and she was very proud of her two sons. She taught them to be brave and manly and always to stand up for the people.

One day a rich lady, while on a visit to Cornelia, showed her some magnificent jewels. When they had looked them over, the lady said:

"These are my jewels; now let me see yours."

Just at that moment Tiberius and Caius, who were then boys, came into the room. As soon as she saw them, Cornelia called them to her and, putting her arms around them, said:

"These are my jewels."

When Tiberius and Caius grew up to be men, they took the side of the people in a quarrel that had been going on for a long time between the plebeians and the nobles. The quarrel was about land. Whenever the Romans conquered a country in war, they took possession of a portion of the land of the conquered country. Such land was called public land, and for many years after the founding of the city, the custom of dividing parts of the public lands among all the citizens was strictly observed.

But in later times this custom was changed. Instead of part of the public lands being divided among all the citizens, it was divided among only the nobles, and the plebeians got none at all. The lands were tilled by slaves, and all that was raised went to the nobles. So the poor soldiers who won the lands by hard fighting were without farms to till, and some of them were even without homes. They continually demanded that the old law, for a fair division of the lands among all the citizens, should be carried out. The nobles laughed at the demand.

But Tiberius Gracchus came forward boldly as the champion of the poor. He declared that the nobles should give up the lands they had unjustly taken and that the people should have their fair share. His words made the nobles very angry, and they became his bitter enemies.

But the people honored Tiberius and made him one of their tribunes. The tribunes were supposed to look after the people's interests, but sometimes they were not faithful to their duty. As we have already said, they had a great deal of power. They could sit at the door of the Roman Senate, and when a law was proposed that they did not like, they could say, "We veto it!" and the law could not be passed.

Whenever the tribunes wanted a law passed, they proposed it at the meeting of all the people in what was called the Assembly of Tribes. The common people had a great deal of power in this assembly, and any law proposed by the tribunes was generally passed. Then the tribunes had the power to compel the consuls to carry out the law.

Not long after Tiberius Gracchus became tribune, he proposed a law that each noble might have 500 acres of public land for his own use and 250 more for each son, and that the remainder of the lands should be equally divided among the poor citizens.

This law was passed, and then the nobles had to give up a large part of the lands they had seized. So the poor citizens got good farms.

About this time At′ta-lus, the king of Per′ga-mus, a country of Asia, died, leaving all his money to the Romans. The nobles tried to get this money for themselves, but Tiberius had it divided among the poor citizens.

Of course this made the nobles still more angry with Tiberius, and they resolved to get rid of him if they could. So on election day, when the people were voting to make Tiberius tribune for a second term, some nobles went to the voting place and raised a disturbance. But the friends of Tiberius drove them away. Then the nobles started a report that Tiberius was trying to induce the people to make him king.

Afterward they gathered their friends and slaves and began fighting with the people. No arms were used, but stones were thrown, and sticks, broken benches, and other things, hastily caught up, served as weapons. There was a dreadful tumult for a while, and many persons were killed.

Tiberius was in the midst of his friends bravely defending himself against an attack by a party of nobles when suddenly he stumbled and fell to the ground. In a moment the nobles rushed upon him. One of them struck him on the head with a piece of wood and killed him. Then they took his body and threw it into the Tiber.

Tiberius was now out of the way, and the nobles began to seize the lands that had been divided among the people. But Caius Gracchus suddenly appeared in Rome and declared that he had come to take his brother's place as the friend of the people. He had been with a Roman army in Spain when Tiberius was killed.

Tiberius Gracchus (circa 164-133 BC)

The verb *vetō, vetāre* means "to forbid." When the tribunes felt that a proposal was unfair to the common people, they had simply to declare: "Vetō!" (I forbid it!), and the proposal could not be made into law.

Historia

Caius Gracchus (died 121 BC)

The people now elected him tribune, and he began to carry out his brothers plans. For this reason the nobles hated him as much as they hated his brother. They said that he was a dangerous man and was planning to make himself king. One day as he was passing through the Forum, a strange man said to him: "I hope you will spare the Republic!"

The friends of Caius were angry at these words, and they fell on the man and killed him.

The nobles and their followers then armed themselves. The plebeians also gathered in great numbers, ready for a fight. Caius was asked to lead them, but refused. He did not want them to fight with the nobles. He knew that the nobles would be satisfied with his own death, so he ordered a slave to stab him to the heart. The order was obeyed, and thus perished the last of the Gracchi (121 BC).

VI – Sexta Lectiō: Marius (*Famous Men of Rome* XVIII.1-2)

Caius Marius (157-86 BC)

At the time of the death of Caius Gracchus, there was in Rome a great man named Caius Ma´ri-us. This man came forward and said to the people that if they would elect him tribune, he would get them their rights.

The people elected him tribune, and, true to his word, he did everything he could to improve their condition. He was afterward elected consul seven times, and for a long while he was the greatest man in Rome.

Marius was a tall and very powerful man and had a strong will. When he said he would do anything, he would do it in spite of all difficulties. He was a very great soldier. Many people thought him the best of the Roman generals.

He succeeded in a war against Ju-gur´tha, king of Numidia, after other generals had failed. He took many cities from Jugurtha and at last captured the king himself and all his treasure.

Jugurtha was brought to Rome and compelled to walk behind the chariot of Marius in a grand triumphal procession. He was afterward put into a foul dungeon and left there to die.

The nobles did not like Marius. He was the son of plebeian parents, and he had taken the side of the plebeians against the nobles. Therefore the nobles hated him, and they would have done anything they could against him, only that they needed his help to protect Rome from very dangerous enemies.

A host of barbarian people, called Cim´bri, Teu´to-nes, and Am-bro´nes, had left their homes on the shores of the Baltic Sea and invaded the southern lands. They were strong, fierce men, and they laid waste every country they passed through. They defeated several Roman armies that were sent against them. Some of the tribes of Hel-ve´ti-a (the country now called Switzerland) joined them and killed a Roman consul and made his army pass under the yoke.

Historia

The Romans were therefore very much frightened. They thought that the barbarians would soon be in Italy. So Marius was appointed to go against them with a great army. He crossed the Mediterranean into Gaul and met the Teutones and Ambrones near the city of Arles on the River Rhone. The Cimbri had already gone to Italy.

Marius first made a strong entrenched camp. He wanted to give his men time to get accustomed to the manners of the strange enemy before attempting to fight them. The Roman soldiers had shown fear at sight of the barbarians. They had never before seen such people.

The Teutones were like giants. They had large, wild, staring eyes and long hair, and they made terrible war cries. The Ambrones and the Cimbri were as savage in appearance. The king of the Teutones was very tall and so active that he could leap over six horses placed abreast.

When the barbarians saw that the Romans would not fight, they began to taunt and insult them. They walked up and down in front of the Roman camp day after day, calling the soldiers cowards.

"Why don't you come out and fight us like men?" they cried. "Are you afraid? Come out, come out; we are in a hurry! We are going to Rome after we kill you!"

Marius had hard work to keep his men from rushing out upon the barbarians. He did not yet want to fight, but he said to his soldiers:

"When the proper time comes, we will give these savages all the fighting they want."

One day a gigantic Teuton chief, with a long shield and spear, came up to the very entrance of the Roman camp and called loudly for Marius himself to come out and fight. The great general laughed heartily at the impudence of the barbarian, and he sent out a gladiator to fight with him in order to give sport to the Romans.

Gladiators were men who fought one another in the shows at Rome for the amusement of the people. They were usually slaves and were very strong, active, and well-trained fighters.

It did not take the gladiator long to defeat the Teuton. In a few minutes he laid the savage giant low, and the Romans shouted with joy at the sight.

After the Teuton was killed, the Romans still remained in their camp. Marius was not yet prepared to fight. At last the barbarians got tired of waiting, and they started off to march to Italy.

So great was the number of the barbarians that it took them six whole days to march past the Roman camp. When all had passed, Marius left his camp and followed them by slow marches. Before long, the two armies arrived at the city of Aix on the south coast of Gaul.

Marius now thought it was time to fight, so he led out his fine army against the Ambrones. They astonished the Romans with their war cry. They held their shields upright and at a little distance from their mouths and shouted: "Ambrones! Ambrones!" as if to terrify the Romans by letting them know who they were. Then they rushed furiously across the field.

The Romans met their charge with wonderful courage. Their lines were scarcely broken. Three times they drove back the enemy, and then they themselves moved steadily forward with their whole force. They cut down the Ambrones by thousands, took many prisoners, and sent others fleeing away in terror.

Next day there was another battle. The Teutones and Ambrones together attacked the Romans, but the Romans were again victorious. When the battle was over, it was found that more than 100,000 barbarians had been killed or taken prisoners.

Marius now turned his attention to the Cimbri, who had gone to Italy. They had encamped on a beautiful, fertile plain near the River Po and were enjoying the warm Italian sun and the sweet fruits of the country.

But Marius was not very long in reaching the same place with his victorious army. When the Cimbri saw the Romans marching on to the plain where they were encamped, they were astonished. To gain time they sent a messenger to Marius to ask him to give them lands to live on in Italy.

"Give us," said the messenger, "lands in Italy for ourselves and for our friends, the Teutones and Ambrones, and we will all live at peace."

"Never mind the Teutones and the Ambrones," said Marius, "They have lands already. We have given them some which they will keep forever. We will give you the same."

Then a battle began between the two great armies. The foot soldiers of the Cimbri were formed into an immense square, and the men in the front ranks were chained to one another by iron chains so that they could not run away. There were 15,000 horsemen, wearing on their helmets the heads of wild beasts.

The battle was a hard one for a while, but it did not continue long. Time after time, the Cimbri were driven back, and at last they were put to flight. Thousands of them were killed and thousands made prisoners.

When Marius and his soldiers returned to Rome, they got a splendid reception. There was a parade through the streets, and a great feast was given to the people. A large sum of money was divided among the soldiers to reward them for their brave conduct.

Marius was now in high favor at Rome. The nobles did not dare to speak a word against him. He was elected consul seven times, so that he was master of the Republic for a long time.

VII – Septima Lectiō: Marius (*Famous Men of Rome* XVIII.2)

90-88 BC
The Social War

Allies and peoples friendly to Rome were called *Socii*, and the war between these peoples and Rome is called the Social War.

In the sixth year that Marius was consul, the war called the Social War broke out. It lasted for three years. It was a war with some of the nations of Italy which Rome had formerly conquered. The people of those nations did not want to separate from Rome, but they wanted to have the right of voting as the Romans themselves had. Rome refused to give them this right, and at last they resolved to go to war.

All the greatest Roman generals of the time took part in this war. One of them was a young noble named Sul´la. He was a very successful soldier and won a number of great victories. The nations were defeated in the war, but Rome soon granted them most of the rights they had asked for.

Lucius Cornelius Sulla (138-78 BC)

The nobles gave great praise to Sulla for his victories in the Social War. They declared that he was a better general than Marius. So many fine things were said about the young noble that Marius became jealous and did a very foolish thing. He suddenly left his army in the field and came back to Rome. He complained that he was nervous and shut himself up in his house and refused to see any of his friends for weeks.

The nobles then started a story that Marius was getting silly and weak-minded from old age. He was about 70 at the time, and the nobles said that he ought to retire from the army. This made the old hero angry, and he declared that he was as strong in mind and body as any of the young Romans.

One morning he went to the place where the young men of Rome used to practice athletic sports, and for two or three hours he wrestled and ran and leaped with as much skill and strength as anyone. Some of the nobles who happened to pass by saw him and were very much amused.

About this time Sulla was elected consul on account of his victories in the Social War. Shortly afterward Rome declared war against Mith´rida´tes, King of Pontus in Asia Minor, who had cruelly put to death a number of the citizens of a Roman province in Asia.

The Senate appointed Sulla to command the Roman army in this war. But as soon as he left Rome with his army, one of the tribunes proposed that the command should be taken from him and given to Marius. The Assembly agreed to this, and Marius accepted the appointment. He sent word to the army, which was not far from Rome, that he would come in a short time to take command.

When Sulla heard this, he became very angry. He called his soldiers around him, told them what had been done, and asked them if they would submit to be the slaves of Marius and his party.

"No, no!" cried the soldiers, "We will not submit. We want you for our general."

"Then follow me to Rome," said Sulla. "We will teach Marius and his friends that they must not insult us."

So the soldiers marched quickly back to Rome with Sulla at their head. They declared that they would take the city out of the hands of rebels, as they called the friends of Marius. When they entered the city, they were met by Marius and his followers, and there was a battle, in which Marius was defeated. Then a law was passed declaring Marius a traitor and that he should be put to death.

88-82 BC
The Civil War

But Marius fled from Rome with some friends and went down the Tiber in a boat to the Mediterranean. He sailed along the coast and then he and his companions went ashore to seek for food. They wandered through the country for some time without seeing anyone. At last they met a farmer, who gave them something to eat. He told them that horsemen from Rome were riding through the place searching for Marius.

They were frightened at this, and they ran into a thick wood where they stopped all night. But while his companions were downcast, Marius was cheerful and hopeful.

"This bad state of things," he said, "will last only a short time. I know it, because the gods have revealed to me that I shall be once more consul of Rome!"

But next day Marius was taken by horsemen. he saw them coming and waded far into a great marsh and hid himself among some high, thick reeds. The horsemen rode into the marsh and found him, and they put a rope around his neck and dragged him to the shore. Then they shut him up in a hut and began to think what they should do with him.

At last they decided to put him to death at once. They thought this would please Sulla and that perhaps he would reward them for it. So they gave a sword to a slave and sent him to kill Marius. The slave entered the hut and stood for a few moments looking at the great general. Marius glared at him like a wild beast and said in a stern voice:

"Slave, will you dare to kill Caius Marius?"

The slave started back in terror and ran out of the hut. Then he threw down his sword at the feet of the soldiers and cried out that he could never have the courage to slay Marius.

It was now decided to send Marius out of the country. So he was taken to a ship and carried to Africa. After going ashore, he wandered through the country until he came to the place where Carthage once stood. Nothing now remained of the famous city but a mass of gloomy ruins, for the Romans had entirely destroyed it a few years before in the Third Punic War. In these ruins Marius lived for a short time. One day a soldier came to tell him that the governor of Africa wanted him to leave the country.

"Go to your governor," answered Marius, "and tell him that you saw Caius Marius sitting on the ruins of Carthage."

Not long afterward, when Sulla was away fighting king Mithridates, there was great trouble at Rome. One of the consuls, named Cin'na, aided by many of the plebeians, attempted to get control of public affairs but was defeated by the nobles. Then Cinna and his followers were forced to leave the city. They organized an army among the Italians who had been complaining of not getting their rights from Rome, and they sent to Africa for Marius to come and be their commander.

When Marius arrived, he made an attack on Rome and soon captured it. Then he marched in through the gates at the head of his army and took possession of the city. At the next election the people elected him consul.

Marius now resolved to have vengeance on the nobles who had driven him from Rome. For several days the old Roman, surrounded by a guard of freed slaves, went through the city seeking the nobles in their houses, in the temples, in the Forum, and everywhere that they could be found, and killing them without mercy.

These were dreadful days. Some of the noblest men of Rome were put to death. None of Sulla's friends was spared. Even his wife and children were harshly treated and forced to leave the city.

Marius did not stop the bloody work until he had killed all his enemies that he could find. But his triumph was short. He died in a little more than two weeks after he had become consul for the seventh time.

VIII – Octāva Lectiō: Sulla (*Famous Men of Rome* XIX)

We have said something of Sulla, but there is much more to be told about him, for he was a very remarkable man, and he did remarkable things in Rome. His full name was Lu´ci-us Cornelius Sulla. He belonged to a very noble family. When he was a young man, he was very fond of study and became an excellent scholar. He was also a good speaker and often made eloquent speeches in the Forum on public affairs.

He was a large, strong man, with red hair and a ruddy face. He was a very great soldier and one of the greatest of Roman generals. They called him "the Lion." He was so successful in war that he also got the name of *Felix*, a Latin word which means *happy* or *fortunate*.

One of the greatest wars that Sulla was in was a war against the Greeks. Rome had conquered Greece some time before, and the governors of many of the Greek cities were Romans. These governors were very cruel to the Greeks; therefore, the people hated them. Mithridates, King of Pontus, knew this, and he offered to send armies to Greece to help to drive the Romans out of the country. The Greeks were very glad of this, and they prepared for war against the Romans.

Sulla arrived in Greece with a strong army and began a march through the country. He captured several of the cities and compelled them to submit to the Roman governors. Then he marched on to Athens, the capital city of Greece. But he found that it was occupied by Ar-che-la´us, one of the generals of King Mithridates, who had brought from Asia Minor an army to help the Greeks.

Athens at this time was one of the most strongly fortified cities in the world. Its walls were 70 feet high, and they were made of huge, thick blocks of hard, smooth stone. It took thousands of men many years to build these massive walls. The city was also well supplied with food, so that it could hold out against a siege for a long time.

For several weeks Sulla attacked Athens furiously day by day, but it was all in vain. He could not take the city. His soldiers tried many times to mount the high walls, but they could not do it.

At last Sulla had battering rams made. These were engines for breaking down the walls of towns. They were long, heavy beams of wood, with iron at one end, formed like the head of a ram. This was why they were called battering rams. At first they were worked by men with their hands and bodily strength. In later times they were hung from a cross beam, so as to swing back and forward, and the iron end was made to strike against the wall with great force.

When a number of battering rams were ready, Sulla began another attack on Athens. But at dead of night, a party of Athenians came out of the city and burned all the battering rams. Sulla quickly had new ones made, and after months of hard labor, the Romans at last succeeded in breaking down the walls and taking Athens. They plundered the beautiful city and destroyed many fine works of art. It is said that they carried off more than 600 pounds of gold and silver.

Sulla remained in Athens only long enough to establish Roman authority there once more. Then he departed with his army and marched to Chaer'o-ni-a, another town of Greece, where there was a force of 120,000 men, which King Mithridates had sent to help the Greeks.

The Romans numbered only about 40,000 men, but Sulla was not afraid to fight the immense army of Mithridates. By placing his troops in good positions at the beginning of the battle, and afterward by moving them skillfully from one point to another, he was able to win a great victory.

This was a remarkable battle in one respect. Although there were furious charges and hand-to-hand combats, in which thousands upon thousands of the soldiers of Mithridates were slain, the Romans lost only a few men. We are told that, when the roll-call of the Roman army took place after the battle, only 12 men failed to answer their names! The army of Mithridates had lost 110,000 men; the Romans only 12!

But perhaps we ought not to believe that so very few Romans were killed, for it seems hardly possible that it could have been so. It is certain, however, that Sulla gained a great victory. He also defeated another army sent by Mithridates soon afterward.

Then Archelaus, the general of the army of Mithridates, begged for peace. Sulla made terms that were very good for Rome, and Archelaus and Mithridates had to accept them. Mithridates had to give the Romans a large sum of money and 70 ships of war and to promise to be the friend of Rome in future. Thus the war with Greece ended.

Sulla now prepared to return to Italy. He had heard how his friends in Rome and his wife and children had been treated by Marius. He was greatly enraged, and in his letter to the Senate, telling them of his victories in Greece, he said:

"In return for my services, which have brought honor and glory to Rome, my wife and children have been driven from their home, my house has been burned, and my friends have been put to death. I am now going back to punish those who did these things."

When the letter was read to the senators, they were very much alarmed, for they knew that if Sulla did as he threatened, it would cause a dreadful civil war in Rome. In reply to Sulla, they begged him not to make war on his own countrymen, and they promised to do their best to bring about a friendly understanding between him and the followers of Marius.

Sulla answered that he did not want any understanding with them.

"I want no friendship with my enemies," he said. "I am able to take care of myself. It will be well for them if they can take care of themselves."

Soon afterward he set out for Italy with his army. Rome was then under the power of the Marian party. This party was led by Cinna and by Marius the Younger, the son of the great Marius. When they heard that Sulla was coming, they raised an army and went forth to drive him back. Young Marius said:

"Now it will be decided who shall be the master of Rome!"

A battle was fought between the two armies. It was long and severe, and for a time it seemed as if the Marians would win. Even Sulla himself had no hope of victory. But soon very bad blunders made by the Marians turned the tide of battle in his favor, and he was victorious. He took six thousand prisoners.

Sulla now entered Rome as its master, and cruel master he proved to be. He first got himself appointed dictator for as long a time as he wished to hold the office. Then he commanded that all the followers of Marius should be slain. So they were hunted out of their hiding places and all put to death without mercy.

When every person who was known to have been connected with the Marian party was killed, the people thought Sulla would cease his murderous work, but he did not. He went on killing this and that one – now a poor man and then a rich man – until at last the Romans became dreadfully frightened. "When will he stop?" they said to one another in trembling tones.

One day a senator had the courage to ask Sulla if he would please say whom he intended to spare from death. Sulla coolly answered:

"I have not yet made up my mind, but if it is the wish of the Senate, I will shortly make out a list of persons who must die!"

And Sulla really did make out a list of persons he intended to kill. It was called a *proscription list* and was hung up in the Forum. Oh, how anxiously the poor, terror-stricken Romans went to that list to read the names! And if a man saw that his name was not there, he went away with joy in his heart. But if his name was there, he covered his face with his toga and ran off to hide himself.

The next day another and longer list of proscribed persons was hung up, and the day after still another list. Anyone who killed a proscribed person got a large reward in money, but if anybody helped a proscribed person to escape, he was punished by death. This dreadful work was continued until many thousands of people in Rome and throughout Italy were slain.

Then Sulla had his Triumph in the streets of Rome. It was the most magnificent procession that had yet been seen in the city. There were hundreds of beautiful horses drawing bright, golden chariots; there were long lines of soldiers in glittering armor; there were wagons containing gold and silver and other precious things, which Sulla had gotten in Greece after his victories over Mithridates. The dictator himself rode in the most splendid chariot of all. He seemed like a king, and indeed was a king in power, though not in name. This was what was called a Triumph.

Sulla, for his own protection, had a bodyguard formed of slaves who had belonged to the people he had proscribed and put to death. This bodyguard is said to have numbered 10,000 men, and they were called Cornelii, after Sulla's family name.

Under the rule of Sulla, his own will was law. He could do whatever he pleased. But he did not remain dictator a long time. In about a year after his Triumph, he seemed to have gotten tired of ruling and resigned the office. Then he left Rome and went to reside in his country house on the beautiful Bay of Naples. Here he spent the rest of his life, passing his time partly in feasting and merriment and partly in study. He died in 78 BC.

IX – Nōna Lectiō: Pompey the Great (*Famous Men of Rome* XX)

Not long after the death of Sulla, a new enemy to Rome appeared upon the Mediterranean Sea. A large number of people who lived on the coasts of Asia Minor built and armed fleets of ships, sailed along the shores of Italy, and attacked and plundered Roman vessels.

The searovers, or pirates, as the Romans called them, had more than a thousand well-built, fast-sailing ships. Many of them were adorned with richly gilded bows and sterns, purple sails, and silver mounted oars. They seized trading vessels, robbed them, and killed every person on board.

Often, too, the pirates committed robberies on land. A boat's crew from a pirate ship would go ashore, put to death all the farmers in the neighborhood, and lay waste their farms. So in a short time, the pirates made themselves masters of the Italian coasts and kept the people in constant excitement and terror.

But at last the Romans resolved to make war upon the robbers and selected a very popular young man named Cne´i-us Pom´pey to be the general. The people had great confidence in Pompey. They said that he was the only one who could put down the Mediterranean pirates and demanded that he should be sent to do the work.

Pompey was a fine-looking man, with very pleasant manners. He had made himself famous as a soldier by brave deeds in wars in Spain and Africa and was generally called Pompey the Great. His father had been a great commander, and the boy had lived in camps and taken part in wars almost from childhood. He had had many adventures during his army life and had always shown the qualities of a hero. He fought on the side of Sulla in many battles against the Marians, and he was thought to be one of Sulla's greatest generals.

The Roman Senate therefore, yielded to the demand of the people and appointed Pompey to go forth against the pirates. He accepted the

Pompey the Great (106-48 BC)

command and promptly set to work to carry out the important undertaking.

He gathered 14 powerful fleets. He kept one for himself and put the others under the command of good officers. Then he divided the Mediterranean into 13 districts, and sent a fleet to each district to hunt the pirates.

With his own fleet he sailed as far as the Strait of Gibraltar and then turned back toward Italy. On the way he chased the pirate vessels before him as he met them, until they were stopped and seized by some of the 13 fleets stationed here and there all over the Mediterranean. The pirates were thus caught in a trap. Thousands of them were killed in battles with the different fleets, and their vessels were burned. The remainder soon surrendered to the Romans, and in three months the sea was cleared of pirates.

Pompey was much praised for this great work, and the people said he was just the man to take charge of the war against Mithridates. This king had again attacked a Roman province in Asia, and the Romans resolved to punish him. But Mithridates was a very powerful man. He had great armies; he was a skillful general, and he defeated the Romans in many battles. The Roman people therefore resolved to send Pompey against him. Pompey was much pleased to be placed in command of a great army, and he proudly started off with his soldiers for the eastern lands.

Pompey remained in Asia several years and won many great victories. He conquered a number of countries and put Roman governors over them. Then he came back to Rome, bringing kings and princes as prisoner and an enormous amount of gold and silver and other valuable things to enrich the republic and himself. He was welcomed in a magnificent manner and he had a Triumph such as was given to great and victorious generals.

But Pompey now began to think of making himself master of Rome during his life time. He had greatly pleased the people by his victories in war, and they were praising him on every side. How to keep their favor, and by it to get power, was what now occupied his mind. He had been consul before, but he was now elected again; then he set about providing various sorts of amusements for the people. He believed that if the people were amused, they would be less likely to object to his taking the powers of the government entirely into his own hands.

He built a theatre large enough to seat 40,000 persons. This was the first great theatre erected in Rome. It was of stone and very strongly made. It had no roof, and the rows of seats rose one above another in a half circle. At one end there was an immense stage on which all the performances took place.

In this grand theatre Pompey gave some very wonderful exhibitions from time to time. He had lions, elephants, and other wild animals brought from Asia and Africa at great expense. These animals were let loose upon the stage, and gladiators fought them in full view of the people in the theatre.

There were also thrilling combats in the theatre between the gladiators themselves. They fought each other savagely until one was wounded and fell upon the stage. Then the victor would turn toward the audience to find whether they wished him to kill the wounded man. If the people wanted this, they would stretch out their hands with their thumbs down; if they did not want him killed, they would hold their thumbs upward. If he had shown skill and courage and fought well, they would give the sign to let him live, but if he had not made a brave fight, they would turn down their thumbs, and the unfortunate man would be instantly killed.

Slaves and prisoners taken in war were taught to be gladiators in schools established for the purpose. There were hundreds of these trained fighters always ready for the combats. The Romans were very fond of such amusements, and great crowds of men, and women too, attended the theatre whenever there was a fight of gladiators.

By giving the people a great deal of amusement of this kind on a grand scale, Pompey became the great popular favorite in Rome, and while the people were entertained at his theatre, he managed the government to suit himself.

At this time the Romans ruled a vast territory, which included not only all Italy, but Greece, Spain, Syria, Egypt, Turkey, Switzerland, and parts of France and Germany. Country after country had been conquered during a long series of years, and millions of people of different races and languages were subjects of Rome.

Rome itself was a city with a population of about half a million. It covered a very large area, including the famous seven hills. Its streets were narrow and crooked but well-paved and clean. In the center of the city were a number of large squares in which there were handsome buildings. There were magnificent temples and baths, and the houses of the nobles and wealthy plebeians were very large and splendid. Many of the fine houses were built of marble, with great pillars in front. Elegant furniture and handsome carpets and rugs filled the rooms.

There were many rich men in Rome at this time. Most of them had obtained the greater part of their wealth by plundering the conquered countries. They lived in a very magnificent manner, gave splendid dinners and entertainments, and had hundreds of slaves to attend upon them.

The slaves were a large class who were brought to Rome from many nations conquered in war. Many of them belonged to high families in their own country and were well educated. Some of them were physicians, and others were good scholars and could read and write for their masters. The best cooks, builders, tailors, and farmers were slaves. In fact, it was by slaves that nearly all the skilled work in Rome was done.

There were markets in Rome where slaves were sold. The slaves to be sold were placed on a platform. Labels hung from their necks, showing their age and what they were able to do.

The Roman children were taught to read and write Latin, which was their own language. They were also taught arithmetic and history. Most of the teachers were well-educated slaves.

Rome, then, was very rich and very powerful in the time of Pompey, and for many years Pompey was very popular. At one time he became dangerously ill while visiting Naples. Then the people showed their great love for him in many ways, and when he recovered, there were public thanksgivings throughout Italy. On his journey home, great crowds came out to greet him as he passed through the towns, and when he arrived at Rome, he was received with unbounded joy.

Pompey had now a very strong hold on the affections of the people, so he cared little for the efforts made by a very ambitious Roman named Ju'li-us Cae'sar to win public favor. But Caesar was a man of strong will and great energy. He had resolved to be the ruler of Rome, and he spared no labor to accomplish his purpose. Pompey at last became alarmed by Caesar's efforts, but it was then too late. He was defeated by Caesar in a great battle and soon after lost his life. How these things came about we shall learn in the next story.

X – Decima Lectiō: Julius Caesar (*Famous Men of Rome* XXI.1)

Of all the Roman heroes, the greatest was Caius Julius Caesar. He was a very remarkable man in many ways. He was remarkable as a soldier, statesman, scholar, and as an orator. He wrote a history of his own wars which is one of the best ancient histories that have come down to us. It is called *Caesar's Commentaries*, and it is used as a textbook in all schools where Latin is taught.

Julius Caesar (100-44 BC)

This famous Roman was tall, handsome, agreeable in his manners, and of a lively disposition. He liked songs and stories, and even when he was a great general, he often was as merry and frolicsome as a boy. Sometimes however he was stern and cruel instead of kind and forgiving.

Caesar was a member of the Julian family, which was one of the first families in Rome. Four Caesars of this family had been consuls of Rome in one century.

The aunt of Julius Caesar was the wife of the great leader Marius. Naturally, Sulla was Caesar's bitter enemy and did all he could against him. "In that young man there is many a Marius," Sulla is reported to have said. However, by keeping out of Rome, Caesar was able to escape the traps laid for him at Sulla's orders. As soon as Sulla died, Caesar returned to Rome.

Although he was a rich noble, Caesar became a friend of the plebeians and always supported their cause. He spoke a great deal in the Forum upon political questions, and the people looked upon him as their champion. They elected him to several public offices, one after the other, and thus his influence and power were much increased. At last he was appointed governor of Spain, which was then ruled by the Romans.

On his way to Spain, he stopped for a night at a little village among the mountains. One of his companions remarked that perhaps in that small place the people had their contests and their jealousies, just as people in large cities.

"Poor as this village is, I would rather be first here than second in Rome!" said Caesar.

Caesar was very successful in Spain, and the Romans were so pleased with his conduct that when he came home, they made him consul. During his consulship he had many good laws passed. When about 40 years old, he was given command of an army, and for some years he followed the life of a soldier with wonderful success.

The Roman armies were formed of regiments called *legions*. Each legion contained over 3,000 men, who were sometimes called legionaries. The weapons of the legionary were a short sword and a long spear called a *pilum*.

Besides spears and swords, the Roman soldiers used slings for hurling stones against the enemy. They also had a machine called a *ballista* for throwing stones too heavy for handslings.

The military standard of the Romans was a figure of an eagle borne on the top of a pole. Each legion had one of these, and the soldier who carried it was called the *eagle-bearer*. Other standards also were used by the *cohorts* or companies into which the legions were divided.

58-51 BC
The Gallic War

Caesar's first great battles were in Gaul. The Romans called all the inhabitants of that country Gauls, although they were of many nations and spoke different languages. The Gauls were brave, but Caesar proved to be a great general, and in a few years he conquered all Gaul.

The Roman soldiers had great confidence in Caesar. When he led them, they believed victory was certain. He was strict in his discipline, but very friendly and pleasant with the men, and often gave them praise. He himself shared in their hardships. Day after day he marched on foot at their head through heat and rain and snow and fought with them in the front ranks.

On one occasion Caesar built a very remarkable bridge. He wanted to get across the River Rhine with his army to punish some German tribes who were in the habit of attacking the friends of Rome in Gaul. There was no bridge. The Germans used to get over in small parties by swimming or in small boats. But a large army could not cross in this way without a great deal of trouble and loss of time, so Caesar resolved to build a bridge. He quickly set his men to work, and they finished the bridge in ten days, though all the wood had to be cut down in the forests and carried to the riverside.

One of Caesar's greatest victories in Gaul was the taking of the town of A-le´si-a. This town had very strong walls all round it, and it was defended by a great army of Gauls commanded by a brave chief named Ver-cin-get´o-rix. Caesar surrounded the town with his army and prevented food from being sent in to the inhabitants. He also defeated an army that came from other parts of Gaul to help the Alesians.

Vercingetorix then had to come out from the town and give himself up to Caesar.

After many conquests in Gaul, Caesar sailed over with an army to the island of Britain, now called Great Britain. The natives were a wild, fierce people, and they fought bravely against Caesar and his army. But the Romans were victorious, and they took possession of Britain, and for over 400 years the island was a part of the Roman empire.

55-54 BC Invasion of Britain

XI – Ūndecima Lectiō: Julius Caesar (*Famous Men of Rome* XXI.2)

Caesar was engaged eight years in his wars in Gaul and Britain. It is said that during these years he conquered 300 tribes or nations, took 800 cities, fought battles with 3,000,000 men and made 1,000,000 prisoners. He obtained immense quantities of treasure in the conquered lands, and he himself, as commander of the victorious armies, kept a large part of it as his own share, so that he became very rich.

Caesar's wonderful victories made him a great man in Rome. The plebeians rejoiced at the success of their leader and favorite and were ready to welcome him with the highest honors whenever he should return to the city.

But Caesar had now made up his mind to become the master of Rome. So he began to plan and to work to destroy the power of Pompey, who at that time ruled public affairs in Rome almost completely.

In order to gain still greater favor, Caesar sent a number of his friends to Rome to spend immense sums of money in various ways to please the people. They got up splendid games and feasts; they divided large quantities of corn among the poor; and they paid the debts of hundreds of men who had influence among the plebeians. The people knew that all this was done at Caesar's expense, and they praised and loved him for his generosity.

Pompey, with a great show of authority, now ordered Caesar to disband his army and send the soldiers to their homes, for he said that Caesar had no need of an army any longer, as he had finished his work in Gaul. But Pompey, too, had an army at this time in Spain, and Caesar said to him:

"If you will disband your army, I will disband mine."

This made Pompey very angry, and he got the Senate to pass a law declaring that Caesar was a public enemy and must be put down. One senator asked Pompey what he should do if Caesar should come to Rome with his army.

"What should I do?" cried Pompey, in a tone of contempt. "Why, I have only to stamp my foot and thousands of men will spring up to march under my orders."

At this time Caesar was with his army in the northern part of Italy. When he heard what the Senate had done, he called his soldiers together and made an eloquent speech. He told them of the injustice that Pompey and the Senate had done to him, and he concluded by saying:

"This is my reward for all that I have done for my country. But I shall go to Rome and establish an honest government of the people, if you, my brave soldiers, will be faithful to me."

The soldiers answered with a loud shout, saying:

"We shall be faithful to you. We will stand by you to the last."

Caesar then started with his army and marched rapidly through northern Italy until he came to the banks of a little river, at that time called the Ru′bi-con and known as the southern boundary of Gaul. What river this was no one can now exactly tell, but it is supposed that it was one of several small rivers which flow into the Adriatic Sea south of the River Po.

Caesar halted his army at the Rubicon and forbade anyone to cross it until he gave the order. He stood for some time on the banks in deep thought, as if trying to decide whether he should cross the river and proceed or give up his dangerous undertaking. He was still within his own territory as commander of Gaul; if he should cross the Rubicon, he would be on territory directly under the government of the officers at Rome. By law it was made an act of treason, to be punished with death, for any Roman general to enter this territory with an army without permission of the Senate.

"We can retreat now," said Caesar to some of his officers who stood near him, "but once across the Rubicon it will be too late to draw back."

While Caesar was talking, a shepherd came along from a field close by, playing lively music on a reed pipe. The soldiers gathered around him to listen to the music, and some of them began to dance. One of Caesar's trumpeters stood among the soldiers with his trumpet in his hand. The shepherd saw the trumpet, suddenly seized it, and waded to the bridge over the Rubicon, which was but a few steps off. Then he put the trumpet to his lips, sounded the stirring notes for an advance of the troops, and began to march across the bridge.

"A sign from the gods!" shouted Caesar. "Let us go where we are thus called. The die is cast!"

So saying, he turned his horse right into the stream and rode across the Rubicon, followed by his army. It was a daring thing to do, and the phrases "he has crossed the Rubicon" and "the die is cast" are now often used to mean that a bold or dangerous step has been taken from which there is no drawing back.

There was no one to oppose Caesar as he marched through Italy. On the contrary, city after city surrendered to him. There was very little fighting. In most places the people seemed glad to have him as their ruler, and gave him a warm welcome and feasted his soldiers. He had only words of kindness for everyone, even for those who were against him, and he won hosts of friends and supporters all along the route.

There was great alarm at Rome when it was learned that Caesar was advancing toward the city. The supporters of Pompey became terrified,

49 BC
Caesar crossed the Rubicon and began a civil war.

The Rubicon was the boundary between the province of Gaul and the land of Italy. Caesar had authority to command an army only in Gaul, and to cross the Rubicon with his army was illegal and an act of war against his own country.

and the rich nobles gathered up their money and other valuables and fled. Pompey could do nothing to defend the city against Caesar, and at last he too ran away. He went to Greece to raise an army to fight Caesar.

When Caesar arrived at Rome he met with no opposition. He entered the city amid shouts of welcome from the people. He harmed no one, but he set up a new government and organized a new Senate. He was now the master spirit of the republic.

After arranging everything to his satisfaction in Rome, Caesar went to Spain and defeated Pompey's generals there. Then he came back and turned his attention to Pompey himself.

In the meantime, Pompey had been very busy gathering an army in the eastern countries controlled by Rome. In one way or another, he collected 50,000 men. They were stationed on the coasts of Macedonia and Greece. There they waited for Caesar and his army to cross the Adriatic Sea to give them battle.

Caesar had a great deal of trouble getting across the stormy sea with his army of 40,000 soldiers, but at last a landing was made in Greece. Then the two armies had some skirmishing but no great battle.

This continued for months. Pompey at one time would gain the advantage, and Caesar at another time. But it was evident that neither of the great rivals was in any hurry to risk the chance of defeat in a general battle. They know well that such a defeat would entirely ruin the one who was defeated.

But at last the two armies met for battle on the plain of Phar-sa´li-a, in Thessaly, a district of Greece. The soldiers on both sides were armed with spears and broadswords. Some carried slings to hurl large stones, and others had bows and arrows. The greater part of the fighting however was done with swords.

48 BC
Battle of Pharsalia

80,000 men were engaged in the battle, about 40,000 on each side. It was a brave heroic struggle and lasted for hours. Both armies fought splendidly, but in the end Pompey's army was forced back to its camp after dreadful slaughter. For a few minutes the camp was bravely defended against the attacks of Caesar's soldiers and then had to be abandoned. The battle did not last long after this. Pompey's great army was utterly beaten.

Pompey himself, with a few followers, fled to the seashore and sailed across the Mediterranean to Egypt. There he was treacherously murdered by order of Ptolemy, the Egyptian king.

XII – Duodecima Lectiō: Julius Caesar (*Famous Men of Rome* XXI.2)

Caesar gained a splendid victory at Pharsalia, but he was not yet master of the Roman Empire. The rich nobles and senators formed armies to fight him in Asia Minor, Africa, and Spain. Caesar went with an army to Asia Minor, attacked his enemies, and won a great battle at a place called Ze´la. This victory was so quickly gained that in sending news of it to

47 BC
Battle of Zela

Rome Caesar wrote the famous dispatch, "*Vēnī, vīdī, vīcī,*" which is, in English, "I came, I saw, I conquered."

He had equal success in Africa and Spain. In a very short time he destroyed the armies opposed to him. Then he returned to Rome and had the grandest Triumph ever seen in the city.

The celebration lasted four days, and during that time Rome was in a high state of pleasant excitement. Thousands of persons from the surrounding country came to the city to witness the magnificent show.

On each day there were splendid processions, in which there were great numbers of gorgeous chariots, drawn by beautiful horses and filled with Caesar's principal officers. Behind them marched hundreds of soldiers bearing banners on which were pictured scenes from Caesar's important battles. Herds of elephants and camels from Asia and Africa appeared in the procession, and there were also long lines of prisoners carrying valuable articles obtained by Caesar in the lands he had conquered.

In addition to the processions, many kinds of entertainments were provided for the people, such as plays, circus exhibitions, combats between gladiators, wild-beast hunts, and chariot races. There were also feasts served to all the people of the city. It was a time of unbounded enjoyment and delighted the Romans so much that they became very devoted to Caesar.

There was now no opposition to him. Both the nobles and the plebeians were willing, and even glad, to have him as their ruler. He was chosen dictator for life and put in command of all the armies of the Empire. He was called *imperātor*, which means *emperor*.

The people gave him the title of *Father of his Country*. Statues of him were erected in the public buildings and squares. A grand chair, made somewhat like a throne, was placed in the Senate chamber, and whenever he came to listen to the debates, he sat in this chair as if he were king.

Caesar now had laws passed making many improvements in the government. He also carried out a number of plans to make Rome of more importance as a commercial city. He erected magnificent buildings, made aqueducts to bring plenty of water to the city, established a great library, and did many other things which were of much benefit to the people.

45 BC
The Julian Calendar

One of the most useful things he did was to make a new calendar. Before his time the Romans had not a very clear knowledge as to the length of a year. At one time they had only ten months in their year. Afterward they had twelve, but they only counted 365 days in every year. They did not know or they did not give attention to the fact that the real length of a year is 365 days, 5 hours, 48 minutes, 50 seconds. They did not reckon the extra hours, minutes, and seconds, and so their calendar got quite wrong in the course of a number of years. Caesar corrected the error by making one year in every four have 366 days, and the calendar thus corrected was called the *Julian Calendar*.

Caesar now possessed all the glory and power of a king, and it began to be believed that he wanted to be a king in reality. The Romans had not had a king for 500 years and would not have one. Their feeling against kings was so strong that none of the men who had ruled Rome, at times with almost kingly power, had ever dared to call himself king.

One day an intimate friend of Caesar saluted him in public as king. Caesar replied: "I am not king, but only Caesar."

Some of the nobles however felt certain that he meant to make himself king, and they formed a plot to kill him in the Senate house on the Ides of March, that is, on the fifteenth of March. The Romans had certain days in their months which they called Kalends, Nones, and Ides.

One of the persons who made the plot against Caesar was Junius Brutus, a highly respected Roman. It is said that he was a descendant of the Junius Brutus who, five centuries before, had helped to overthrow the tyrant King Tarquin. Brutus was an intimate friend of Caesar, but he thought that Caesar intended to destroy the Republic by making himself king, and therefore he joined the plot against him.

As the Ides of March drew near, the plan for putting Caesar to death was carefully arranged and settled. An augur, or fortune teller, one day stopped Caesar in the street and said to him, "Beware the Ides of March!" but the great conqueror laughed at the warning.

Mar. 15, 44 BC
the death of Caesar

On the day appointed, the plotters met in the senate chamber, ready to do the wicked deed they had planned. When Caesar entered the chamber, all present rose to greet him. He bowed and smiled pleasantly to the people and took his usual seat. Now was the fatal moment.

As had been arranged, one of the plotters went up to him with a request for the pardon of a prisoner. Then the rest crowded around his chair as if to urge him to grant the request. Caesar seemed somewhat alarmed at the crowd and rose from his chair. At this moment, he was stabbed in the side with a sword. Then there were loud outcries in the chamber, and all was excitement and confusion.

Caesar used his stylus to defend himself. The stylus was an instrument made of iron, with a sharp point on one end for writing on wax tablets, and with the other end smooth, for rubbing out a word when necessary. For writing on parchment or paper, a pen made of reed was used. Educated Romans carried their stylus and tablet in their pockets. From the name of the instrument, the word *style* is now used to mean a particular manner of writing.

Caesar had nothing but his stylus with which to defend himself. He fought bravely until he saw his friend Brutus coming to strike him. Then he cried out, "You, too, Brutus!" and made no further resistance.

They stabbed him until he fell dead. Then they went out of the Senate and through the streets of Rome with Brutus at their head. They told the people what they had done and rejoiced at the deed. They said the death of Caesar saved the Roman Republic.

But the people were very angry and threatened to put to death those who had killed Caesar. They would have done this, only that Brutus and his friends fled from the city.

The famous English author William Shakespeare wrote a play named *Julius Caesar*. In the play Caesar fights off the assasins for a while, but when he sees Brutus among them, he asks "*Et tū, Brūte?*" which means "And you too, Brutus?" But the historian Plutarch says that Caesar's last words were Greek: *"kai su teknon?"*, which means "And you too, my child?"

There was a grand funeral service in honor of Caesar. The body was laid in the Forum, and a famous Roman named Mark Antony made an eloquent funeral speech over it. He praised Caesar and spoke so bitterly against Brutus and his party that the people were now more angry than ever. This Mark Antony was afterward a very powerful man in Rome.

Caesar died 44 years before Christ was born. Of course his death did not save the Roman Republic. It had, indeed, already ceased to exist in all but the name. Rome was no longer a republic, but an empire, and as we shall see, the family of Caesar gave it its first emperor. All the emperors adopted the name of Caesar as part of their title.

XIII – Tertia Decima Lectiō: Cicero (*Famous Men of Rome* XXII)

Cicero (106 – 43 BC) was one of Rome's greatest authors, orators, and statesmen. He was just a few years older than Caesar.

Marcus Tul′li-us Cic′e-ro was a prominent man at Rome for some time in the latter years of the Republic. He was a great orator – one of the greatest the world has ever known. His principal speeches have been preserved and are read and studied at the present day.

He often spoke in the Forum before large audiences, and by his wonderful eloquence, he delighted all who heard him. Both the nobles and plebeians admired him for his learning, his oratory, and his manly qualities.

Cicero was a tall, graceful man, with an intellectual and rather handsome face and very bright black eyes. He was so great a favorite that he was chosen to fill several public offices and at last was elected consul.

63 BC the Catiline Conspiracy

In the early part of his year as consul, there was a mysterious plot formed in Rome by some nobles of bad character, old soldiers, and others ready for any mischief. What their real object was no one seemed to know. But it was said that the conspirators wanted to overthrow the government and set up a new one of their own.

There was a senator named Ser′gi-us Cat′i-line, and many believed that he was at the head of the plot. He had a bad reputation, and for some time, the other senators had looked upon him with suspicion. There was no proof however that he was engaged in any unlawful proceedings, so no charge could be made against him.

But one day a young woman named Ful′vi-a came to Cicero and gave him some important information about the plot and Catiline's part in it. She said that she had a lover who was one of the plotters and that he had told her some of their secrets. She was greatly frightened, for she thought that there might be bloodshed in Rome if the plot went on, and she felt it her duty to tell Cicero about it.

Cicero immediately went to the Senate and made a powerful speech. He charged Catiline with being the leading person in a plot to overthrow the government. There was great excitement at his words. Catiline was present, and he boldly denied the charge and defied Cicero to prove it.

"If Consul Cicero is afraid of my doing harm in Rome," said he, "I am willing to place myself as a prisoner in the hands of any senator."

"I do not think it is safe to have you in the city," replied Cicero, "and do you expect anyone to take you into his house?"

After a great deal of exciting talk, the Senate laid aside the charge against Catiline for a while.

A few weeks later, in a city near Rome, there was an uprising of the people against the public officers. This caused a great deal of alarm, and Cicero said it was the beginning of the plot that he had charged Catiline with forming.

Then Cicero hurried to the Senate, where Catiline was, and made a great speech against him. He called him a traitor to his country. Catiline turned pale and began to tremble. He attempted to speak, but the senators shouted and hooted and hissed him. Those who sat near him got up in disgust and took seats in another part of the chamber, leaving the conspirator sitting by himself. At last Catiline ran out of the Senate, furious with anger and threatening revenge. Then he mounted a horse and rode quickly out of the city.

Shortly afterward Cicero learned the names of nine Roman citizens who were leaders in the plot, and he had them arrested. He declared in the senate that they had planned to murder the senators and the high officers and to burn Rome. The senators declared at once that the nine must die, and so Cicero had them put to death.

> Five years later, in 58 BC, Cicero was exiled because he approved the execution of these nine conspirators. Cicero's enemies argued that he had illegally put citizens to death without a fair trial – a right guaranteed to citizens by Roman law. A year later, Cicero was acquitted and allowed to return to Rome.

Catiline now fled to the mountains called the Apennines and there raised a force of 20,000 men. Two armies were sent against him from Rome. A battle took place, in which Catiline's army was defeated and he himself killed.

Thus ended what was known as the Catiline Conspiracy. Cicero's action in helping to destroy it greatly pleased the Romans. In the Senate he received much praise and honor. It was even declared that he was the "Father of His Country."

Antony did not like Cicero, and when the Triumvirate was formed, the great orator was put to death by Antony's order.

XIV – Quarta Decima Lectiō: Augustus (*Famous Men of Rome* XXIII)

The first of the long line of Roman emperors was Oc-ta′vi-us, called in history Au-gus′tus. He was the grandnephew of Julius Caesar. Although he was scarcely 20 years old when Caesar died, he was very ambitious. He often said that he should one day be at the head of the Roman Empire.

"I shall rule Rome like Caesar," he would say to his companions. "You may laugh at me now, but the time will come when I shall be master of the Romans."

Shortly after Caesar's death, Octavius began to take an active part in political affairs. At this time, Mark Antony was in control of Rome and was managing everything to suit himself. He had been an intimate friend of Caesar and had commanded one of his armies. He obtained a great deal of power, but he was not liked very much either by the nobles or the plebeians. He was a bad ruler, and nobody trusted him.

Once Antony tried to prevent Octavius from being elected a tribune of the people. "I will be a tribune in spite of you," Octavius said, and he set to work with all his energy to get the office. There was a severe struggle on election day, but the boy was successful.

After this Octavius hated Antony and planned in secret to bring about his downfall. And he succeeded in all he attempted to do. From a tribune he advanced steadily, step by step, to more important offices. At last he obtained command of an army and marched his soldiers to northern Italy, where a war was going on. While in this region, he met Antony with his army. The two began to quarrel and at last came to blows. Then the army of Octavius fought the army of Antony, and the northern plains were reddened with the blood of the soldiers.

When the fighting had gone on for some time, Octavius sent to Antony and asked him to stop it. He pretended that he was very sorry he had begun to fight with Antony and asked for his friendship. "Let us be friends and work together," he said to Antony. "By joining our armies we shall be able to do some good."

The fighting was then stopped, and the two generals had a meeting. They agreed to unite their armies, and to invite another Roman general, named Lep′i-dus, who had a large army, to join them. Lepidus accepted the invitation and came to have a talk with Antony and Octavius. They agreed to a plan by which they themselves were to rule Rome together. This rule, or government, was called a *triumvirate*, and Octavius, Antony, and Lepidus were called *triumvirs*, a word which means *three men*.

After making all their arrangements, Antony, Octavius, and Lepidus started for Rome with their armies and took possession of the city. Then they began to kill those whom they thought were their enemies. More than 2,000 Romans were slain. They would have killed Brutus, only that he was then in Greece, where he had gone after Caesar's death to raise an army to fight Antony and his friends. Antony and Octavius now went with an army to Greece to fight Brutus. Both armies met at Philippi, in Macedonia, and then there was a battle in which the army of Brutus was defeated. After the battle, Brutus requested one of his slaves to kill him. The slave refused, but when Brutus still pressed him to do it, he held out his sword, and Brutus killed himself by falling upon it.

It is told that some time before the battle of Philippi, as Brutus was sitting one night in his tent, a vision or spectre appeared to him and said, "I am thy evil genius, Brutus; we shall meet again at Philippi." It is also said that the spectre again appeared to Brutus on the night before the battle of Philippi and told him that his death was at hand.

There was no one now to interfere with Antony, Octavius, and Lepidus, and they managed everything in Rome as they liked. They pretended all the time to have great respect for the Senate and officers of government who had been elected by the people.

---

43 BC
The second triumvirate was formed by Mark Antony, Lepidus, and Octavius, who agreed take control of the government at Rome and share their power with each other.

NB – The first triumvirate had been formed by Julius Caesar and his allies in 60 BC.

42 BC
The Battle of Philippi

After a short time, Antony went to some of the Eastern countries that were a part of the Roman Empire, and Lepidus went to Africa. Octavius was left in Rome to attend to its affairs. He then began to plan to get rid of Antony and Lepidus, so that he might rule Rome himself. With this object, he raised a great army and determined to make war on his rivals.

Sextus Pompey, a son of Pompey the Great, was at this time in control of the island of Sicily. He was always making trouble for Octavius, and he was aided by Lepidus, who had come from Africa to Sicily with his army. One day Octavius sailed over the Mediterranean Sea to Sicily with thousands of soldiers, destroyed the army of Sextus, and induced the army of Lepidus to leave him. Lepidus was then taken prisoner.

"Now to put an end to the power of Antony!" said Octavius to himself, when he returned to Rome from Sicily. So he went to the Senate and accused Antony of treason in Asia and Africa and asked that war be declared against him. The Senate declared war, and Octavius began to make great preparations for it.

Antony was in Egypt when he heard of the declaration of war. He laughed scornfully at the idea of Octavius being able to beat him. Then he gathered an army of more than 100,000 men and a fleet of several hundred warships and set out to meet Octavius. He had with him Cle-o-pa´tra, the beautiful queen of Egypt, whom he had married, and she had a fleet of her own, numbering 60 ships.

Octavius had about as many soldiers and ships as Antony. The two fleets met near a place called Ac´ti-um, on the coast of Greece, and fought a battle. For several hours the fight went on bravely, but neither side gained any great advantage. Suddenly Cleopatra sailed away with her fleet, and Antony quickly followed her with a few ships. Thus he deserted his men while they were fighting.

31 BC
The Battle of Actium. The end of the Roman Republic and the beginning of the Roman Empire.

The sailors and soldiers of the deserted fleet kept on fighting for a short time and then surrendered to Octavius. A few days later, a part of Antony's army, which was encamped on the shore near Actium, also surrendered.

Antony went back to Egypt with Cleopatra. His friends and supporters then left him, and his power was gone. Soon after, he stabbed himself and so died. It is said that Cleopatra died from the bite of a poisonous serpent called an asp, which she placed on her arm on purpose to kill herself.

Octavius continued to fight in different parts of the Empire until he defeated everyone who dared oppose him. Then he went back to Rome with a great deal of glory and riches and let it be known at once that he intended to be the master of the government. Although he pretended to protect the rights of the people, he made himself consul and also assumed other high offices, which greatly added to his power. Thousands of soldiers were at his call, and finally he became very much like a king.

Historia

27 BC
Octavius granted the title "Augustus."
The end of the Roman Republic and the beginning of the Roman Empire.

"The accumulation of all powers, legislative, executive, and judiciary, in the same hands . . . may justly be pronounced the very definition of tyranny."

James Madison, *Federalist* 47, 1788.

The Senate asked him if he would wish to be appointed dictator for life, but he thought it wise to refuse this office. The Senate then gave him the name of Augustus, which meant that he was worthy of respect. The word *augustus* in the Latin language means *sacred*. He called himself emperor, and, as Emperor Caesar Augustus, he ruled the Romans all the rest of his life, a period of about 27 years. And when Augustus became emperor, the Republic of Rome was no longer in existence.

What were known as the Prae-to′ri-an Guards were organized by Augustus to protect himself and uphold his authority as emperor. These guards were about 10,000 in number, and they were composed of the most trusty soldiers of the Empire. Each soldier had high rank and large pay and had to serve for many years. Whenever Augustus appeared in public, he was attended by some of the Praetorian guards, and they looked very imposing with their handsome uniforms and glittering swords and spears.

Augustus made many good changes in the government. He very much improved the condition of the plebeians. His principal ministers were two able men named A-grip′pa and Mae-ce′nas, who gave him very valuable assistance.

Whenever these wise men saw that the Romans were getting uneasy and beginning to grumble, they would advise the emperor to distribute corn or money to the poor or to give the people grand exhibitions to amuse them. Augustus would follow the advice and by so doing, made himself very popular.

During his long reign, Augustus had many splendid palaces, temples, and other buildings erected in Rome, and they made the city very beautiful. Augustus also founded cities in various parts of the empire. He encouraged literature and art and was himself an author. In his time, the famous Roman poets Hor′ace, Ver′gil, Va′ri-us, and O′vid lived, and also the great historian Li′vy, who wrote the history of Rome from the earliest period down to his own time. Vergil was the author of a celebrated poem called *The Ae-ne′id*, which tells of the wanderings and adventures of the Trojan hero Aeneas, whom the Caesars said was their ancestor.

Circa 1 AD
The birth of Jesus

It was in the reign of Augustus that Jesus Christ was born in Bethlehem, a town of Palestine, or Judea, in southwest Asia. Judea was then part of the Roman Empire.

14 AD
Emperor Tiberius

XV – Quīnta Decima Lectiō: Tiberius, Caligula, Claudius, Nero
(*Famous Men of Rome* XXIV.1-2)

Circa 33 AD
Crucifixion, death, and resurrection of Jesus Christ

On the death of Augustus, in the year 14 AD, his stepson Ti-be′ri-us became emperor. He was a cruel tyrant. He put to death a great many people only because he thought they were his enemies. A Roman emperor could put to death anyone he pleased. If he did not like a person, he would charge him with some crime and order his soldiers to kill him. Tiberius had many people killed in this way, but he was himself killed by the commander or general of the Praetorian Guard.

The next two emperors were Ca-lig′u-la and Clau′di-us. They also were tyrants and put many people to death without just cause. It is said that Caligula once wished that all the Roman people together had but one head so that he might cut it off with one blow.

But the next emperor was a still greater tyrant. His name was Nero. He became emperor in the year 54 AD. He was the son of a wicked woman named Ag-rip-pi′na. This woman married Claudius and got him to appoint her own son, Nero, his successor, instead of his own little son Bri-tan′ni-cus. Then she killed Claudius by poison, and Nero became emperor.

Nero was a tall, strong, good-looking, bright youth. He was fond of games, and could play several musical instruments. When he first became emperor, he seemed to be affectionate and kind-hearted, and he did a number of good things. Once, when he was asked to sign a warrant for the execution of a man condemned to death, he exclaimed:

"I wish I had never learned to write, for then I shouldn't have to sign away men's lives!"

Then the people around him cried:

"What a noble young man our emperor is! What a good heart he has!"

But in a very short time it was found that Nero was not at all kind or merciful, but that he was a cruel and wicked man.

Nero's mother, Agrippina, expected that when her son was emperor, she herself would be the real mistress and would rule the Roman Empire as she pleased. Nero was only a boy, she thought, and he would not want to take upon himself the cares and burdens of government.

And for a while Agrippina did rule Rome. She had a woman she hated put to death, and she punished several other persons who had offended her. She made some of the richest Romans pay her large sums of money. But Nero soon put an end to his mother's power. One day he said to her:

"I, not you, am the ruler of the Empire. You have no right to take any power upon yourself, and you must not do so again. Whenever you want anything done, you must ask me to do it for you."

"Ask you?" cried Agrippina in a rage. "How dare you talk this way to me, who made you emperor? You the emperor! You are not the rightful emperor. The true heir to the Empire is your stepbrother, young Britannicus, the son of Claudius!"

Then there was a fierce quarrel between Nero and his mother, and at last he turned her out of his palace and ordered her never to appear there again.

But what she had said alarmed him very much. He feared that Britannicus might be made emperor, and therefore he determined to get him out of the way as soon as possible.

At this time there was in Rome a dreadful woman named Lo-cus′ta, who made poisons and sold them secretly to anyone who wanted them. Nero went one night to this woman and said:

37 AD
Emperor Caligula

41 AD
Emperor Claudius

54 AD
Emperor Nero

Historia

NB – Nero's guests might have been deceived by his lie because the effects of the poison would have appeared very similar to an epilectic seizure or "fit."

"Make me a strong poison – so strong that it will kill a person like a flash of lightning!"

Locusta made the poison and gave it to him. He tried it on a pig, and it killed the animal in a few moments.

"Ha!" said he, "this will do the work."

Now Britannicus lived in the palace with his stepbrother and next day, when dinner was served, Nero put some of the poison into a cup of wine which he knew the boy was to drink. The moment Britannicus drank it, he fell to the floor dead. Then Nero said to the guests who were at the table:

"Do not be alarmed. It is nothing. My poor stepbrother always was subject to fits."

The attendants carried the body of Britannicus out of the room, and the dinner went on gaily.

A little while after he had poisoned his stepbrother, Nero made up his mind to get rid of his mother also. He was afraid that as long as she lived, he would not be safe as emperor. She might stir up the people against him any day. So he went to see her and pretended that he was sorry he had ill-treated her. He kissed and caressed her so affectionately that she was entirely deceived.

Then the cruel son made a plan to drown his mother. He had a ship so built that by pulling out certain bolts and pins, it would suddenly fall to pieces and sink. He then hired a wicked captain and crew to do his bidding and got his mother to take a sail in the ship down the Tiber.

Agrippina took a maid with her and went aboard. She was in a happy humor, because her son, as she thought, was so kind to her. When the ship came to a certain place in the river where the water was very deep, the sailors pulled out the bolts and pins. Then the ship began to fall apart and to sink.

The sailors sprang into the river to swim to the shore, and Agrippina and her maid jumped overboard. The maid was killed by a sailor, but Agrippina was picked up by the crew of a fishing boat.

59 BC
Agrippina murdered

Nero was greatly troubled by his mother's escape. He believed that now she would certainly try to have him removed from the throne. So he sent some men to kill her in her house, and they did so in a most cruel manner.

XVI – Sexta Decima Lectiō: Nero (*Famous Men of Rome* XXIV.3-4)

None of the emperors before Nero lived so grandly as he did. He had a splendid marble palace at Rome, containing immense quantities of beautiful furniture, gold and silver ornaments, and works of art of the finest kind. On the pleasant shores of the Mediterranean Sea, he had several houses where he lived in the summer and autumn months. Wherever he went, he had, as his court or companions, three or four hundred richly dressed men and women, with many slaves to wait upon them. They traveled in chariots covered with ivory and gold and drawn by beautiful horses.

Nero was famous for the splendid dinners he gave in his palace. The rarest and most costly food and wines were spread upon the tables in great plenty, and when the feasting was over, troops of actors and dancers would give performances which lasted until late at night.

Sometimes at these dinners, Nero would play the harp or flute. Sometimes he would act portions of plays or recite poems which he himself had composed. He was a very clever musician and actor, and he wrote very good poetry.

One evening a fire broke out in Rome and raged furiously for a week. Half the city was burned, and hundreds of people lost their lives. Some of the Romans said that Nero had started the fire and had prevented it from being put out. Most of the six days during which the fire lasted, he spent in a high tower, enjoying the sight. He played on his harp, sang merry songs, and recited verses about the burning of the ancient city of Troy.

64 AD — Rome burned; Nero blamed the Christians.

After the fire was put out, Nero said that it had been caused by the believers in the religion of Christ. At this time, there was a very large number of Christians in Rome. But most of the Romans still worshipped their old pagan gods, and they hated and ill-treated the Christians.

When Nero declared that the Christians had caused the great fire, the people began to persecute them in a dreadful manner. Many of the Christians were hanged, some were covered with pitch and burned, and others were hunted to death by savage dogs. During the time of this persecution, the Apostle Paul was beheaded, and the Apostle Peter was crucified, as Christ had been crucified 31 years before.

63 AD — St. Peter and St. Paul martyred at Rome.

After a short time, Rome was rebuilt in greater magnificence than before. Nero built for himself an immense and splendid palace on the famous Palatine Hill. This palace contained so many ornaments of gold that it was called the Golden House.

In governing the Empire, Nero was very harsh and cruel. He often put innocent men and women, and even his own friends, to death. He killed his wife in a fit of passion. He did so many wicked things that at last the Romans got tired of having such a tyrant to rule them, and they formed a plot to dethrone him and make someone else their emperor.

But the plot came to nothing, because a slave who had heard of it went to Nero and told him all about it. The Praetorian Guards seized the leading plotters and put them to death. Nero then became more wicked than he had been before. He even accused his old tutor, Se´ne-ca, and the famous poet Lu´can, of taking part in the plot against him, and he sent them an order to put themselves to death. Seneca was a very good man and a great writer. When he received the cruel order from Nero, he knew that if he did not obey it, the tyrant would send someone to kill him, so he had the veins of his arms cut open, and he died after much suffering. Lucan also obeyed the tyrant's order. While dying, he repeated lines from one of his own poems.

65 AD — Seneca and Lucan die by Nero's orders.

Historia

This wicked emperor had reigned for 14 years. But at last there was a rebellion against him, and the soldiers elected Gal´ba, the Roman governor of Spain, to be the new emperor.

Then Nero acted like a miserable coward. He was afraid to stay any longer in Rome, for most of the people hated him and favored Galba. So he mounted a horse and rode out of the city to the home of a trusty slave. But while he was there, he received word that the Senate had condemned him to death and that horsemen had been sent out to capture him. "Now dig a grave for me," he said to the slave, "and I will kill myself!" At this moment the galloping of horses was heard.

"Hark! They are coming to kill you," cried the slave. "Use the dagger while it is time and save yourself from disgrace!"

With trembling hand, Nero placed his dagger at this throat but did not have the courage to use it. The slave then seized it and plunged it into the emperor's throat, and the wicked Nero fell dead.

XVII – Septima Decima Lectiō: Galba, Otho, Vitellius, Vespasian, Titus (*Famous Men of Rome* XXV)

69 AD
The year of the four emperors: Galba, Otho, Vitellius, and Vespasian

During the two years that followed the death of Nero, there were three emperors: Gal´ba, Ot´ho, and Vi-tel´li-us. They were generals of Roman armies and were made emperors by their soldiers. But they reigned only a few months each, and they did nothing of importance.

Vitellius was a glutton. He took pleasure only in eating and drinking. He would often visit the houses of rich Romans without invitation and take breakfast with one, dinner with another, and supper with another. After breakfast he thought only about dinner; and when dinner was over, he began to think of what he would have for supper.

69 AD
Emperor Vespasian

66-63
The Jewish Revolt

The next emperor was Titus Fla´vi-us Ves-pa´si-an, commonly called Vespasian. He also was an army general. When he was made emperor by his soldiers, he was in Palestine. He had been sent there by Nero with an army to punish the Jews who had rebelled against Rome. As soon as he was declared emperor, he returned to Italy and left his son Titus Flavius, called in history simply Titus, to carry on the war against the Jews.

70 AD
Jerusalem and the temple destroyed, fulfilling the prophecy in Matthew 24:2 "Jesus said unto them, See ye not all these things? verily I say unto you, There shall not be left here one stone upon another, that shall not be thrown down."

Titus captured Jerusalem after a siege of six months, and his soldiers took possession of all the valuable things they could find. Then they burned the city to the ground. The famous temple was also destroyed and thus was fulfilled the prophecy of Christ that not one stone of the building should be left upon another. When Titus returned to Rome, he had a grand Triumph, and a beautiful arch was built in his honor. This arch is still in existence.

79 AD
Emperor Titus

Vespasian died in 79 AD, and then Titus became emperor. One of the remarkable things Titus did during his reign was to finish the Colosseum, which had been begun by his father. The Colosseum was the largest theatre in the world. It had seats for over 80,000 people. It was first called the Flavian Amphitheatre, from the family name of the emperors who built it. Inside, it had seats all round the ring or arena, and as the word *amphi* means *around*, they called the great building an amphitheatre. In later times, it got the name of Colosseum. The Greeks used the word *colossus* as a name for any very large statue, and because the Flavian Amphitheatre was so large, it was called the Colosseum. In our own language, we use the word *colossal* to describe anything of immense size.

In the Colosseum they had many kinds of amusements. When it first opened, the shows and games lasted for 100 days, and 5,000 wild beasts were killed in the arena by gladiators. The arena was a vast space fenced round about with a strong wall, and around it were circular tiers or rows of seats, one behind the other, like steps of stairs. Sometimes the arena was turned into a lake by letting water flow into it from pipes. Then they put ships upon it and had sham fights in imitation of a battle at sea. This sort of show was called a *naumachia*, which means a fight with ships. It was first introduced into Rome by Julius Caesar, who had a lake dug for the purpose in the Campus Martius.

The Colosseum is still in existence, but it is partly in ruins. Yet from its ruins we can still form an idea of how grand a building it once was.

Besides finishing the Colosseum, the Emperor Titus also built splendid baths. They were called the Baths of Titus. The Romans were very fond of baths. Wealthy citizens used to bathe several times every day, and often they spent the greater part of the day at the baths, where there were finely furnished rooms.

It was in the reign of Titus that the cities of Pom-pei´i and Her-cu-la´ne-um, in the south of Italy, were destroyed by an eruption of Mount Vesuvius. A famous Roman author, Pliny the Younger, saw the eruption from a distance and wrote a description of it. He tells that a fiery cloud of cinders, stones, and ashes burst from the top of the mountain and rained down upon the country all round, destroying towns and villages and people. The ruins of Herculaneum were accidentally discovered by workmen in 1709, and the ruins of Pompeii were discovered some years later.

Titus was a very good emperor. He always did everything he could for the welfare and happiness of the people, and he was so much liked by everybody that he was called the "Delight of Mankind." It is said that one night he thought he had done nothing during that day for the good of any person, and that he cried out, "I have lost a day."

XVIII – Duodēvīcēsima Lectiō: Domitian, Nerva, Trajan (*Famous Men of Rome* XXVI)

On the death of Titus, his brother Do-mi´ti-an became emperor. He was a very bad man and took pleasure only in doing cruel and wicked things. It is said that one of his amusements was catching flies and sticking them with pins. Once when a visitor called and inquired whether

---

80 AD
Colosseum completed

NB –Nero had once erected an enormous bronze colossus, or statue, portraying him as the sun god Helios. This colossus stood next to the site where Vespasian and Titus later built their amphitheatre. The statue was still standing until Medieval times. For this reason, we now call the amphitheatre built by the Flavians the "Colosseum."

79 AD
Eruption of Vesuvius

81 AD
Emperor Domitian

Historia

there was anyone with the emperor, the servant answered:

"No, not even a fly."

It is not to be supposed that such an emperor could have been liked by the people. Even his soldiers hated him, and at last they formed a plot against his life and killed him in his own palace.

96 AD
Emperor Nerva

Ner´va, who had been a favorite of Nero, was the next emperor, but he was an old man and died after a reign of two years. He was succeeded by his adopted son, Trajan, who became emperor in 98 AD and reigned for 19 years.

98 AD
Emperor Trajan

Trajan was a good man and a brave soldier. At the time he became emperor, he was governor of one of the Roman territories or provinces in Germany along the banks of the Rhine and he resided at Colonia, now called Cologne.

101-106 AD
Dacian Wars

Not long after his return to Rome, Trajan was engaged in a war with the King of Da´ci-a. This was the name of the country lying north of the Danube River. The greater part of it is now called Hungary. The Dacian king, whose name was De-ceb´a-lus, had frequently made raids into neighboring countries which belonged to Rome and had robbed and killed many of the people. Trajan resolved to punish Decebalus, and so he set out with a large army and marched into Dacia. The war continued three years, for the Dacians were brave and skillful fighters; but at last Decebalus was defeated in a great battle, and he had to come to Trajan and humbly beg for peace. He agreed to be a vassal of Rome, that is, to hold his kingdom subject to the control of the Roman emperors.

But in less than a year, Decebalus again attacked his Roman neighbors, and Trajan had again to march against him with an army. The Dacians were once more defeated in a great battle, and Decebalus, after failing in an attempt to escape, put an end to his own life. Dacia was then made a Roman province. During this year, Trajan built a remarkable bridge across the Danube. Before that time, bridges were built of wood, but in the bridge over the Danube, Trajan used stone for the piers, which were of great size. The bridge had 22 arches, and its ruins, which are still to be seen, show what a wonderful work it was.

When Trajan returned to Rome after his victory over Decebalus, he had a grand Triumph, and there were games and shows in his honor which lasted 120 days. It is told that during these celebrations 10,000 gladiators fought in the amphitheatre, and 11,000 wild animals were killed in the arena.

A marble column was erected in honor of Trajan's victories in Dacia. This monument is still standing in Rome. It is called Trajan's Column. Many scenes showing battles and other events in the Dacian war are engraved upon it from the base to the top.

Trajan also had wars in Asia, and he won many victories. He conquered Armenia and Mesopotamia and added them to the empire. But he did not live to return to Rome. He died in a town in Asia Minor, which, in honor of him, was afterward called Trajanopolis.

Historia

The Romans were much grieved at the death of Trajan, for he had been a good emperor and had done much to benefit the people. He built fine roads and canals and bridges in Italy and the provinces. He greatly improved and beautified the Circus Maximus. This was the place in which the Romans had their horse races and chariot races. It was built in the hollow between the Palatine and Aventine hills, and it had seats for 250,000 people.

Trajan also made a forum in Rome, which was called, after his name, the Trajan Forum. In the center of this forum Trajan's Column was built, and around it were temples and libraries established by the good emperor. For a long time after Trajan's death, the people of Rome, whenever they got a new emperor, used to wish that he would be "as great as Augustus and as good as Trajan."

Some great writers lived in Rome in the time of Trajan. One of them was Plu´tarch, who wrote the famous book called *Plutarch's Lives*. This book, which you will perhaps someday read, contains an account of the lives of many great men of Greece and Rome. The historian Ta´ci-tus, the poet Ju´ve-nal, and Pliny the Younger, already mentioned, also lived in the time of Trajan.

Pliny the Younger was so called to distinguish him from his uncle, Pliny the Elder, who lived in the time of Nero and was the author of a celebrated work on natural history.

XIX – Ūndēvīcēsima Lectiō: Hadrian, Antoninus Pius, Verus, Marcus Aurelius (*Famous Men of Rome* XXVII.1)

The next emperor was Trajan's cousin Ha´dri-an. He was a good ruler and did a great deal to improve the city of Rome. He traveled through many parts of the empire to see that the people were justly governed and that the public officials were doing their duty. He visited Britain, which was then a Roman province, and he caused a strong wall to be built from sea to sea across the country near Scotland, to prevent the fierce tribes of the north from making raids upon the Roman settlements in the south. Some remains of this wall can still be seen.

117 AD
Emperor Hadrian

Hadrian also built a great tomb in Rome, which was called Hadrian's Mole. He and many other Roman emperors were buried in this tomb. It is now known as the Castle of St. Angelo.

When Hadrian died, a very good man named An-to-ni´nus was made emperor. He showed so much filial regard for Hadrian by building a temple in his honor, that he was called Antoninus Pi´us. Under the emperors who ruled before his time, the Christians were very cruelly treated. They were not allowed to have churches or places of worship, and numbers of them were put to death in the most shocking manner. Often Christians were thrown into the arena in the Amphitheatre and devoured by wild beasts.

138 AD
Emperor Antoninus

NB – The adjective *pius, -a, -um* means *loyal, faithful,* or *reverent.*

In those times the Christians of Rome held their religious meetings in passages dug under the city for burying places. These Catacombs, as they were called, extended under all the Seven Hills of Rome, and were hundreds of miles in length. Along both sides of the tunnels were openings, one above another, in which the dead were buried. Many of the Catacombs have been explored in recent times. They are among the sights which visitors to Rome are always eager to see.

Antoninus Pius was very friendly to the Christians. He gave orders that they should be allowed to practice their religion and that anyone who interfered with them should be punished.

161 AD
Co-emperors
Marcus Aurelius and
Lucius Verus

The next emperor of Rome was a very remarkable and a very good man. His name was Marcus Au-re´li-us. He governed the empire justly and well for nearly 20 years. He began to reign in the year 161 AD. He was the adopted son of the good emperor Antoninus. For some time before the death of Antoninus, he held a high office and helped to govern the empire.

As soon as he became emperor Aurelius invited a young man named Ve´rus to share the throne with him. Verus had also been adopted by Antoninus. The generous act of Aurelius surprised everybody. Never before was there a Roman emperor who wanted to give half of his power to another person, and it seemed strange to the people that Aurelius should do so. But Aurelius said:

"I think my adopted brother has a right to be emperor with me."

And so Verus was made emperor with Aurelius, and for the first time Rome was ruled by two emperors. Verus had great respect for Aurelius. He seldom attempted to do anything in matters of government without asking his advice. But he did not have much to do with public affairs. He cared very little about being emperor and generally spent his time amusing himself. He was not a good young man, and his conduct gave Aurelius a great deal of sorrow. After nine years, Verus died, and Aurelius was the sole ruler during the rest of his life. In his youth Aurelius studied under the best teachers in the empire and so had an excellent education. He always had an eager desire for knowledge and was constantly learning. Even in war times, when he was fighting in the field, he carried a library with him and could often be seen in his tent engaged in study. He was one of the most learned of the Roman emperors, and his intimate friends were scholars and authors.

169 AD
Emperor M. Aurelius

When a boy of only 12 years Aurelius joined the Sto´ics. These were followers of a famous wise man or philosopher of Greece called Ze´no. This man taught that the people should act according to reason and virtue and should keep an even temper and a brave heart under all circumstances. He also taught that men should show neither joy nor sorrow but control their feelings and passions and submit without complaint to what could not be prevented.

The followers of Zeno were called Stoics, from the Greek word *stoa*, which means a roofed colonnade or porch. It was in a roofed porch at Athens that Zeno taught his doctrine.

The Emperor Aurelius was one of the best and most earnest of the Stoics. He carefully trained himself to control his feelings at all times and to do his duty honestly and faithfully. The Romans never had a purer or nobler emperor or one more respected and beloved. His style of living was very simple. He had no idle courtiers at his house, and he kept only a few servants. He gave no costly dinners and entertainments. He spent much of his salary to improve the condition of the poor and to provide good schools for their children.

Aurelius used to walk through the streets of Rome in plain clothing, attended only by a favorite slave. He returned the greetings of the people with bows and pleasant smiles. Anyone could go to him and talk freely, and he encouraged the people to tell him about their troubles so that he might understand how to help them.

Aurelius gave the Senate a great deal of power which he thought it ought to have, and gave back to the people many rights and privileges which former emperors had taken away from them. No wonder the Romans loved him and called him a good man.

XX – Vīcēsima Lectiō: Marcus Aurelius (*Famous Men of Rome* XXVII.2-3)

But the reign of Aurelius was full of troubles. Early in his reign, the Tiber overflowed its banks, and the waters swept away a large portion of Rome, destroying many lives. After this, there were dreadful earthquakes, very destructive fires, and other serious misfortunes.

There were also many wars. There was a war with the Parthians, a brave, warlike nation in Asia, that destroyed a Roman army and then invaded Syria. Large armies were sent against them, and they were soon conquered and forced to pay homage to Aurelius.

The Parthian horsemen had a strange way of fighting. They were armed with bows and arrows and small spears called javelins and were mounted on very swift horses. They would make attacks on the rear lines of the Romans, and when the Romans turned to attack them, they would lash their horses and ride off as fast as the wind. And while their horses were going at full speed, they would turn in their saddles and cast their javelins or shoot their arrows with wonderfully accurate aim.

After the Parthian War, there were wars with a number of wild tribes living in the countries now called Austria and Hungary. The tribes there rebelled against their Roman governors, and Aurelius had years of hard fighting before he could subdue them. He was himself a remarkably brave and able general and gained many splendid victories. So at last he taught the barbarians to respect and obey the Romans who governed them.

Once, when Aurelius was fighting a tribe called the Qua'di, his soldiers were hemmed in by the enemy in a small rocky valley and suffered greatly from thirst. Suddenly the sky darkened, and rain fell in torrents. The thirsty soldiers collected the water in their helmets and drank it eagerly.

While the soldiers were drinking and their lines were in confusion, the Quadi suddenly attacked them in large numbers. The Romans would have been cut to pieces, but there came a violent hailstorm, with lightning and thunder, which stopped the battle. When the storm had ceased, the Romans, much refreshed by the rainfall, boldly fought the Quadi and won a great victory.

Some of the Romans believed that the sudden storm which relieved them so much was caused by the magical power of an African wizard who was with the army at the time. But there was also with the army a legion of soldiers, some 3,000 in number, who were Christians. The Christians had prayed for rain, and they believed that the rain came in answer to their prayers. They said that it was a miracle sent by God to prove the truth of Christianity.

Now Aurelius was a pagan. Some of his Christian soldiers had tried to convert him to their faith, but they had not succeeded. He lived and died a believer in the pagan gods and goddesses. After the strange storm, however, he seemed to have a greater respect for Christianity, and he named his Christian legion of soldiers the "Thundering Legion."

Once the commander of the Roman armies in Asia, a man named A-vi´di-us Cas´si-us, planned a rebellion against Aurelius. When everything was ready, Cassius declared himself emperor and started with his army to Rome to take possession of the city. Aurelius collected his troops and went to meet Cassius, but no meeting took place, for Cassius was killed by own soldiers, and the rebellion quickly came to an end.

Those who had aided Cassius were brought before Aurelius for punishment. But the emperor would not punish them.

"No, I will not punish them," he said. "I think I have governed the empire too faithfully and liberally to fear plots. I can afford to forgive traitors. Let all the friends of Cassius go free; they are to be pitied rather than punished."

Aurelius was always very industrious and would never waste any of his time. It was a part of his duty as emperor to attend the games and sports in the Colosseum and Circus. Aurelius cared nothing for such sports, and whenever he attended them, he always spent his time at some useful occupation while sitting in the splendid chair of state provided for him. Sometimes he would study his favorite books and make notes from them, and sometimes he would dictate letters and government orders to a secretary. Thousands of excited Romans around him would be shouting their delight at the sports in the ring, but Aurelius would go on calmly with the work he had in hand.

"I do not like to waste my time by sitting here doing nothing," he would say. "To waste time is one of the greatest of crimes."

And so by never allowing himself to be idle, Aurelius was able to do many useful things. He established good schools and hospitals in Rome and other cities of Italy. He introduced new trades so that the poor people could get a much better living than before.

Aurelius always gave great encouragement to art and literature. He welcomed authors and artists to Rome and was always their friend. He established libraries and halls of paintings and statuary. He himself wrote several books.

It is said that with all his virtue, the life of Aurelius was not a happy one. He had serious troubles at times in governing the empire, and the cares of a ruler often weighed heavily upon him. His wife, whom he dearly loved, behaved very badly and caused him much anxiety, and his only son was a very bad young man. So in the later years of his life, Aurelius always appeared melancholy. A smile was seldom seen upon his face. He died at the city now called Vienna, in Austria, in 180 AD.

XXI – Vīcēsima Prīma Lectiō: Diocletian (*Famous Men of Rome* XXVIII)

After the death of Marcus Aurelius in 180 AD, there was a long, dreadful period in Rome's history. For 100 years there was great confusion. Emperors came and went almost every year. They were very weak and selfish, and other government officials often refused to do what the emperors ordered (because the emperor who gave the order might not be emperor for very long).

180-285 AD
Military Anarchy

The army placed most of the emperors in power. If the emperor did anything that displeased the soldiers, or if the emperor could not give them enough money or land (which happened frequently), the army named a new emperor. For this reason, the period from 180-285 AD is often called the "Military Anarchy."

As you might expect, the empire did not prosper during the period when it was ruled by the army and weak emperors. Many of the governors, mayors, judges, tax collectors, and other government officials became quite corrupt and wouldn't do their jobs unless given large bribes.

The emperors and governors kept raising taxes, which became more and more difficult for ordinary people to pay. To make matters worse, prices for everything went up rapidly every year. Many of the old sturdy Roman middle class of farmers and tradesmen lost everything they had and became poor.

For the first time in a long while, it was no longer safe to travel from city to city in the Empire. Pirates attacked ships in the Mediterranean, and thieves robbed travelers on the roads between cities.

The wild German tribes in the north and the fierce Parthians in the east attacked more and more frequently and seized large parts of some Roman provinces.

Di'o Cas'si-us, a Roman historian who wrote during the Military Anarchy, described it like this:

"Our history and the affairs of the Romans descend from an age of gold to one of iron and rust."

Historia

285 AD
Emperor Diocletian

In 285 AD, the soldiers named yet another of their generals, Di-o-cle´ti-an, as emperor, but Diocletian was different from the many other men the soldiers had made emperor in the previous 100 years. He vowed not to let the soldiers remove him from office once he took over. He was descended from Roman nobility. He had been born in the Roman province of Illyria. He had been a successful general, leading his troops against invading tribes in the north. And he knew something about organizing and leading people.

293 AD
The Tetrarchy

NB – *Tetrarchy* is a Greek word that means "a government with four leaders."

Diocletian was convinced that the empire was too large for one man to govern, so he divided it into two parts, the Eastern Roman Empire, with a capital at Ni-co-me-di´a, which he ruled himself, and the Western Roman Empire, with its capital at Mi-lan´. He named another general, Max-i´mi-an, as co-emperor, to rule the Western Roman Empire. To prepare for a peaceful succession (not one dictated by the army), each co-emperor named a vice emperor. The co-emperors planned to resign eventually and to be succeeded by their vice emperors. The new emperors would then name new vice-emperors, thus solving the problem of succession and keeping the army from interfering.

The great armies of many legions were broken up into smaller units so that they would be less able to threaten the emperor. The commanders of these armies had been powerful generals. Diocletian hoped that with fewer men under the command of each general, the armies would no longer be able to remove the emperor if they did not like what he was doing.

Diocletian is best known for his reform and reorganization of the Roman government. Because he thought the Empire had become too large, he divided almost every province and every office between two officials so that each would be responsible for a smaller area. Diocletian hoped that this would result in better government with less corruption. With each new official having less power, he hoped that it would make them more willing to obey the emperor. In some cases the reforms worked, but in many cases, they did not. The new officials usually obeyed the emperor, but they were often just as corrupt as the old ones.

Finally, Diocletian created a new branch of the government called the inspectorate, which was supposed to inspect local officials and catch those who were stealing or taking bribes. Unfortunately, the inspectorate soon became corrupt itself, and the inspectors began using their powers to demand bribes from the officials they were supposed to be investigating.

303 AD
Christians persecuted

Diocletian is also remembered as the last emperor under whom there was widespread persecution of Christians. Diocletian himself did not seem to have ordered the persecution or to have had any special hatred for Christians. Many of his new officials, however, did not like Christians and thought their religion was somehow not Roman. In many provinces, Christians were imprisoned and sometimes executed because they would not worship the official Roman gods. If Diocletian was not responsible for ordering the persecution of Christians, it is also true that he did nothing to stop it.

Diocletian did try to do something about the economic hardships suffered by the Roman people, especially the farmers, tradesmen, and middle class. He was troubled by the yearly increases in the price of food, houses, land, and everything else. In 301 AD, he issued an Edict of Prices, which fixed uniform prices for nearly everything. No one was supposed to charge any more than the official price in the edict, but Diocletian found that one couldn't give orders to merchants and traders the same way he could to soldiers. Almost everybody ignored the edict, and prices continued to go up.

Diocletian managed to control the army and make some progress in stopping the corruption of government officials. However, the vice-emperors he and Maximian had named were not as capable as they were, and so his reforms did not endure. It seems as though Diocletian may have been right when he said, "The Empire is too large to be ruled by one man."

Diocletian's plan for selecting new emperors when the old emperor died or resigned sounded good, but it never really worked. It was a new idea with no tradition or authority behind it, and the vice-emperors were not as strong and able as Diocletian. In 305 AD, after ruling as co-emperors for 20 years, Diocletian and his co-emperor Maximian resigned and were succeeded by their vice-emperors. Within five years, there was a civil war between five men, each claiming the title of emperor. One of the men was Maximian's son. Another was a general named Constantine, who was in charge of the legions in Britain and Gaul.

305 AD
Abdication of Diocletian and Maximian

XXII – Vīcēsima Secunda Lectiō: Constantine (*Famous Men of Rome* XXIX.1)

For more than 100 years after the time of Marcus Aurelius, none of the Roman emperors did anything great or remarkable. They were nearly all bad men, and many of them were put to death for their evil deeds.

In the year 307 AD, the empire had been divided up through many quarrels and wars between generals of armies. Often an army would declare its commander an emperor, and he would set himself up as a ruler of part of the empire. So in this way there came at last to be six persons who claimed to be emperors.

None of these three emperors was in any way remarkable except the emperor Con´stan-tine, called Constantine the Great. He was the son of a former emperor named Con-stan´ti-us. When Constantius, died the army chose Constantine to be emperor. But he did not go to Rome to be crowned. He remained in Gaul, for he learned that five others had taken the title of emperor in different parts of the empire.

After a while, however, Constantine got messages from people in Rome, begging him to come and relieve them from the cruel government of Max-en´ti-us, who was acting as emperor there. But Constantine was

> NB – Maxentius had tried to provoke a fight many times before, but Constantine did not respond. Then Maxentius sent an unsealed letter. The message (and its insult) public for anyone to read. Constantine could no longer overlook the insults and attacked.

> 312 AD
> Battle of the Milvian Bridge

a wise man. He thought it would not be good for him to leave Gaul and enter into a fight with Maxentius, so he paid no attention to the messages.

At last Maxentius openly insulted Constantine and threatened to kill him. Then Constantine was aroused to anger, so he gathered a great army of good soldiers and set out for Rome. He marched over the Alps and in a short time was fighting the army of Maxentius on the plains of Italy.

The first battle took place near Turin. The soldiers of Maxentius were clad in steel armor, but Constantine's men fought so fiercely that their armor was of little use to them, and they were speedily defeated. There was another battle at Verona, where Constantine was again the victor.

The third battle took place on the banks of the Tiber, near Rome. Maxentius led more soldiers than Constantine, but he was not a good general, so he was easily beaten. He himself was drowned while fleeing across the Tiber.

After the battle, Constantine entered Rome amidst the cheers of the people. A little while afterward, he told an interesting story to a Christian bishop named Eu-se´bi-us. He said that while he was marching through northern Italy, on the way to Rome, he was constantly thinking about the Christian religion. It had been spreading in every civilized country for more than two centuries, and Constantine thought that he too should become a Christian and no longer worship pagan gods. But he could not make up his mind to do so.

One day while Constantine was in front of his tent, with his officers and troops around him, there appeared in the heavens an enormous cross of fire. A little on one side of the cross were these words in the Greek language, "By this, conquer." The words are sometimes given in the Latin form, *In hōc signō vincēs*, the translation of which is, "Through this sign thou shalt conquer."

Constantine was astonished at the wonderful vision, and he gazed at it until it faded away. He could not understand what it meant and was greatly troubled. But that night, he dreamed that Christ appeared to him in robes of dazzling white, bearing a cross in His hands, and that He promised him victory over his enemies if he would make the cross his standard.

Constantine now declared himself a Christian and had a standard made in the form of a cross, with a banner attached to it bearing the initial letters of the name of Christ. This banner was called the *Lab´a-rum*, and it was afterward the standard of the Roman emperors.

When Constantine became a Christian himself, he began to take Christians into his favor. He made some of them high officers of the government; he built Christian churches and destroyed the pagan temples. He also made the Christian religion the religion of the empire, and he had the sign of a cross painted on the shield and banners of the Roman armies.

Thus after many, many years of terrible persecution, the Christians were befriended by the Roman emperor, and soon they became very powerful. Thousands of Romans were converted to Christianity, and the

> 313 AD
> The Edict of Milan permits Christians to worship openly.

Historia

churches were crowded with worshippers.

XXIII – Vīcēsima Tertia Lectiō: Constantine (*Famous Men of Rome* XXIX.2)

Constantine also very much improved the Roman laws and system of government. He put a stop to the dishonest practices of the officers and established just methods of carrying on public affairs. He disbanded the famous Praetorian Guards, which had been an evil power in Rome for centuries. Many other reforms were carried out by Constantine, who seemed anxious to do what was right and what was for the best interests of the people.

Under Constantine's rule, therefore, Rome was happy and prosperous. To show their gratitude to him for his noble deeds, the people erected in his honor a grand marble arch in the central square of the city and inscribed on it:

"To the founder of our peace."

Four of the six emperors who had at one time ruled the empire were now dead. But in the east, there was one emperor named Li-ci'ni-us. Constantine attacked him, scattered his armies, and took away from him the greater part of his territory.

The two emperors then became friends, but after some time, they had a quarrel and went to war again. Each had a large army and a fleet of warships. Two great battles were fought, and Constantine won both. Licinius soon afterward died.

Now for the first time Constantine was sole emperor, and for more than 14 years he ruled the immense Roman Empire. He built the most magnificent palace Rome had ever seen. He surrounded himself with hundreds of courtiers and lived in great splendor.

324 AD Emperor Constantine

After a time, Constantine resolved to move the capital of the Empire to a more central place than Rome. He selected Byzantium, an ancient city of Thrace, at the entrance to the Black Sea. To this city Constantine sent numbers of workmen to make alterations and improvements, and he changed its name to Constantinople, which means "City of Constantine." He spent vast sums of money erecting gorgeous buildings, making aqueducts, constructing streets and public squares, and doing the many many other things proper to be done in a capital of a great empire. The finest statues and other works of art that could be obtained in Greece, Italy, and the countries of Asia were brought to make Constantinople beautiful.

330 AD Constantine made Byzantium capital of the empire but named it Constantinople.

When everything was ready, Constantine, with the officers of his government removed to Constantinople. He lived for about seven years afterward. There were no more wars, except for a slight conflict with a tribe called the Goths, and the people of the empire were contented and prosperous.

Historia

Constantine died in Constantinople at the age of 63, after a reign of nearly 31 years. He was the first Christian emperor of Rome.

XXIV – Vīcēsima Quarta Lectiō: The End of the Western Empire
(*Famous Men of Rome* XXX)

Most of the Roman emperors after Constantine were either cruel tyrants or very worthless persons, who spent their time in idle pleasure and neglected their duties to the people. A few, however, did some remarkable things and therefore deserve to be mentioned among the Famous Men.

360 AD
Emperor Julian "the Apostate" attempted to revive pagan religion

One emperor, whose name was Ju'li-an, is called in history Julian the Apostate, because he gave up the Christian religion and tried to establish the worship of the pagan gods again in Rome. Julian also attempted to rebuild the Temple of Jerusalem which, as we have seen, was destroyed by Titus. There was a Christian prophecy that it would never be restored, and Julian thought of rebuilding it to prove the theory false.

A story is told that as soon as the men began the work, balls of fire burst from the ground close by them, and they had to stop. They tried again and again, and the same thing happened, and at last they had to give up the work altogether.

Not long after he became emperor, Julian set out with a large army to conquer Persia. For a while he was very successful and defeated the Persian king in many battles. But one day he was shot in the breast by an arrow, and he died soon after. It is said that while he lay wounded, he cast a handful of his blood toward heaven, crying out, "Thou hast conquered, O Galilean." By Galilean he meant Christ, who is sometimes called the Galilean because He was brought up in Galilee.

364 AD
Emperor Valentinian divided the Empire. He ruled the west and Valens ruled the east.

Not long after the reign of Julian, there was an emperor named Val-en-tin'i-an. He made his brother Va'lens emperor of the eastern part of the empire while he himself ruled over the western part. And for many years afterward the empire was ruled in this way by two emperors, one called the Emperor of the East, and the other the Emperor of the West.

392 AD
Emperor Theodosius

On the death of Valentinian, his son Gra'ti-an became Emperor of the West, and a talented soldier named The-o-do'si-us became Emperor of the East on the death of Valens. Gratian was weak and unfit to rule, and he was killed by a Spaniard named Max'i-mus, who made himself Emperor of the West.

Theodosius fought Maximus and defeated him and afterward had him put to death. Then he made a son of Valentinian Emperor of the West as Valentinian II and gave him, as his advisor, a chief named Ar-bo-gas'tes. But Arbogastes was soon the real master of the Western Empire. One day Valentinian was found dead in his bed, and Arbogastes then made Eu-ge'ni-us, a teacher, the emperor. Theodosius, who well knew that Valentinian II had been murdered, made war on Eugenius and Arbogastes and defeated them, and until his death a few months afterward,

Theodosius was emperor of both east and west.

Theodosius had been a wise ruler, but he did one very bad thing. The people of Thes-sa-lo-ni´ca, a city of Macedonia, a country north of Greece, had killed their governor because he had put one of their favorite circus riders in prison. When Theodosius heard of this, he was very angry, and he gave orders that they should be invited to a show in the circus and there be put to death. This cruel order was carried out. The citizens of Thessalonica were invited to come one day to the circus to see a grand show. Thousands came, and as soon as they had taken their seats, a troop of soldiers under the command of one of Theodosius' generals entered the building and massacred them all without mercy. More than 6,000 men, women, and children died.

Theodosius resided in Milan, a city in northern Italy. A bishop named Am´brose, a good and holy man, also lived in Milan. When Ambrose learned of the massacres at Thessalonica, he was shocked. He severely reprimanded Theodosius and would not permit him to enter the doors of the church until he had done penance for the sin he had committed in so cruelly killing thousands of innocent people.

Theodosius' successor as Emperor of the West was his son Ho-no´ri-us, who reigned for 29 years. However, the actual ruler during all that time was a soldier named Sti´li-cho, the emperor's guardian. Honorius was a simpleton and had no desire or ability to attend to the affairs of the government.

395 AD
Emperor Honorius

The Goths and Vandals and other barbarous tribes from the north and east of Europe began to overrun the Western empire and to threaten Rome itself. Twice the great city was actually captured and plundered, the first time by the Goths under Al´ar-ic, and next by the Vandals under a bold warrior named Gen´ser-ic.

410 AD
Goths sack Rome.

455 AD
Vandals sack Rome

To defend the seat of their Empire against the attacks of its enemies, the Romans were obliged to withdraw their forces from several outlying provinces, including Britain, which was then left to its native inhabitants. For more than 50 years, a number of men who had little ability took part in ruling what was left of the once mighty Empire. One of these had the high-sounding name of Romulus Au-gus´tu-lus. He was the son of O-res´tes, the general of the army of Italy, and had been made emperor by his father. He was the last of the Western emperors.

476 AD
The last emperor, Romulus Augustulus

Among the Italian soldiers there was a huge, half-savage man named O-do-ac´er, who belonged to a wild northern tribe. He was a favorite of the army because of his courage and strength. He resolved to be the ruler of Italy, so with the army supporting him, he put Orestes to death, took Romulus Augustulus prisoner, and forced him to give up the title of emperor. Then Odoacer became king of Italy in the year 476 AD.

By this time the world had nearly entered that period which is known as the Middle Ages, and many of the other countries which had been parts

476 AD
Fall of the Western Roman Empire

1453 AD
The Byzantine Empire fell with the capture of Constantinople.

NB – After the fall of the Ottoman Empire, Constantinople was renamed Istanbul in 1933.

of the Roman Empire were either ruling themselves or defending themselves against new invaders. Gaul was invaded and conquered by the German tribes called Franks, from whom the country subsequently got the name of France. Britain, abandoned by the Romans, was soon after conquered by other German tribes. And so at last the great Roman Empire had crumbled to pieces, and Rome, so long the Mistress of the World, as she was called, had fallen from her proud position of grandeur and power to that of a second- or third-rate city.

But the empire of the East continued to exist for centuries afterward, with Constantinople as its capital. It included many of the countries of Asia, Africa, and Eastern Europe which had formerly belonged to the undivided Empire. In course of time, the power of the Greeks, aided by the influences of the Greek division of the Church, became supreme at Constantinople, and so the Empire was also called the Greek Empire, and sometimes the Byzantine Empire, from the ancient name of the capital.

In the fourteenth century, the Turks, or Mohammedans, then very powerful in southwestern Asia, began to make inroads on the empire. They conquered and took possession of several of its provinces, and in 1453 they captured Constantinople, which has since been the capital of the Turkish, or Ottoman, Empire.

www.ingramcontent.com/pod-product-compliance
Lightning Source LLC
Chambersburg PA
CBHW080912170426
43201CB00017B/2298